ACCIDENTAL EDEN

ACCIDENTAL EDEN

EDEN

Douglas L. Hamilton
and Darlene Olesko

HIPPIE DAYS on
LASQUETI ISLAND

CAITLIN PRESS

CONTENTS

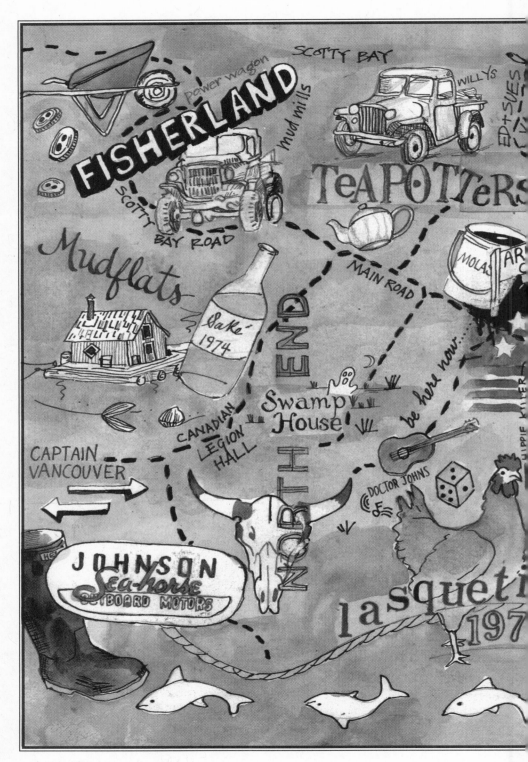

Map illustration by Darlene Olesko.

This book is dedicated to our horrified parents.

ACKNOWLEDGEMENTS

So many people helped us to write this book with their contributions of stories, photographs, advice, technical assistance, and more. We'd like to thank you all for being part of our dream of recording the most adventurous decade of our lives, we enjoyed working with you. We have also really enjoyed working together and collecting these stories

We extend much gratitude to Elda Mason who inspired us with her book, "Lasqueti Island, History and Memory".

We would like to thank Tom Wheeler, Barry Churchill, Merrick Anderson, Dianne Bump, Howie Siegel, Wendy Schneible, Ken Whitman, Bob Schroeder, Bruce and Gordon Jones and Kevin Monahan for sharing their old photos with us.

We also thank Gordon Lafleur for doing a great job cleaning up many of Tom's old photos so they would reproduce well, and Martha Holmes for providing us with many of Rand Holmes paintings and cartoons to select from for this book.

To all those who shared their stories with us, and to those who allowed us to quote them in this book, and the list is huge, we thank you as well.

To all the wonderful, dearly departed people that we wrote character sketches about, it was an honour to remember every one of you in this book. Thank you for being such colourful, independent people, and for gracing our Island lives here with your presence and memorable character. We have loved remembering you.

And our thanks to Sheila Harrington and Adam Enright for both their encouragement and technical assistance.

We both thank the wonderful, talented people at Caitlin Press; Vici Johnstone, Holly Vestad, Andrea Routley, Kathleen Fraser, Rebecca Hendry, Patricia Wolfe and Benjamin Dunfield for taking a leap of faith with us.

Accidental Eden is the result of almost twenty years of slowly collecting the stories of people who were happy to share their memories of living on Lasqueti Island in the 70s. Without all these offerings, we wouldn't have much of a book.

Opposite: Winter shoreline, with wooden boats in Cocktail Cove.

INTRODUCTIONS

—*Doug*

Lasqueti Island has gone through a lot of changes over the past forty years. In the early 1970s it was largely abandoned—sparsely populated and heavily logged, with much of the land held by absentee property owners. The back-to-the-land movement of the 1970s forever changed the island by growing a thriving community of artists, writers, musicians, freethinkers and social activists. Lasqueti also became a place that celebrated eccentricity and encouraged people to let it all hang out. Tolerance for extreme personalities, odd characters and strongly held beliefs all melded to create a fascinating and sometimes bizarre social milieu. Although things have toned down a bit in recent years, I feel so lucky and honoured to have been part of the remarkable changes that have taken place here.

Today there seems to be a new interest in those forgotten hippie days. We can see it again in today's youth and their struggle for environmental sanity and human equality. The so-called counterculture is not quite dead, although we are still treated to an endless barrage of obituaries from the media. Our journey needs to be remembered both for nostalgic amusement and as an example for future generations.

Long live local history!

Opposite: Dianne Bump, sitting on stacked hand-milled lumber, 1975. Photo Tom Wheeler.

Previous spread: Angus Ellis, "Crabber Bob" and Ritchie Stewart at the Teapot fence, 1972. Photo Merrick Anderson.

—Darlene

Arriving here on a dark, windy afternoon in 1971, I remember thankfully stepping off the *Captain Vancouver* ferry, walking up the wooden ramp and viewing the scene: just a few aging homes and the Sea-Shell Store and Marine. That was all that stood in False Bay in those days. Heading south, through the back windows of Shirley Mann's Volkswagen I saw the sagging, beige Royal Canadian Legion building and, on the other side of the road, the Church of the Good Shepherd. Other than a few homes that were out of sight from the road, there was nothing more but forest until False Bay School and the Teapot House. And then, more stretches of forest in both directions, and only occasionally I saw little house lights shining through the trees.

The overall tone of the island was one of economic downslide, illustrated clearly by the abandoned shacks and empty, rundown houses, the mysteriously deep forests and romantically overgrown fields, the tumbledown farms and vacated homesteads that still held potential for agriculture. Yet these were seen as assets in the eyes of dozens of mostly young people who were looking for a way out of a politically uncomfortable, culturally uptight, cash-centred urban existence. We saw only a landscape of luscious possibility where we could completely live out our visions of self-reliance, creative self-growth and financial independence. This was the back-to-the-land movement, and we were part of this movement that changed the island.

In these stories and chapters we try, in both our voices and the voices of others who have contributed, to recall, retell and relive the beautiful, strange and important events that took place here in the 1970s. If no one writes about those years, the stories and memories may just disappear in time.

Opposite: Musical couple Alan DiFiore and Bonnie Olesko, at the Douglas Field for the May Day Picnic. Photo Tom Wheeler.

PART ONE: HOW IT ALL BEGAN

Opposite: Alan DiFiore takes a break from his morning work on an Alaskan mill, 1974. Photo Tom Wheeler.

SETTING THE STAGE

—Doug

Lasqueti Island, or "The Rock," as residents know it, lies in the middle of the Georgia Strait between the snowy peaks of Vancouver Island and the mainland, seventy-two kilometres north of Vancouver. It is well isolated on both sides by nineteen kilometres of treacherous waters. Twenty-one kilometres long and five kilometres wide, it hosts eight major bays along a rough rocky coastline. A strong rain shadow makes the island one of the sunniest and driest along the coast, and there are even isolated patches of prickly pear cactus on the south end. The climate of the Sunshine Coast has long been considered the warmest and most pleasant in all of Canada.

An unpaved road snakes down the length of the island with a dozen overgrown side shoots leading off to the sea. It remains among the least developed of the major Gulf Islands, and the civilized amenities that many take for granted are few. Public services are sparse—no hydroelectric hookup, a very rudimentary phone line, no public water system, no sewage disposal, no building zoning, almost no paving and no RCMP detachment. Essential public services include a school, a small passenger ferry, a couple of small stores for groceries and gas and a post office that delivers mail three times a week. Today, Lasqueti hosts around five hundred full-time residents, but the number doubles during the summer months.

The island remained lightly settled until the 1930s and then experienced an economic boom after the Second World War. There was a vibrant social life and full employment. Although the population may have reached a thousand, prosperity was fleeting. Most of Lasqueti's land was soon logged and flogged, leaving little of value. By 1956 only a couple of logging operations remained, and Lasqueti entered into what some have called a "depression."

In fact, this kind of cyclical economic downturn was typical of the entire region during the twentieth century. And British Columbia's coast, home to a hard-drinking, mining, fishing and logging culture, periodically underwent a series of slow-motion population fluctuations. As the great extractors thinned out and their insatiable appetites moved north and east, families left the bush in droves, courting better job opportunities and the easy conveniences of modern life.

A 1973 piece in *Raincoast Chronicles 4* (Harbour Publishing) described this mass exodus. Lester R. Peterson's "British Columbia's Depopulated Coast" estimated that ten thousand fishermen and shore workers lost their jobs between 1925 and 1972, and that 7,500 permanent residents between Lund and Kitimat surrendered their farms and homesteads to move back to civilization. He claimed that forty general stores, forty post offices, dozens of sawmills and canneries and five hospitals also shut down. Peterson even mentioned Lasqueti by name, calling for a regeneration of farming and ranching on the island to ease pressure on Fraser Valley farmland.

Most residents left without fanfare, but the effect was devastating. Anyone who travels the inner and outer coasts of British Columbia today will uncover haunting and forgotten relics of an earlier occupation in nearly every bay and cove—overgrown farms, crumbling dormitories, rusting machinery and ancient garbage heaps. Over and over, it was the same old story. Coastal communities would experience a sudden boom of resource prosperity after settlement, which proved unsustainable in the long run.

Although it is difficult to imagine today, Lasqueti became a very empty place after this mass exodus. Most of the island was held in large parcels by absentee owners and logging companies waiting for a land boom and a regrowth of the forest. The terrain was littered with downed virgin Douglas fir and western red cedar cut and then abandoned after the bottom fell out of the market and timber prices plummeted. The population was barely seventy— mainly made up of a few old-time families still clinging to their homesteads in a stripped wasteland. Rusting logging donkeys and dead cars littered the landscape. Farmers' fields lay in a thicket of fallen fence posts entangled in page wire. Flocks of feral sheep roamed the countryside, remnants of various unsuccessful livestock operations dating back to the 1850s. Ramshackle houses were available for the asking—rent-free, although the roofs leaked and chimneys smoked. Logged-over landscapes went for fifty dollars an acre or less, but few cared to buy. Who would ever want to live on this island of stumps, muddy logging roads and broken timber?

As it soon turned out there were a lot of people interested in doing exactly that. In one of those odd, inexplicable twists of history, the population tide abruptly turned again. In fact, the early 1970s brought an unexpected demographic influx to all of rural British Columbia. But it was fostered by neither

Bonnie Olesko. In the late 1960's the back-to-the-landers sought out the simple life. Kerosene lights, handmade tools and wood stoves for heat and cooking were preferable to the comforts of modern life.

resource extraction nor real estate. The revolution of the late 1960s had metamorphosed into the back-to-the-land movement with hordes of young flower children abandoning the city for the country. A whole new crowd of enthusiastic young people (of which I was one) abruptly arrived to colonize those abandoned farmsteads, picturesque beaches and just about any place one could throw up a shack or cabin.

Country life was idealized—peace, simplicity, living in balance with nature and spending as little money as possible trumped career, wealth, education, class and all the other trappings of conventional North American life. Kerosene lamps replaced bright electric lights, wood stoves were used for heating and cooking, and people walked or boated to their destinations rather than driving. Self-sufficiency and economy were everything. There was a reverence for the "old ways," ancient hand tools, and First Nations food and medicinal plants. Castoff building materials, an ancient spinning wheel or loom, unfashionable clothes from the Salvation Army and a large, productive organic garden became status symbols. One took pride in using as little as possible. Nobody had a pot to piss in, and that was just fine. Be Here Now! Live in the eternal present and forget about society's expectations and an uncertain future.

Looking back on it now, it all seems so insanely pure. (But was it? In another curious turn of the wheel, many of today's twenty-somethings seem to be following a similar path, choosing to move back to rural areas—but that is another story.)

A powerful pessimism consumed many in the seventies. Ecological disaster, earthquakes, economic depression and nuclear war seemed to be on everyone's mind. Life in the country became a refuge from nasty world events that never seemed to materialize. It was also a time of disillusionment. The rallying cry of "Power to the People" had brought little. The sixties revolution was based on a solid core of anarchy, and this is probably why so little was accomplished. People were disgusted with the futility of it all and looked to life in the country as a way of changing society by example rather than by confrontation. We all felt that we were somehow altering our first-world pattern of life into something that made a lot more sense, ecologically, psychically, financially and socially.

There were suddenly alternative groups sprouting up in every rural nook and cranny, trying out all manner of personal and social experiments. The variety, abundance and daring of these attempts were staggering. Many of these groups chose names that were both whimsical and evocative. Chickencrest (Qualicum Beach); Mother's Vision (Victoria); Moonstar Family (Hagensborg); Catface Community (Tofino); the Shire (Hornby Island); Treefrog (Mayne Island); Rainbow Family (Cortes Island); Applespring (Lillooet); Pepperland (Williams Lake); Cosmic Debris (Vancouver) and countless others. Some of these groups were urban, but most were steadfastly rural or planning to be in the near future.

The communal/back-to-the-land movement also spawned a number of BC magazines like *Community* and *Open Circle* and organizations like the New West Co-op and the Community Alternatives Society. The province, long known for its assortment of oddballs, visionaries and utopians, now had a new distinction: it had become a mecca for the counterculture. It seemed everyone you talked to in Berkeley or NYC or Toronto in 1970 was planning to hitch out to BC and find that mellow, communal farmstead at the end of the rainbow.

Driftwood beach shacks sprang up like mushrooms from Long Beach to Haida Gwaii. We were the new hunter-gatherers, cheerfully content to scrape by on a pittance in exchange for the leisure to pursue our own agenda—be it art, the intellectual world of books, music, personal relationships or just living on the earth. Many were squatters on vacant land. The societal conventions governing marriage, career, money, diet, recreational drugs and much else were pointedly turned on their heads.

Not surprisingly, some viewed the influx of searchers with fear and loathing. Echoes of this attitude can be found today in many histories and popular books of the time. Most did not paint a pretty picture. *The Eden Express* relates in frightening detail Mark Vonnegut's mental breakdown at a commune on Powell Lake. *Apple Bay*, by Paul Williams, describes a selfish world of sexual experimentation, jealousy and tension in a commune located near Galley Bay in Desolation Sound. Sadly this negative portrayal of the back-to-the-landers has become part of today's culture wars. It seems that anyone foolish enough to "drop out" must endure a life of degrading promiscuity, rampant drug use, crushing poverty and vapid idealism.

I would have to disagree with this bleak assessment. For me the 1970s was a time of profound happiness, positive growth and personal discovery. It was like going back to school all over again, but this time the subject matter was practical carpentry, gardening, gathering and creative improvisation. However, it is certainly true that the sudden transformation of a deserted rural infrastructure into a thriving social experiment led to some misunderstandings and confusion. One has only to peruse the editorial pages of our local paper, the *Parksville–Qualicum Beach Progress*, to gain a sense of the immense culture shock felt at that time. Here is a letter to the editor of the *Progress* written by a longtime Lasqueti resident in November 1972:

> We have been going to Lasqueti Island on boat trips etc. for some 20 years and because we found it to be such a lovely, quiet and peaceful spot with friendly people everywhere, we decided to buy property and hoped one day to retire there. We're not so sure that we want to any more.
>
> At that time you could spend days wandering about the island enjoying the scenery and the wild animals, visit the local residents and in turn have them visit you. There were always picnics, wiener roasts etc. where everyone joined together for a day of good clean fun. The last Saturday night of each month is a night of fun at the old community hall half-sponsored by the

Legion. We enjoyed a few games of bingo, some dancing and singing, a midnight lunch brought in by local residents and a visit with folks you had not perhaps seen for some time. Many tourists docking in the bay joined in the fun.

The last couple of years have seen an end to that. One hardly dares to take young children for a swim at the "old Swimming Hole." You are likely as not to run into a bunch of long haired, dirty, bearded, naked, so called "native residents." Picnics and Saturday Legion nights are impossible to attend if a person has any self respect. These "native residents" sit around smoking pot until the stench of it reaches your nostrils from half a block away from the hall. If someone has to go to the bathroom, they haven't the decency to "head for the bush" and conceal themselves. "Johnny on the spot" seems to be their motto. Their mode of dress seems to be "the dirtier the better." You feel itchy just standing next to them …

These "native residents" claim "their doors are open." Yes—they probably are, but the real native residents have had to lock theirs.

But this unsigned letter was more the exception than the rule.

Was this watershed change in values a return to some kind of primitive communism, a counterculture delusion or a practice session provided by kindly fates for a difficult future? Historians will be pondering this question for a while yet. Certainly the ideas and values of the counterculture revolution have demonstrated a surprising viability, despite a long litany of contemptuous obituaries.

Perhaps because of the isolation, the generations got on well here on the "Rock" and still do. On many of the Gulf Islands, two community halls had to be constructed in the seventies—one for the older residents, the other for the longhairs. That did not occur on Lasqueti. Most welcomed us with open arms as a therapeutic antidote to the boredom of an empty landscape. Social and economic life was rejuvenated. Friendships between the two cultures were made that abide to the present day. And now we are the stodgy oldsters writing a book about it.

LASQUETI'S ANCIENT HISTORY

—Doug

Although some think of West Coast history as beginning with James Cook's third expedition in 1776, the region's past has much deeper roots. Lasqueti Island has seen a number of distinct occupations over the ages. Artifacts found on the island suggest that it was first visited at least eight thousand years ago, after sea levels stabilized in the early postglacial age. By that time many other areas of the British Columbia coast were already populated. We know little of these earliest settlements, or in fact much of Lasqueti's archeological history, since there has never been a formal excavation conducted on the island. These early settlements were likely composed of small family groups.

But by two to three thousand years ago, First Nations people were using large parts of the island. Middens of mollusc shells and other archeological material can be found in most of the coastal bays, and today's residents regularly turn up artifacts farther inland.

In the more densely populated areas like False Bay and Marshall's Beach, large, flattened house sites near the water still stand out. It is likely that many of these village sites were inhabited continuously for over a thousand years.

Bones and shells eroding out of middens suggest that people were hunting deer, seabirds and sea mammals as well as gathering the shellfish and fish that were once plentiful. In False Bay, Tucker Bay and Marshall's Beach, one can still see the remains of large and complex stone fish traps. The island also abounded with plant edibles like salmonberries, huckleberries, salal, wild crabapples and a variety of wild lily bulbs including blue camus. There was trade in high-value objects like nephrite jade and obsidian—neither of which can be naturally found on the island. Ancient stone artifacts are surprisingly abundant if you know where to look, and what to look for. It is a bit like developing an eye for sighting mushrooms.

There must have been times of considerable instability and strife.

Defensive works can be found far from the water, complete with fortifications and lookout posts. Based on archeological work immediately to the north, many of these fortified sites may date to only five hundred years ago, sometime after the Spanish arrived in eastern North America.

When European settlers first arrived in the 1870s, there were few obvious signs of Native life—no poles, houses, villages or settlements, though small groups of First Nations families came to Lasqueti to gather resources. In fact, some families from the neighbouring First Nations identify Lasqueti as their ancestral home. Sliammon Native elders still refer to the island as Xwe'etay, meaning "strong wood"—a possible reference to the yew wood found there. Despite this and the abundant archeological evidence, the conventional wisdom about Lasqueti and most of the Gulf Islands has been that "there is no evidence of permanent Indian settlement ever having been on the Island." What, then, happened to all those people who lived on this island for several millennia prior to the late nineteenth century?

When the Spanish conquistadors arrived in Mexico in the early sixteenth century, they brought with them the germs of what has been described as "the greatest demographic catastrophe in human history." These new European killer diseases included measles, syphilis, typhus, influenza, whooping cough, smallpox and others. Of all these, smallpox was the worst, and there is some conjecture that there was a hemispheric epidemic as early as the 1520s, originating in Mexico. In any event there were well-documented smallpox epidemics on the British Columbia coast in 1775, 1801, 1836–38, 1853 and 1862. Every few years this ghastly plague would run rampant, killing up to 90 percent of those infected. By the 1870s, the populations of the northern Coast Salish peoples had been decimated, and this would explain the emptiness of Lasqueti when the Europeans arrived. Based on the number of large and small settlements in Lasqueti's archeological record, the island was populated by several hundred people prior to the European-introduced epidemics.

The next wave of settlement had its roots in the late eighteenth century, when the northwest coast suddenly became an object of fascination for the world's great powers. France, Spain, Russia, Great Britain and the United States all found themselves in a race to establish a permanent presence here. Sparking their interest was the vastly lucrative fur trade with China in sea otter pelts. There was also hope that the elusive and fabled Northwest Passage might eventually be revealed. Many at the time felt that Vancouver Island held the key, and the wide Juan de Fuca Strait must be the entrance.

Spain had sent a number of explorers to investigate and possibly occupy a piece of territory at Nootka. Among them was a naval group of two ships:

the schooner *Santa Saturnina*, under José María Narváez, and the packet boat *San Carlos* under Francisco de Eliza. In the summer of 1791 they were the first Europeans to enter British Columbia's inner coast, surveying the Rosario Strait, Haro Strait, Nanaimo Harbour and the Strait of Georgia to Texada Island. Eliza's 1791 chart shows an outline of Lasqueti Island with the name "Lasquety." George Vancouver accepted Eliza's place name, and Lasqueti Island remains in use to the present day.

The island remained unoccupied by Europeans until the mid-1800s, when the Royal Navy began conducting more detailed surveys for coal and minerals. There were promising signs of copper, silver and trace gold, but not enough to warrant construction of a mine. It was only in 1875 that J.O.W. Carey spent two and a half months laying out the sections and quarter sections for settlement. Rock cairns marked the corners, and details including springs, marshes, lakes, hills and stands of timber were outlined on waxed linen. He recommended the island be used for sheep farming and claimed it should be able to support ten thousand animals.

In fact, there were already two settlers with two hundred sheep each—Captain Pearse and Albion Tranfield. Harry Higgins and several others soon followed. All three were refugees of the so-called "Pig War," a volatile squabble between Great Britain and the United States over the position of the border and ownership of the San Juan Islands.

From the start, life on Lasqueti was anything but conventional. Higgins promptly ordered himself a child bride of fourteen, Mary Ann—not that unusual, as eligible women were hard to find during those early days. The two got on well and struck up a friendship with another settler couple, William and Margaret Rous. It was such a happy foursome that the two men decided to amicably trade wives. Although such an arrangement seems more out of the 1970s than the 1880s, the realignment worked well and resulted in two long-lasting unions.

Then, as now, the island remained isolated from the mainland and Vancouver Island by nineteen kilometres of treacherous water. Valuable resources were plentiful, but there were serious problems in getting them to market. Logging by the Rat Portage Lumber Company out of Boat Cove was only successful after a complicated series of log skids was constructed in 1898. After the gigantic trees were cut, the enterprise dissolved in 1911, and the land was put up for pre-emption.

Salmon fishing had enormous potential, but again, distance to markets was a major impediment. In 1915 a cannery was built in False Bay, which created jobs, brought prosperity and enlivened social life. The war drove prices up even further, and the population boomed to over one hundred, with twenty students attending the school at Centre Road. The cannery tripled in size and immigrant workers were introduced, including Chinese crews and a contingent of Scottish women to make scotch-cured herring. Then it all came tumbling down when the war ended abruptly in late 1918. At least fifteen Lasqueti Islanders had left the island to fight in the Great War—amazingly, none were killed.

The postwar period, sometimes referred to as the "Golden Twenties," brought in a whole new crowd of fresh faces bearing names that remain familiar island place names today—among them Douglas, Livingston, Hadley, Weldon, Conn and Kurtzhals. More schools opened: False Bay at the north end in 1917, and Maple Grove on the south end in 1923.

The popular Presbyterian reverend George Pringle brought religion to the island in 1922. He was a perceptive observer, and one of the few to describe the island in the 1920s. "If you stand on the Cliffs of Point Grey you can see the haze of Lasqueti. This leads me to speak of this settlement, one hundred and forty people live there including fifty children. They are mostly homesteaders and are good folks. I doubt if you could find on the island any two shacks within sight of each other, hence their lives are lonely enough in all conscience. There are no roads deserving the name, only bush trails."

The island got its first introduction to electricity when Charlie Williams set up a kerosene generator in False Bay in 1928. Union Steamships began to call intermittently in 1923, and the post office was moved from Anderson Bay to Tucker Bay, a much more central location. These improvements occasioned some bad feeling, as roads were rudimentary and it could take hours to pick up the mail and get kids to school. The shape of the island is long and narrow, and this has always affected social relationships and services. It has also increased isolation and created distinct social "pockets" or neighbourhoods. There is no central place with easy access to all, and a round trip from the north to the south end can be over thirty-two kilometres of travel. The arrival of the telephone, radio and automobile in the late 1920s reduced the seclusion and made things easier.

Along with the influx of people came a number of alien animals. Oblivious to the dangers, most were introduced deliberately to generate income. The first were the sheep, cattle and goats, which drastically changed the flora by overgrazing. Some, like foxes, nutria, lobsters and muskrats, never really took hold and vanished soon after their introduction. Others, including raccoons, mink, beaver, bullfrogs and rats, have caused unbelievable environmental damage and made the life of the farmer and homesteader miserable. Even today, new species will suddenly appear to remind us of how fragile an isolated island environment can be. They include the carrot rust fly, the clothes moth, the black slug, clubroot, the catfish and too many others to mention.

In contrast to the Golden Twenties, the thirties were a time of economic contraction. Still, the population continued to grow, surpassing three hundred by 1940. Hard times drew people together, and many preferred to weather them in a tight community rather than an anonymous city. The depression destroyed jobs—fish and timber prices plummeted—but the island was always able to feed itself. There were extensive clam beds, orchards, vegetable gardens, berries, fish, sheep and deer, so no one ever went hungry, but there was little left over for luxury, and the fare could get to be quite monotonous. Not surprisingly, the deer population crashed, and rustling became a problem.

Government assistance, which paid people to work on local projects, was a lifesaver that benefited the entire community. Many found this much preferable to being on the dole, with its overtones of failure and sloth. On Lasqueti the big work project was improving Main Road, which ran nineteen kilometres from False Bay in the north to Squitty Bay in the south. A few side roads like Centre Road and Gline Road were also expanded. In some places they were little more than rough wagon trails. As more and more applied for these limited positions the regulations became much stiffer. Single men were sent off to a relief camp to work on the mainland. Married men with ten dependants could put in nine days a month on the island road and receive twenty-seven dollars. The number of hours of work was based on the number of dependants. Each man was issued a wheelbarrow, rake and shovel, as almost all the work was done laboriously by hand. But in order to collect their paycheques, men had to declare themselves "indigent"—a humiliating adjective.

Women over twenty-one were in a particularly difficult position. They could not claim dependency on their parents, could not go to a relief camp, could not work on the road and could not ride the rails as hoboes. Government inspectors regularly arrived on the island to enforce the rules and interrogate recipients. Draconian, yes, but a wonderful road was created that serves our needs to the present day.

For those with a sense of adventure and daring, there were alternatives to government employment. Illicit production and sale of alcoholic beverages was highly profitable during both BC Prohibition (1917–1925) and American Prohibition (1920–1933). Every Gulf Island had at least one large still. In the late 1920s, Lasqueti's George Hadley built his famous Teapot House with two distinct chimneys—one shaped like a teapot and the other like a sugar bowl. Hadley was adept at brewing more than tea, but was careful to sell his product only to friends and trusted business partners. The man was a gifted inventor who never seemed able to turn a profit on his ideas, but he was able to produce a superlative grade of moonshine.

One late-November night there was a knock at Hadley's door. A bedraggled fisherman hauled himself in with a sad tale of a sunken boat and financial ruin. He had heard that George produced the best in the west, and just wanted one little bottle to help him through the loss. Hadley was apparently suspicious at first, but the story was convincing. He finally relented, and with good wishes parted with a bottle—a serious blunder. The next day the BC Provincial Police arrived in force. Hadley was arrested for selling to an undercover operative. His booze was confiscated and his large still dragged down to the dock and loaded on a barge for Nanaimo. Sentenced to six months at Oakalla Penitentiary, George never returned to Lasqueti Island.

Although the economic situation remained dire throughout the 1930s, there were slow signs of improvement. Wages improved, salmon runs began to pick up, Main Road was completed and island women went through a flurry of organizing—producing a Women's Auxiliary, a Women's Institute and the Golden Rule Club, which sponsored good works and enlivened the isolated social scene.

The outbreak of World War II drastically altered everything. Suddenly there was well-paid employment for anyone who wanted it. Thirty-two island men joined the military, twice as many as signed on during World War I. Women were enlisted to work in the factories and offices, taking on men's jobs. At home, the Golden Rule Club began to sew "shelter quilts" for use in Britain's bomb shelters.

After the shock of Pearl Harbor at the end of 1941, it seemed to many that a large-scale invasion of the sparsely populated areas of the West Coast was a certainty. When Japanese submarines shelled the Estevan Point lighthouse and Fort Stevens on the Columbia River in June 1942, the war suddenly seemed very close. Jittery observers spotted imaginary Japanese aircraft over Vancouver, Victoria and Lasqueti. Some claimed to see cryptic messages etched on mountainsides to aid in enemy bombing raids. Spies were mistakenly reported at every turn. Japanese immigrants (and their descendents, known as *Nisei*) who had lived for years on the coast were suddenly treated as an advanced guard for the invasion, and tens of thousands lost property and were deported to Japan or resettled as far east as Ontario. Island residents were told to block out their windows with blankets, stockpile food and prepare an escape route to the interior.

The Pacific Coast Militia Rangers (PCMR) was organized in 1942 as an irregular militia for coastal areas, and around twenty Lasqueti men enlisted.

All were either too old or too young for regular military service. Fresh-faced thirteen-year-old youngsters found themselves serving with grizzled veterans of South Africa's Boer War (1899–1902). Uniforms were rudimentary to save money and keep things simple. To encourage as many as possible to join, there was no age or health limit. As long as the commanding officer found you fit and capable of "ranger work," you were in.

There was also no regular pay unless the force was called into active service, and the men were issued hunting rifles, which became their own at the war's end. One Lasqueti ranger described the manoeuvres, or "schemes" as they were called, as a "hell of a lot of fun in the woods." And there was always the possibility of "a bit of meat for the pot" thrown in for good measure. Another assured me that large caches of Japanese invasion supplies still lie hidden on remote islands of our north coast. According to him, some even know where these tools of war lie hidden, still covered in grease and cobwebs. Paranoia reigned supreme, even though it later turned out the Japanese never intended to invade British Columbia.

Following the end of the war in 1945, rationing ended and the island prospered. A new wave of people arrived, and logging took off following the rising price of lumber. By the early 1950s there were fourteen operations using seventy vehicles on the island. The new road made transport infinitely easier, and the availability of modern equipment—chainsaws, logging trucks, Cats and yarders—opened up further opportunities. It was the most prosperous time in Lasqueti's history, but the boom was surprisingly brief.

By 1958, it was clear to all that Lasqueti's forests were just about played out, so Peter Forbes, Tom Millicheap and Treant Wamer pooled their resources to start the Lasqueti Fish Company. Their first boat, the *Lasqueti Fisher*, proved a resounding success, and several more boats were added to the business. The company remains one of Lasqueti's most successful enterprises.

But once the trees were gone, the profitable fishing industry was just not enough to sustain the population of the island. This set the stage for the great exodus, and within a few years most of the homesteads, gravel roads, orchards and farmers' fields were deserted.

It was almost as if a benign providence had deliberately set about clearing the slate in preparation for a whole new occupation—one with very different goals, values and view of the world than had ever been seen before on Lasqueti Island.

ISLAND NEIGHBOURHOODS

—Darlene

During the 1970s, Lasqueti had about a half-dozen or so distinctive "neighbourhoods" where newcomers lived in fairly close proximity to each other. They were pretty much determined by the geography of the land, available housing and, in some cases, the common origin of the settlers. Some of these neighbourhoods were occupied by actual landowners, and some were occupied by squatters or people in a rental agreement.

THE MUDFLATS

The Mudflats were home to wanderers, artists of all sorts, boatbuilders and sailors. People living on land or water in the Mudflats had life skills of a different type than inland people.

Starting at the island's north end, there were about five floathouses in the Cocktail Cove and Mudflats area, and a few live-aboard boats, bayside cabins and shacks as well. The Mudflats are a shallow bay that covers a large area out between Lasqueti and Wolf, Olsen and Higgins islands. When the tide was out, people would meet and dig for clams and oysters, visiting and catching up with neighbourly news while working. Travel and social interactions depended on the wind and the tides. Potluck dinners throughout the long winter months were a common way of exchanging news and staying in touch. Boat rides over to False Bay were shared, and people were free to borrow the resident truck that was kept there.

Marianna La Violette, in her essay "The Wind Tells Me So" (printed in the 2012 Arts Festival anthology), reminisces about her friend Lori Haukedal, who built a home called the Wolf House, and recalls her time spent living out on the Mudflats.

> The old Wolf House, on Wolf Island, was located between
> Higgins and Lasqueti. A short walk away when the tide was

Lori Haukedal's house on Wolf Island was a gathering place for making music. Photo Wendy Schneible.

out, or a short row away when weather permitted and the tide was right. In the summer, Wolf House was a swim across—just long enough for your skin to feel the water's coolness.

Great things happened at Wolf House. It was the gathering place for everyone at the north end of Lasqueti. There was a lot of drumming and clanging on pots, tin cans, or a pair of spoons, wood or metal. In those moments, everyone became musicians.

During the dark and dreary winter, some of us would partake in potlucks at each other's homes. This was our way of keeping contact throughout the winter, as none of us had telephones.

Mathilde Vilas also recalls life in the Mudflats in the early seventies:

On my arrival to this island, I felt that things would be alright. Once I was on the muddy trail that led to the hut and walking through salal as high as my head, I questioned my choice. Here was a shack with no electricity, no water. There was a bed on a wooden floor, and a bit of crude furniture. It was a shack on someone else's property, located across from Higgins Island, and it looked out toward Olsen Island.

Boatbuilders Alan and Sharri Farrell relax on the deck of their floathouse in Cocktail Cove. Tom Anderson Sr. is in the kayak. Photo Merrick Anderson.

I hauled water from a spring nearby. I had to carry it across the rocks in a bucket and I tried not to spill any ... Sea otters also drank from this hole and I had to scare them away. Then I would heat up some of this water on a small fire-pit nearby and have an outdoor shower with all of Vancouver Island looking on.

Our cook-stove in the cabin was an old oil drum with a door made into it, and I cooked on the top of it in a frying pan. I made chapatis and rice, mostly. I grew a small garden in a rock crevasse. I built up some soil by packing it full of seaweed and dirt that I had to haul from the forest. I grew mostly just greens to eat. I was thirty-two at that time, and I was retreating from the pace of my urban lifestyle.

I was doing freelancing audio interviews for CBC Radio at the time. I was paid between seventy-five and one hundred dollars per interview, which was great money to be making in those days. My interviews were used on CBC's *The Morning Show*. I interviewed David Slabotsky, Allen and Shari Farrell, Cynthia, Sabra and all of the interesting people that were around me living interesting lives out on the mudflats.

Laurence Fisher's vision of sharing his inherited land was the beginning of a 39-year-old model of successful co-op living. Photo Tom Wheeler.

Opposite: Kathy Fisher, fresh from L.A. in her new gumboots. Photo Tom Wheeler.

NORTH END: FISHERLAND

As you follow the shoreline close into False Bay, you reach one edge of Fisherland. This neighbourhood, officially known as Magic Mountain Land Co-op, extends north from there, almost to Scottie Bay, then goes south along Scottie Bay Road to the Teapot Intersection and covers some land around Pete's Lake. Fisherland covers nine hundred acres and provides Pete's Lake water to users north of the lake.

In 1971, young Laurence Fisher returned to the island after inheriting his father's portion of shares in a land company that owned a very large piece of property on the island's north end. After selling some of the land to pay off accrued tax debts, he decided to share the remaining nine hundred acres with friends. His early, simple vision of communally shared property eventually grew and developed over the following thirty-eight years into a model of a very successfully structured land co-op.

In those early years, the seventeen members of the co-op lived in handbuilt houses, small cabins and a few floathouses. One narrow dirt road went through the length of Fisherland, with small trails intersecting and criss-crossing throughout the forest. Down the trails were small homes where co-op members lived.

A sawmill, Mud Mills, was run by Laurence, Trey Carey and Gordon Bissett. They cut the cedar and fir planks that were used for many land co-op cabins, boatsheds and early buildings.

A woodworking shop, the Button Factory, employed a dozen or more people. The Button Factory started off as just that, a place that made wooden buttons from cedar, fir and arbutus limbs gathered from the Magic Mountain land co-op forests. As the years passed, the button factory grew into Wildwood Works, a much larger woodworking shop that now manufactures a variety of wood-based products.

At the Mud Mills, sawyers Grover Foreman, Gordon Bissett, and Laurence Fisher take a break for a photograph. Photo Merrick Anderson.

Laurence and Kathy Fisher spent many years in a tenthouse that overlooks a large pond and wetland area. They lived there along with their three daughters, Sarah, Meghan and Kate, and Laurence's mother, Judith Fisher. They kept goats and a donkey, and Kathy grew a big garden. Any extra income they had went into machinery and building and upgrading the factory, and it was years before they were able to build a "real house."

Entering Magic Mountain Road from Scottie Bay Road, there is a large cedar tree that was once called the "Telephone Tree." It had a BC Tel phone installed on one side of the trunk, and everyone in the co-op shared it. Quite a sight, on a dark and rainy winter night, to be walking down the Magic Mountain trail through the pitch-black forest and see a little headlamp and hear a conversation carried on the wind.

Like so many early co-ops, land groups and communes, the Fisherland members were one big family. Thanksgiving and Christmas were lively affairs—houses were packed with co-op members and their children, maybe a few relatives, fellow islanders and old friends from the city. The homes were cheery, candlelit havens warmed by old wood cookstoves. The mingled scents of baking meats, hot apple and plum pies, pungent homemade wines, wool coats and leather boots drying near the fires were carried throughout the wooden buildings and out into the frosty night air.

Fisherland children travelled the paths through the forest, slept out under the stars on summer nights, swam among the small islands out in Cocktail Cove, dug clams and picked oysters with their parents. On late nights after parties they were bundled up, put into wheelbarrows and wheeled home down the long dirt trail. Their seventies parents made a pact that, in the event of an earthly cataclysm, be it a tidal wave, global collapse or earthquake, they would all meet at the base of the big cedar tree so that they could all be together.

The big cedar tree still stands tall and healthy, and the Magic Mountain Land Co-op remains a large shared property with thirty-one members.

NORTH END TEAPOT HOUSE

The Teapot House land group settled all of the lower southwest corner of section 28. They were among the first of the newcomers to arrive on Lasqueti. Randy and Sue Taylor were living at Crescent Beach in 1969 but were looking for a more rural environment. The back-to-the-land movement was rapidly gaining steam and, like thousands of others, they were hoping to escape civilization and find a place in the country.

The couple was on Hornby Island for a recreational weekend retreat when they were advised to take a look at Lasqueti. Rumour had it that the

The Teapot House as it stood in 1970. Broken windows, crumbling chimneys and climbing blackberry vines were soon replaced, fixed and eradicated. Photo courtesy Merrick Anderson.

island was full of logged-off forest and abandoned farms, with a population of only about fifty—perfect for an island the size of Manhattan. The land would be cheap, and much of it was already cleared for farming. The couple took the evening ferry from French Creek and arrived in False Bay without proper shoes, clothing or a map. Their first act was to build a campfire on the beach near False Bay at one of the driest times of the year. Longtime resident Ian Laing came to warn them of the fire dangers, and remained to chat about land. He told them the old Teapot House might be for sale.

The property was a 160-acre quarter section with an old ramshackle mansion built by moonshiner George Hadley and his sons. He had been busted in a police undercover operation in the early 1930s, and after a stint in jail he had never returned. The building was badly in need of repair and was scheduled to be torn down, but the distictive shapes of the chimneys—a teapot and a sugar bowl—enchanted the visiting couple.

They immediately wrote a letter to property owner Lance Johnson asking if it was for sale. Surprised that anyone would want the property, Johnson replied that it could be had for twenty-eight thousand dollars. Randy and Sue set about the difficult task of finding like-minded partners. Eleven people were

"The Teapotters." L-R back row: Dennis McBride, Marci Lyon, Barbara McBride, Randy Taylor, Noel Taylor, Merrick Anderson and Ritchie Stewart. Foreground: Janet and Peter Lironi. Sue Taylor and John Cantrell are missing from photo, 1970. Photo Tom Anderson Sr.

eventually enlisted—Dennis and Barbara McBride, Merrick Anderson and Noel Taylor (Randy's sister), Ritchie Stewart, John Cantrell and Marci Lyon and Peter and Janet Lironi. Each of the six couples had to put up $4,600 and they received twenty-five acres, with the ten acres around the Teapot House itself to be held in common. The building was later completely restored and rebuilt and is now a heritage building. Shares were divided up in a novel fashion: lots were drawn on an aerial photograph and picked out of a hat, with the option of change or exchange if someone was unhappy with their piece. No one was.

For the first year or two all the partners lived together in relative harmony in the Teapot House, but after that everyone wanted their own place and soon moved out to their share, where most remain today.

Pigs and cows were purchased, fences were repaired and gardens planted, and the group settled back to enjoy life in the country. Word soon got out in the counterculture underground, and within a year large numbers of people began to arrive seeking their own little paradise on Lasqueti. The Teapot House generously extended hospitality to one and all, and in the summer, guests at dinner often totalled twenty-five or more.

The house had a big rock fireplace in the living room and a farmhouse-style kitchen. There were two bedrooms downstairs as well as a large, open room upstairs.

Ritchie Stewart in front of the Teapot House looking at the future, 1970. Photo courtesy Merrick Anderson.

One Teapotter recalls the first winter spent upstairs, after a few small bedrooms were walled in. When it became obvious that the winter wind blowing from the southeast could really suck the heat out of the old building, everyone hustled to put insulation in the exterior walls and ceiling in order to keep the heat in the house. One member flatly refused to insulate his room, saying he loved to look up at the underside of the old cedar shakes above him. The frigid winter air whistled right through his door and into the rest of the upstairs, chilling the whole upstairs right back down to zero. When January came, he and his wife flew to San Diego.

The house hosted many big holiday dinners, gatherings and parties. Often the guitars would come out, there'd be singing around the fireplace and the big Teapot hookah would be passed around. In summer, the whole house would be open, and parties spilled out onto the big front lawn and throughout the moonlit orchard.

The Teapot area goes roughly from the Teapot House on Main Road south to Pete's Lake (where it meets Crown land) and east, up the hills, toward the Texada side. Six original members still remain, and a few adult children—the new Teapotters—have homes and gardens up on "Teapotland."

Young Lazarus DiFiore and his uncle, Harold Macy, relaxing at Arnie's Corner, 1972. Photo Tom Anderson.

CENTRE ISLAND: ARNIE'S CORNER

Arnie's Corner, Doctor John's log house and the panabode made up the centre-island hippie cluster. There are a few small homes at the crossroads of Main and Lennie, and Arnie Porter lived in the first one nearest the road. Today we call it Jody's Corner, but in the seventies it was Arnie's Corner. Arnie's Corner has a big grassy orchard and an open field, and it was a fun party house. Arnie was originally from California, and some of his guests came from there, adding interesting travellers to the flow of people passing through the island.

> Dazy Drake recalls visiting Arnie on Lasqueti in the seventies:
>
> Zootie and I came up from California to see Arnie, whose sister was Zoot's ex-wife. We planned to stay only about a week, but the weather got so bad that the ferry didn't run for a few days, and somehow we ended up staying for about two weeks. It was so great and mellow, and we were amazed at how people just came by the place with homemade bread and home brew, played music and generally hung around to visit. Nothing like Marin County!

Bonnie Olesko recalls how once she came over to Arnie's house in the morning and found him standing at the side of his front room, laughing at a huge, shiny black stain that covered the floor. "Last night I tried to pour some molasses out of this bucket," he said, "and it wouldn't pour out—I think it was too cold—so I turned it upside down, put it over that bowl and I guess I forgot about it. God, when I woke up, I thought I was hallucinating!" He laughed.

During the night it had softened and proceeded to empty out completely. The floor looked like brand new blackish linoleum had been laid down. "When I walked in, he was standing there staring at this mess, just laughing away," she told me.

A bit farther down Lennie Road was the old Livingstone house. It was a small, pinkish-coloured wooden house surrounded by holly trees and wild plums. It had low ceilings, painted fibreboard walls and an old linoleum floor in the kitchen. Various tenants stayed there including Molly McKinna, Val and Indian Bob and Luella.

Near Arnie's Corner, and up what we now call Dump Road, was the old Lenfesty place, a big, rambling log house probably built in the thirties or forties. John Mitchell moved into the house after living in the panabode for a few months. "Doctor John," as he was known, hosted regular music jams sometimes, and the old house was full of people singing and playing guitars.

CENTRE ISLAND: THE PANABODE

I was part of the panabode group that lived in … what else? A panabode is a pre-fabricated wood house that was popular in the 1960s. The house was on Main Road.

Before we came to Lasqueti, we were all just hanging out in Kitsilano, looking for somewhere in BC that we could all go to and begin homesteading. One day in the late summer, a woman we knew named Norma ("Abnormal Norma") passed through the big old house where a few of us were living in Vancouver. She told us about a beautiful little island she'd stumbled onto not far from the city. She said that we should check it out, so we did, and somehow found the panabode. It was for rent for eight hundred dollars a year, and had three bedrooms, so it looked good to us. I made the sixth person living there when I arrived in February of 1971, moving in with Alan and Bonnie Olesko, Gordon and Annette Bissett and Ray Purcell.

Ginger Gilchrist, 1974. Photo Tom Anderson.

John Mitchell lived in the big old Lenfesty place, and Steve and Audrey MacDougall were building a cabin up at the Stump Farm. Tom Wheeler and Ginger Gilchrist had moved into a log cabin up the road, at the old Waymer place. I remember that our every move—both honest and otherwise—was seen by Shirley Mann and her large family, who lived right across the road. Shirley had great patience with us, letting us use her telephone for months until we got our own. She would even send her daughters over to let us know that someone had called for us.

The panabode group were pretty much all from Portland, Oregon, and eastern Washington. We were living under the radar with no visitor's permits. You didn't need a passport then.

We were resourceful and earnest about being in the back-to-the-land movement. We grew a garden out in the front yard in a raised bed made from logs. We got some chickens and tried unsuccessfully to raise a young wild goat. There were wild goat herds on the island then, as there still are on Jedediah Island. We washed our clothes in a cast iron bathtub that was propped up in the yard. It had a hand-wringer clamped to the side walls of the tub.

Tom Wheeler was thankfully rarely seen without his camera, 1974. Photo Tom Anderson.

Inside the panabode house it was dark, probably because the old interior walls were wooden and the site faced north. We lit candles and kerosene lamps in the evenings so it felt cozy. There was a tin heater in the kitchen area, and a propane stove. On those early dark winter nights we'd play guitars or just lie around and read. There was a small black and white television in the house, which we powered with a noisy Briggs & Stratton motor. We had a real love/hate relationship with it because no one could agree to the same program. One night when there was yet another disagreement going on over what to watch, one of the guys—probably Ray—unplugged it, took it outside and shot it dead.

Sometimes we'd go out to Conn Bay to dig for clams and gather oysters. In winter the low tides are usually very late at night, so these were walks down dark gravel roads, usually carrying the kids. We'd walk out onto the moonlit beach and scrape away the top layer of sand, then feel for the round Manila clams that lay just below the surface. Once our bucket was full, we'd go lower down the beach where the oysters lay and gather up a sackful of them.

Spring of 1972 came, and following the usual pattern of groups of young people living communally, we all decided to "go nuclear," finding places of our very own. The panabode slowly changed occupants. But since the rental arrangement at the panabode was year by year, we still had use of the house for months afterward and stayed there when we needed to.

THE STUMP FARM

In the sauna at the Stump Farm. L-R front row: Wendy Schneible, Lindsey Loch, Darlene Olesko, back row is Barry Kurland.

The Stump Farm group lived up Richardson Bay Road, adjacent to Lambert Lake and not far from the Douglas Farm. Initially purchased by Californians Steve Parent and Larry Myers, the Stump Farm had a large garden and a winding creek that ran down from Ogden Lake, and the Stumpers built a roomy sauna that was the place to be on Sunday afternoons. It had a clay-banked pond right outside the door, just perfect to jump into, rub yourself up with a handful of clay, submerge to get it off and then try to climb out and up the slippery clay bank. Sometimes called the "Hollywood Hippies," the first Stumpers included former Los Angeles

Art and Carol Huston building their cabin near Mt. Trematon. Photo Johnny Osland.

residents Larry Myers, Steve Parent, Kathy Fisher and Jamie Wellner. Kathy recalls that Larry Myers would get out of Los Angeles every summer and travel around, often to find new places on the West Coast. One summer, he phoned down to LA and told Kathy, "I've found Paradise!"

Through word of mouth, they were told to contact George Douglas, and so they travelled to Vancouver to see him about a large piece of property that he had on Centre Road. They found him there, mending his fish nets. Kathy, Steve and Larry had just sixteen thousand dollars between them, and they were exuberant when he accepted their offer. They shortly left Los Angeles and moved into a small wooden cabin on the Stump Farm.

Soon others came to live on the Stump too. Kathy said that living on the Stump Farm was a lot like going back to school: "I figured out how to make bread and beer, and we all got together and dug a big garden and got some chickens, pigs and even a horse."

There were two domes on the Stump Farm, a big old barn and several small outbuildings. The rich valley soil was a great gardening spot, and the old apple trees in the sloping orchard produced lots of fruit. Up from there was the Douglas Farm, and from there, the Trematon Mountain place, brief home of the "Three Dees" (Bingy Follinsbee, Marilyn Stamm and Emily Disher, so called after Tweedledum and Tweedledee, because, in the words of Bingy and Emily's teacher, "You girls look alike, act alike and you're together all the time") and Art and Carol Huston, and one or two other mountain cabins.

Southern brothers Karl and Peter Darwin moving logs. Photo Johnny Osland.

THE SOUTH END

Unlike many other parts of the island, the south end was largely made up of big parcels of land owned by Americans. In general, these absentee landowners were sympathetic to the young newcomers, perhaps because they rarely actually visited the island. What did they care who was living on their land when it was all going to be logged, subdivided or sold anyway? It also made sense to have someone around to keep an eye on things. These parcels included some of the richest farmland and most beautiful bays on Lasqueti.

The first of the new colonizers were refugees from big cities like New York and Los Angeles. What with visitors, water people and the many part-time homesteaders experimenting with the back-to-the-land life, the population of the under-thirties must have reached fifty during the summer months. It was an eclectic mix including American draft dodgers, professionals, revolutionaries and talented improvisers. No one worked a steady job, preferring to slave in the canneries, log savage or fish whenever the money ran low.

There were no serious attempts at communal or group living on the south end, and the population was much less dense than on the rest of the island. Tight couples seemed to make up most of the new back-to-the-landers. It was a squatter's paradise—no one owned land and hardly anyone paid rent. Everyone either built a shack or beach house out of driftwood, or simply moved into a dilapidated shack or abandoned farmhouse. Abundant plywood, shake bolts and milled lumber washed in after every storm, and one could build a durable home with a roll of plastic, a box of nails and a few simple hand tools. Many of these houses were built without permission, and some were constructed on Crown land. In some cases it took years before the landowner realized someone was living on his property. Of course these were not supposed to be forever homesteads; rather it was "be here now" and let come what may. For heat one bought a fifteen-dollar airtight, and for light a kerosene lamp. Electricity was frowned upon except for battery-powered radios, which all were addicted to.

The south end also hosted several long-term families who viewed the newcomers with a mixture of anticipation and skepticism. The Collins, Millers and Darwins had pretty much had the place to themselves for the decade since logging had ended. They were happy to have some new faces in the neighbourhood, especially during the long winter months, but they doubted the staying power of the longhairs. How could they stay if no one had a pot to piss in?

"You'll never last" was how John Collins sadly put it on several occasions. Yet the old-timers were invariably helpful and always ready to share a book or cup of tea. Curiously, most of these squatters later found a home on the island and remain here to this day.

EAST ISLAND: EAST ISLAND SHORELINE

The east-island "water people" lived on and near the southeast shore of Lasqueti, and on smaller islands just offshore. We lived on the ocean and we all got around on boats, for the most part. For those who lived on Bull Island and later on Boho Island, shopping, gas and propane were usually bought in Secret Cove on the Sunshine Coast.

Water people could usually tell who was coming by the sound of the boat engine. Rodger Ramjet had a stuttering Seagull engine that you could hear stopping and starting again several times before he came into view, "Boho Ron" Lawton had a smooth-running Mercury outboard and Ron Pearson had a cranky Briggs & Stratton that lurched a bit.

We all lived in funky beachcombed cabins or floathouses. When water neighbours came by to visit it was often an overnight, especially if the wind came up. Visitors just pulled out the sleeping bags and the bottle of navy rum and settled into those winter nights.

PART TWO:
BUILDING A
COMMUNITY ON LASQUETI

Opposite: Darlene Olesko and son Hoatie Macy, listening to the music jam at Dr. John Mitchell's log house. Photo Tom Wheeler.

THE COMMUNITY HALL BLUES

—Doug

The trouble all began in January 1972, when the newly formed Lasqueti Island Community Association applied for a Canada Fund for Local Initiatives grant of $28,400. The program was known locally as the Local Initiatives Program or LIP, and the money was to go toward the construction of a much-needed community hall for the island. The inspiration for the application had come from the crowd of young back-to-the-landers that had suddenly arrived on Lasqueti, seemingly by magic, just a few months before. It looked like a win-win situation. The federal government was begging for local participation in vitally needed community projects. People would be hired in an area of low employment, and cheap materials would be donated or purchased from local sources. When the job was completed, the workers would be further blessed by generous employment insurance and the knowledge that they had made an important contribution to their community.

Work at the site began in February, but the effort was soon bedeviled by disorganization coupled with an extremely harsh winter. By June, the project was flat out of money, and shockingly little had been accomplished. The site was littered with a disorderly pile of peeled logs, assorted hardware, twenty-two soaked bags of mortar mix and several gigantic foundation pads more suited to the Parthenon than an island community hall. Eight hundred dollars had been spent on logs, two hundred on gasoline, several hundred on concrete blocks and most of the rest on wages for the two dozen workers. What had gone wrong?

The wretched weather during the winter of 1972 had certainly made things harder, but there were also organizational problems. Communication was difficult, with few cars and even fewer phones on the island. Just getting everyone on site on time presented a real problem. The project lacked a trusted foreman and chain of command. These kids were mostly city folk in their early twenties who knew next to nothing about construction. Plans changed with the moment, and working hours were ill defined, to say the least.

In short, the project reflected both the negative and positive sides of the so-called counterculture. Anarchy and disorganization ran parallel with idealism and a generous desire to improve the quality of life for all. Talking today with those workers, who are now in their sixties, it is clear that the project was not entirely a scam. While some wanted to "stick it to the man" to get all they could, everyone genuinely hoped that a hall would somehow be completed. The island really needed some kind of central building for community activities and projects. As

"Work Bee" poster made by Johnny Osland.

time passed, those hopes faded, but everyone kept working.

News of the growing fiasco sent the hippie-hating *Parksville–Qualicum Beach Progress* into raptures of delight, and they soon took the lead in exposing the waste, lack of accountability and general incompetence demonstrated during

Lack of organization, bad weather, and poor access to machinery delayed the project until the late 70s when volunteer labour and local donations finally completed the community hall.

A group of workers at the community hall.

the project. The paper launched an investigation, complaining about the lack of a central architectural plan and work foreman, and employment insurance irregularities. Particularly galling was the statement that "all involved were strongly opposed to the idea of disciplined work." The paper drew particular attention to Americans allegedly working without papers, "ghost" employees collecting employment insurance and lackadaisical working hours.

Not content to vilify the project, the *Progress* actively tried to draw the police and immigration authorities into the investigation. It grandly accused island workers of "a conspiracy to defraud the Unemployment Insurance Commission (UIC)" and contacted George Bevis, the regional overseer of the LIP projects, who agreed and expressed profound disgust. The paper also called on the Department of Manpower and Immigration to deport the illegal American workers. The UIC seized the project's books, and talk radio throughout the province trumpeted the debacle as yet another criminal scam to bilk BC's downtrodden taxpayers. Eventually twenty-six islanders were disqualified from receiving employment insurance for the job. There were no further charges or deportations.

On the island, the project received mixed reviews. Many were embarrassed by the fiasco, and some were blatantly hostile. One anonymous letter to the *Progress* described the workers as "parasites without a conscience," and continued, "Don't let the government hush this up and let it die. You've opened up a can of worms. Now don't settle for anything less than the facts on where this money went or who approved it. I, for one, as a taxpayer, want to know." Other old-time residents were less averse. Workers on the project had set up a transparent shower easily visible from the road, and visitors always seemed to time their visits to coincide with the ladies' afternoon shower break. Even taxi driver Shirley Mann, no friend of the project, was heard to remark that with all that showering those hippies were certainly not "dirty."

The Lasqueti Community Association fought back in a tart letter to the editor entitled "Where is the Cesspool?" It pointed out that much of the information provided to the paper was nothing more than malicious gossip. There were no undocumented Americans working on the project except as volunteers, and terrible weather and marginal transportation made keeping regular hours impossible. "Are we criminals for trying and half-succeeding in a project that was a little too ambitious to begin with? Are we criminals because we did a lot of work by hand that should have been done by machines? For building a road, clearing land, digging three seventy-foot-long trenches four feet wide and four feet deep with accompanying drainage ditches and filling them by hand in rain and snow with stone when all this could have been done for less with a backhoe, a front-end loader and a dumptruck?"

In all fairness, most agree that the money allocated was never adequate for the job—since all of the work was done by hand and that included site clearing, road building and drainage—or for the cost of the materials. There was no way such an ambitious project could be completed for a paltry $28,400. It had always been hoped that further grants and volunteer labour would be forthcoming once the project was under way.

But the story obviously does not end here. Today that same infamous community centre stands tall, providing a central nexus for community life. In a monumental effort involving the entire island, the hall was salvaged and rebuilt with cash donations, volunteer labour and a few small grants in the late 1970s. This time there was no disorganization. Many of the skills so lacking in 1972 were part of a well-oiled routine by 1978. Under the inspired leadership of Dana Darwin, the hall was finally brought to completion and a black mark on the community was erased forever. Considering what we have today, that original grant money was certainly not wasted.

TINY CABINS, AND PLASTIC SHACKS

—*Darlene*

In the 1970s, many new residents of Lasqueti were faced with the challenge of somehow slapping together a place to live: a shack, a cabin or a cozy dwelling that would keep us safe, warm and dry. Few of us had the money to actually purchase the land that we built on, but whatever arrangement we were operating under, rental, shared land or squatting, we had to build our dream castles. Starry-eyed youngsters that we were, we managed to create our first houses with great imagination, salvaged materials, lots of hard work, very little money and usually just a few tools. Swede saws, hatchets, some plastic and a box of framing nails were about all that some of us had arrived with. A working chainsaw was a treasure, and much of the finishing carpentry in the place that I built with my partner, Ray, was done with one.

My first seventies home was not on Lasqueti Island proper but on adjacent Bull Island. Ray and I got permission to live in a small squatter's shack in 1972. It was about 3.7 m by 2.4 m and made from rough beachcombed cedar. It was not insulated, just two-by-four framing with boards slapped on the outside and a shake roof. "Cozy" is an understatement. There was a small wood cookstove inside and a ladder that went up to a sleeping loft. It was totally rustic and basic. There was a small bed against the back wall of the loft where my son, Hoatie, slept, and baby Mopsy slept with her dad and me.

The ceiling was just black tarpaper on rafters, covered with cedar shakes. I'd lie in our bed up in the loft and stare at that tarpaper ceiling. Later, when a young visitor placed a lit candle too near the ceiling, the shack went up in flames. Thankfully, no one was hurt in that fire; the kids went outside and the place burned to the ground.

We had been in that little shack for six months, during the spring and summer, and now we needed a new place to live. We acquired a US Army

Tony and Dede Seaman at their floathouse in Cocktail Cove, 1976. Photo Howie Siegel.

tent, five metres by five metres, as a temporary living space until we figured out what to do next. There was a smashed-up old bunkhouse down in the bay, left over from a hand-logging operation, so we held a work party later that summer and invited all our friends. We had everything necessary for a good demolition party: a batch of homebrew, some dynamite, some red snapper and codfish and lots of weed. Our friends on the water came, as well as lots of Lasqueti people, and we spent four days blowing up the old bunkhouse, passing the reusable timbers and planks in a chain up the trail to the top, building a tent platform and cleaning up the burned-down shack. At day's end, the guitars came out, music would be played as food was cooked over a beach fire and we ate, drank and danced until it got dark. When it was over, we had a nice, solid floor for the army tent.

We lived in that tent for the winter and the following spring and summer. Inside we had our bed, two small beds for the kids, a driftwood table and a tin heater. Our clothes and books were stored in wooden boxes under the beds. A Grundig shortwave radio was our prize possession. With it, we could tune in stations from all over, and we often lay in bed at night listening to music from Seattle, California and Montreal. Once, during a howling southeast storm, "Riders on the Storm" came on the airwaves and I cranked it up as loud as it would go and just danced on the bluffs overlooking the raging ocean.

The army tent had no light inside whatsoever, so one day I cut out a ten-by-ten-inch square in the heavy green canvas and stitched in a clear vinyl square.

I finally had a window! And light! That small beam of daylight totally lifted my spirits, enough to get me through until summer when we lived outdoors nearly all of the time.

When summer was over, we passed that big army tent along to someone else who needed it and moved along to our uptown caretaking cabin on Boho Island.

Marc Hirsch told me of his first home, a place that he resurrected in 1973:

> Ron Lawton and I crossed paths one day, and he told me about a place that I could probably fix up and live in if I wanted to. He and I walked along through the woods down by Sandy Cove, and he showed me the remains of a sturdy log cabin. It was about eight by twelve feet [2.4 m by 3.7 m], with a dirt floor. There was no door and no window on the side of the cabin that faced the sea. It was cramped and dark, but I saw the possibilities.
>
> "You can do this," Ron told me. "You'll have to put down a floor and cut a window into the ocean side. The cabin's small, but you could knock out the triangle under the end of the roof, extend it out and make yourself a sleeping loft ..."
>
> Ron had some leftover six-inch [fifteen-centimetre] tongue-in-groove cedar siding of various lengths and a few bundles of cedar shakes that he said I could have. I got tarpaper for under the floor, under the extended sleeping loft, and under the roof that I had to build over the loft. Ron had stashed two large multi-paned windows, which were perfect for the window in the main cabin and for the side of the loft that looked out onto the Sabine Channel. Ron and I travelled in his rowboat to collect the cedar boards and shakes. He had a small outboard motor on the back. Fully loaded, only surface tension kept the sea from flowing in over the gunwales and swamping us. We moved very slowly through the water.
>
> Ron showed me how to shim each log so that when I cut the window, the cabin would not collapse. I put in the floor, extended the sleeping loft and supported it with two large driftwood logs. The cedar board scraps were used to rebuild the floor, and I used the cedar shakes for the roof. I was very excited to be undertaking such an ambitious project for the first time in my life.
>
> When it was done it was a thing of beauty. It smelled like cedar, and it all looked clean and bright and new. It was a tight

cabin; I stuffed pieces of old clothing in between the logs to keep the wind out and the heat in during the winter. Before that first winter, I went to Vancouver and bought a tin wood-burning stove. It had a firebox, an oven and four removable lids. I baked bread and made granola in it once a week. I jigged for cod from Ron's rowboat, and if I caught nothing I harvested oysters with a hammer and screwdriver or dug for

A true pirate/philosopher, Boho Ron was happiest when he was out on the ocean in his boat, the *Maritimus*. Clever and inventive, he was a helpful and generous neighbour.

clams. I fried everything in a cast iron pan. Drinking water came from a stream, and I hauled in jugs of kerosene for my lamps.

Eventually it was time for me to return to the United States. I was in the Bronx, New York City, visiting my parents, when I received a letter from Ron and his girlfriend, Ida, that my cabin had burned to the ground. A visitor who was staying in the cabin had left the door of the stove's firebox open. Fortunately he was not injured, but we were all very sad about it.

I remembered someone once explaining to me the reason a groom stamps on and breaks the wine glass after he and the bride drink out of it in a Jewish wedding ceremony. The person said it was to remind the couple that joy must always be tempered by sorrow. I thought that sentiment fit the destruction of the cabin that had brought me so much pleasure.

Dianne Bump recalled the house that she and John built:

Our first home was 12 x 12 feet (3.7 x 3.7 metres) with a loft. The first winter the house wasn't really finished—just two walls were insulated. John was off fishing and my son, Shane, and I started chinking the walls and floorboards with moss and some of his old diapers. It being such a small cabin, the wood

John Bump in the old south end orchard, 1973. Photo Tom Wheeler.

cookstove heated it up pretty fast in the mornings, but when we first got up, the water in the five-gallon bucket would be frozen. I made a rug out of different coloured squares of carpet samples and little by little the little house took shape.

Over the next couple of years things got easier and easier as we carved our little homestead out of the woods. By now I had a wringer washer and had given up scrubbing clothes on the old washboard. I learned how to tan deer hides and got a treadle sewing machine. I canned salmon and sometimes we smoked oysters—that is, until the day the whole smokehouse burned down. We got a couple of pigs, but they were pretty smart and kept getting out of the pen because they knew that we would offer them food to get them back into the pen. We played that game for quite a while until we found the tunnel they had dug. We had chickens and fresh eggs, and now we had bacon!

When I got pregnant with my daughter, Julia, I insisted on a larger house, so we got an Alaskan mill and started working on that. John was a bit leery of heights, but I wasn't, so I got up on the roof and nailed the shakes in, measuring the ones around the dormers and tossing them down to John, who would cut them and toss them back up to me. The house was finished before winter and we threw a big party, mainly so people could dance on the sand we had thrown on the floor. Our rough fir floorboards got well polished that night.

LEGION NIGHTS

—Darlene

The present-day Lasqueti Island Arts Centre, with its grassy lawn and surrounding forest, provides a perfect place for the lively summer Saturday market, the new kids' playpark and the summertime arts picnic. The building is in False Bay, on two acres of land belonging to the Powell River Regional District and therefore to the people of Lasqueti Island. But in the 1970s, this very spot was occupied by a different building altogether. This was the site of Lasqueti Branch 166 of the Royal Canadian Legion.

On a typical night at the Legion we would throw together a band and jam. We felt pretty professional on this Halloween night. L-R: Grover Foreman, Ross Hughes and Bonnie Olesko at mic, Steve MacDougall, Sam Marlatt, Zoot (Jim) Drake on bass, 1975. Photo Darlene Olesko.

It was open on the last Saturday night of each month. You entered the hall into a coatroom, then turned left into the main room, where one side consisted of tables and chairs all set up for the bingo games. Ultra-bright electric lighting came from the overhead lights, which were powered by a diesel generator that throbbed from the forest beyond the parking lot.

Ian Cole, the ferry captain, always brought a big pot of chili to share, and the delicious smell wafted in the air. The bar was a little room with a small square opening where you ordered your beer. Beer was a stubby brown glass bottle of Old Style, and it cost fifty cents. The Legion members took turns bartending. Island men in their forties, fifties and beyond, they

Rosa Shumack was a familar face at the Legion Hall bingo game.

Opposite: Merrick Anderson grooving to the crowd at the Legion Hall (note the twig mic stand).

were especially friendly with the young hippie girls. They'd make jokes and tease us as we slid the two quarters across the plywood counter.

The old-timers would play bingo with bingo cards splayed out in one hand and a drink in the other and maybe a cigarette smouldering away in the ashtray. Rosa Shumack would have about five or six bingo cards fanned out on the table, as well as a few in her hand.

"On the B! Eleven on the B!" a big voice would shout out. Round discs would slide over numbers; people would mutter to each other and lean one way or another, trying to see how their neighbours were doing.

On the other side of the room, young people would be setting up to play music. At first, the newcomers were allowed to play music only when the bingo game was over, and after that, a few favourite dance records were played. Then we set up our guitars and our funky little amps, if we had any. Microphones were those little tape-recorder mics, wrapped with electrical tape onto a branch that was set into a stable steel plate, or whatever worked. We shared them, two or three to a mic.

There was a small room, like a kind of kind of closet, at the rear of the hall. If we brought our kids along, and we usually did, we'd sit in there with them, maybe tune our guitars or just play games with them, and then snuggle them into coats and blankets when they fell asleep. Then we'd leave the door open just a crack and go out and have fun. Our throw-together bands had a few singers, a few guitar players, one bass player and a drummer. The drummer had a small, basic set with a very tinny sound, which sounded great to our ears. We played songs like "Hotel California," "Up on Cripple Creek," "Lively Up Yourself" and "Satisfaction," which are many of the same songs we play today at jams.

We'd drink as much of the fifty-cent beer as we could afford and play and dance until about ten or eleven. The mood in the Legion Hall was relaxed and friendly, but there were a few incidents that I can recall. One time, Terry Beck was having a heated argument with Keray Farrell and it came to blows over in the corner. Terry's mother, Ruby Nichols, was standing over the fighters, shrieking, "Kill him, Terry! Kill the son of a bitch!" All of us peace-loving hippies stood by in shock at this violent display, but no one killed anyone.

Another time, Bill Harrison walked into the room, looked around and said in a loud voice, "We're gonna get the RCMP in here and clean this whole place up," directing his baleful glare at us newcomers. But it was all bluster, and everyone got right back to the business of bingo and beer. The place never did get "cleaned up," much to our appreciation.

We continued to enjoy those Legion Saturday nights for several more years, until the Legion was burned to the ground in 1979 by a troubled young local man. He also set fire to the little woodworking building in Mud Bay known as the Scottie Shack, and then made an unsuccessful attempt to burn down the church across the road as well.

The land there became a kind of salvage yard, filled up with old junk cars and trash. That was all cleared out in the nineties, and it sat empty for a while until the island's new regional director, Merrick Anderson, suggested that it be the new home for the arts council building.

Today, only memories of those old Saturday nights at the Legion remain.

SANITATION ETIQUETTE

—Doug

The new-age arrivals to Lasqueti were very comfortable with nudity and frank about bodily functions. Flush toilets were almost non-existent on the island, and outhouses were smelly, filthy, unpleasant places to visit. The situation cried out for creative solutions.

In my first week on Lasqueti in the early seventies I attended a wedding party in beautiful surroundings. The sun was out; everyone was dressed up in their finest; people were drinking green beer, passing joints around and handing out "the sacrament" (LSD). Suddenly, a half-dozen young women dropped their glamorous drawers in unison, squatted down and peed. At first it was a little unclear what was happening—until they artfully pitched their wads of toilet paper into a nearby bonfire.

I confess to having been completely unprepared for public female urination en masse—this is not how they did it at the Quaker college I had attended in Indiana. Should I be titillated or offended?

Actually it turned out to be neither, as this was such a common and unremarkable occurrence for both men and women that it soon ceased to register at all. In fact, it became a pleasant and relaxing way to relate during the pause that refreshes, almost a way of establishing a kind of tribal trust between the sexes—and a way of horrifying the straighter onlookers. It also played on the equality issue. Why should the men have the sole privilege of easy release by turning their backs to piss, while women have to hide themselves in the woods for the same process?

In fact, urine was regarded as a kind of miraculous and precious unguent. We believed it was harmlessly sterile unless someone had a nasty disease. It had been used for millennia as a tonic, skin conditioner and cure-all in many parts of the world. Later on I watched as people drank their own piss claiming wondrous cures for allergies and AIDS and the promotion of general good health. If you did not want to use it for medicinal purposes there was always

HOW TO SHYTE ON LASQUETI

by Douglas Hamilton

The cover of a pamphlet that budding author Douglas L. Hamilton wrote to help Lasquetians develop better sanitation practices. Published by Gut-Ache Press, 1994.

the garden. Urine is very high in nitrogen and has been used as a cheap and easily available fertilizer since time immemorial. Indeed, it is so strong it must be diluted at least by half, or the plants will be burned by the nitrogen. The only problem is the smell, and that can be almost eliminated by making sure to vary the site of the deposit. In other words, never piss in the same place twice.

The problem of what to do with our shit presented a completely different set of problems. The island had (and still has) no public water system, sewer outlets, holding tanks or processing stations, and only had a handful of composting toilets. There were a few septic fields, but if you lived on a rock bluff or swamp a septic system could not be installed, so the annual pump-out was usually just dumped in a nearby field. How sanitary is that? Of course, being squatters we had no money or desire for septic fields in those days, anyway.

I quickly learned first-hand the dangers of dirty water. My partner and I considered ourselves blessed to have found a lovely, isolated beach on the south end of the island. Our nearest neighbour was over a mile away. Two pristine, crystal-clear streams provided ample and delicious water for most of the year. We blissed out in our little paradise for a couple of years, but it soon became apparent that something was not quite right. Nausea, bloating, headaches, gut aches and general malaise gradually intruded into our lives. For me it became a regular twenty-two-day cycle, much like a menstrual period, running on for years at a time. I would automatically know the time of the month by the state of my gurgling gut.

In those hippy-dippy days, the conventional wisdom dictated that such problems were caused by a personal deficiency in attitude. Mellow out and the problem would soon take care of itself. But a question arose: why were we both sick with the same thing at the same time? Finally, some genius suggested we test our beautiful water, and the results were interesting. It was so highly contaminated with coliform that we were told it was not even safe for washing dishes. The truth struck us like a lightning bolt. We had been drinking a rich brew of sheep-manure tea for years.

This was confirmed by looking carefully at the watershed that fed our two streams. Both originated in wet areas that provided excellent pasture in the dry of summer. During winter, the whole area flooded, releasing millions of parasitic ova into our drinking supply.

To remedy the situation we both started to boil our now-questionable water, but that made no difference. Dozens of stool samples made their way to the labs on Vancouver Island, but nothing showed up in them. Several perplexed doctors shook their heads sympathetically and talked soothingly of the heartbreak of hypochondria. Or maybe it was just a touch of stomach cancer? Finally, on a whim, I made my way to the tropical disease clinic at Vancouver General Hospital, which specialized in exotic diseases.

They quickly isolated the eggs of a parasitic worm called *Trichostrongylus* in both of us. This organism is rarely found in humans in North America but is a problem in Iran, Iraq, North Africa and other countries running herds of unmanaged cows, sheep and goats. The affliction was so unusual in Canada that for a while it looked like we might be celebrated at medical conventions and put on display. Drugs were available for cases of extreme illness, but because of toxic side effects were considered a last resort. We were told that the best thing to do was to change our water supply completely and wait it out for six months to a year. Avoid reinfection and give the little buggers time to work their way through the system. We did as suggested, and things slowly got better.

To say that this was a wake-up call is a gross understatement.

It suddenly became obvious just how dangerous raw fecal matter actually was. This amalgam of bacteria, viruses and parasites could not be trifled with. It must be carefully contained and treated. Simply put, what has recently passed from a person's (or animal's) rectum must never find its way back into someone's mouth. We learned too that the unusual bug that plagued us was only one among many—giardia, *Cryptosporidium*, hepatitis B, salmonella and a multitude of others unnamed also had to be contended with.

Although water quality issues had existed on Lasqueti since earliest settlement, the new back-to-the-land element had to relearn the lesson the hard way. It was apparent that my partner and I were not alone in our misery, for almost all of our comrades insisted on drinking unboiled "natural" water from streams and lakes as a matter of ideological pride. And almost everyone had stomach problems.

The worst methods for dealing with human waste were immediately abandoned. No longer did we bury little deposits of poo around the garden as if they were some kind of harmless soil conditioner. Using the ocean as a crapper was also no longer acceptable since Vancouver Island and the mainland already dumped vast amounts of sewage into the Georgia Strait. The solution lay in composting.

Composting your own wastes at home is illegal in North America (except in approved, usually massive and costly composting toilets). Certainly this writer would never dream of encouraging anyone to break the law. But for the low-budget homesteader with a house on a rock bluff or swamp, composting is far superior to outhouses and septic fields, especially on an island like Lasqueti, which has no pump-out facilities. We used a composter that was waterproof, leak free and protected from the rain, and added copious quantities of organic matter—sawdust, spoiled hay, grass clippings, peat, leaves, sawdust, etc.—after each use.

It is amazing how one's health and quality of life can be improved by good sanitation. In North America such things are usually well taken care of—and for good reason. Of all the lessons learned by Lasqueti's alternative community this was one of the most important.

PARKSVILLE IN THE 1970s

—Darlene

Parksville, the closest town to Lasqueti, was referred to as "town," "the little smoke," "the other side," "Parksburg" and even "Peaville." For some, a trip to the other side was necessary once every two or three weeks, but some of us could get away with only going once every six or eight months. After all, didn't we come to the island to get away from noise, traffic, concrete and consumerism?

People would go to Parksville for all kinds of reasons: the fresh food was long gone, the rum was running low, building projects were on hold because of a lack of nails or tarpaper or maybe someone had a toothache or earache that needed to be looked at.

Parksville is about a one-hour ferry ride from Lasqueti's False Bay, depending on the weather. To make it to the eight o'clock ferry to Parksville

You could buy just about anything at Stedmans, which opened in 1973 on Port Alberni Highway. Photo courtesy Parksville Archives.

False Bay Dock, with the *Captain Vancouver* ferry. Cedric Hawkshaw and Dianne Bump, 1970. Photo Johnny Osland.

meant—and still means— getting up from a cozy bed sometime after six, leaving your house by seven twenty if you lived north of the community hall and getting all your stuff and/or kids onto the dock and in the boat by about seven forty-five. In the winter darkness and rain this required forethought, pre-packing and planning.

If you were lucky enough to own a rattly old truck or car, you would make sure the night before that it had some gas in it, the battery was good and none of the tires were flat so you could take right off in the morning. You often had to walk long trails through the forest to get up to the Main Road and to your car, or to where you could thumb a ride.

In the seventies, hitchhiking to the ferry was a common practice, but often cars and trucks full up to the windows with other riders had to drive right past you. It was a toss-up whether to keep walking down the road in hopes of a ride at another intersection or to just stay put so you could go back home when it felt hopeless.

But if all went well, you were on the *Captain Vancouver* by eight o'clock, heading southwest across the Strait of Georgia toward French Creek. The crossing on the old steel-hulled boat could be calm and pleasant or terrifyingly rough and wet. You didn't care, you just wanted to go to town. The morning boat was lively, like a party, with everyone happy to be on board and talking away. Young women greeted each other with hugs and happily examined each

French Creek Harbour with the Lasqueti ferry, *Captain Vancouver*, 1970.

other's babies, grateful for this chance to visit each other. Young, bearded men carried on boxes and maybe a piece of broken machinery or a tool that was going over for repair.

Middle-aged people and a few older folks would be on board, some dressed quite nicely, and there might even be a man in a suit and tie. They would sit in a cluster on one side of the cabin, sharing their own news and gossip. Some women would take off their gumboots and put on the clean city shoes they'd brought along. Boxes and folded shopping bags were shoved and stacked in the front compartment of the steel-hulled boat.

The *Captain Vancouver* would slow down as she entered French Creek Harbour. When the ferry reached the wooden dock, the first mate would leap onto the dock and tie the boat up. Everyone waited to get off, and many made plans to meet for breakfast somewhere. You might hear things like:

"Wanna meet us at the Swing Inn?"

"Yeah, but first I have to go to the bank."

"Anyone got room for me? Just into town?"

"Sure, but I might have to jumpstart my car."

In French Creek, you'd locate your vehicle somewhere in the gravelled parking lot. Hopefully, the battery was okay and it would start. You'd hop in, then head left up Lee Road and onto the Island Highway.

Parksville in the 1970s was the same little oceanside town that it is today, but much smaller and more compact. The Island Highway, as it headed north, returned quickly to forest, small farms and a few little houses as soon as you passed the Temple Market. The biggest store after that was the K&R. Next to the K&R was an old farmhouse with a rickety barn and some outbuildings. It was quite beautiful despite its age and rundown state. It had straight fir wainscoting on the walls and a big, beautiful fireplace built of round river rocks. The farmhouse was a crash pad, a place to stay overnight if the ferry didn't run or if you missed the last one.

Your first stop was often to a bank to get some money out. Anyone with broken tools would take them to the M&M Sales and Service on the Island Highway. Getting that broken-down chainsaw or that seized-up pump out of the car and into their shop was priority so it could be ready by the afternoon.

The fellows at Falcon Lumber were good to Lasquetians, and they had everything you'd need for building: lumber, hardware, tools. And if we were a bit short on money for a purchase, they'd say, "Ah, just bring in the twenty bucks next time you're over."

The Swing Inn was a popular restaurant at the time. The waitresses were pretty old and a bit grumpy, but David Stanhope introduced me to their sardine sandwich and I was hooked. It came on whole wheat toast with onions and was all mayonnaised up inside. I'd have that with a glass of tomato juice and a coffee and I'd be set for hours.

Rennie's Ideal Bakery sold the usual baked goods and quick lunches. If you needed to use the bathroom, you had to go through the kitchen and walk past the big dough-mixing machines and stacked trays of buns, bread pies and sausage rolls. It was the place where the Parksville police all hung out, too, and I had some friends who wouldn't step inside because of that. There was always at least one cop inside having a coffee and a doughnut.

In town, there was Robertson's Food Master, the Red and White grocery store and the Overwaitea right downtown along the highway. The green linoleum floor of the Overwaitea slanted downwards, so when you checked out your groceries, you could ride your cart away, and if you turned hard enough to the right, you could make a clean exit out the door. Usually the cashier would laugh and hold the door open for you. If not, an equally crazy friend would.

The Island Hall Hotel and the Rod and Gun Hotel were about the only places to stay that were located right in town. The Ace Motel on the highway was your option if you were really low on money. It had the worst beds in the world and was damp and old. The TVs hardly worked and sometimes the funky wiring connections were exposed. The Englishman River Court at the south end of the highway wasn't too bad, but it felt far from any action—and spending the night in town usually meant looking for a little action.

The Rod and Gun had two entrances: one for "Gentlemen" and one for "Ladies and Escorts." Sometimes we'd set the kids at a table in the Chinese cafe next to the bar, order them some french fries and then go have a beer. Beer was twenty-five cents and came in a glass that had a white ring at the top so you could see you'd gotten a full glass. The place was dark and stank like ashtrays, old men and stale beer, but you could down a couple of quick ones before making the ferry.

If you needed a new kerosene lamp, some wick, sandpaper or even a tin heater, Noden's Hardware had it. Thelma Farrell ran the place and she always had another woman working with her in the store. You could get just about anything there, and if they didn't have what you needed, they would try to find out where in town you could get it.

Another great place was Logan's Sheet Metal to the south of town. Mr. Logan had his shop adjacent to his house, and you could go in there and have almost anything fabricated. He had lots of tools and sheets of all grades of metal. In his shop display window he had a sheet-metal sculpture of a three-piece band playing instruments, all tin-man-type creations. The kids loved it.

At the Pharmasave there was an old-style lunch counter in the back that had sandwiches, drinks and a few simple hot meals on the menu. Along with Aspirin, you could buy obscure stuff in bulk there too, like lanolin and sodium perborate. They even had leeches, but you had to order them first.

I never had the money to buy anything from Mickey's Ladies' Wear, or from Gene's Apparel, but it was fun to go into those stores and look around. They carried fashions for women, mostly dress-up clothes, sports outfits, accessories, scarves and hats. Mickey herself looked like a movie star. She was a good-looking blonde businesswoman and was easy to spot walking around town.

Chris's Coiffures and the Lady Carol Salon had faded pictures of fashionable women with bouffant hairstyles displayed in their windows. Looking inside, there were women buzzing about in fancy aprons as they snipped, dyed, curled and styled the hair of their clients. I recall my own small kids, Hoatie and Mopsy, being both frightened and curious at the sight of women sitting under those big, shiny, round hair dryers. These places were busy, but they offered services that I no longer needed. We Lasqueti women were all just letting our freak flags fly.

Garner's Natural Health Supply was the place to get smaller amounts of beans and grains, but mostly we shopped there for the herbs that were displayed in big glass gallon jars on shelves that ran along the inside walls.

CHINESE SMORGASBORD

SUNDAYS, 12 noon to 8 p.m. Chinese Food only.

EAT ALL YOU WANT!

Adults $2.10 – Children (under 12 years) $1.50

CLOSED MONDAYS

TUESDAY to THURSDAY – 8:30 A.M. to 11:00 P.M.

FRIDAY and SATURDAY – 8:30 A.M. to 1:30 A.M.

TAKE OUT ORDERS, Hamburgers - Fish & Chips - Ice Cream
Newspapers - Cigars, etc.

Large Menu of Canadian Meals and Specializing
in AUTHENTIC CHINESE FOODS.

SPECIAL DINNER MENU.

HOLIDAY CAFE

Phone 248-6734

The Holiday Cafe on the Island Highway had questionable food but was always open. Courtesy Parksville Archives.

They carried free-run eggs, homemade breads, some organic vegetables and baking supplies, and I remember the store smelling like mint and cinnamon. Joe and Irene Garner ran the store all throughout the 1970s, and it was always busy whenever I stepped inside.

The SOS Thrift Shop was on the second floor of a strangely built triangular building. The Society of Organized Services is a charitable organization that blankets several community-based groups: Meals on Wheels and Time Out for Tots and Moms (now Time in Comfort for Tots and Caregivers) are just two. In 1973, after our shack on Bull Island burned down, we went to the SOS and they gave us vouchers for anything in the store that we needed, as well as food vouchers that were good at any local grocery store.

Grennan's Records was right downtown, and a great place to hang out and look through albums and cassette tapes. It was my way of staying on top of what was going on in the music world, as well as having tapes mailed to me from friends down in the US.

Along the Alberni Highway was Jack Noel's Menswear, with dapper-looking male mannequins in the front window. Jack himself was always well turned out in a smart suit and bow tie. He would wrap your purchase in brown paper, then tie it up with string that was installed up on the ceiling, a common practice of early stores. The big ball was in a holder, and the string ran from it across the ceiling and then dropped down right where it could be conveniently snipped and put to use.

Parksville's government liquor store had a minimal, no-nonsense cinderblock and linoleum interior and when you went inside you would go up to the counter and make a request to the man behind it. One rotund fellow wearing navy blue slacks and a white shirt would write it out on a slip of paper and hand it to the other fellow, who would pack up your order and cash it out for you. They were always in a good mood and invariably made a joke or two. My shopping list was usually a bottle of navy dark rum and maybe a six-pack of Old Style or O'Keefe's Extra Old Stock. It seemed like anyone who spent time in boats or lived on the waterfront in those days had a bottle or two of navy dark rum in the cupboard.

The Park Theatre was where the almost-latest movies were shown. It was a small theatre with the usual popcorn and snacks counter. They had Saturday matinees with a double feature, and the hooting and popcorn throwing from the young kids was wild.

After that, a stop in at Charlie's Exchange and you could bargain with Charlie for an axe, tools, a gasoline container, whatever. He especially appreciated us Lasqueti hippies because we really drove a hard bargain.

Unless you had a bag of clean laundry to pick up from Ennis and Gladys's Coin-Op Laundromat, you could carry on north to French Creek, park the car and make the four o'clock ferry. It would be loaded with boxes of food, a repaired chainsaw, maybe an outboard engine and many bags of animal feed. You'd find a front cubbyhole to put everything into safely, and then you'd go down into the main cabin and find a seat or an empty spot on one of the couches.

But if it was blowing hard and Ian didn't want to make the run, you might have to sleep in the car or go to a motel or wherever everybody else said they were heading and share a room with six other people. There were some nights with at least two people in each bed and a few on the floor in sleeping bags. But they were fun times, with Chinese takeout, pizza, beer, laughter and talking into the late hours as the storm blew outside. It was always a relief to wake up in the early-morning darkness to a quiet day with no sound of wind. Then there'd be takeout coffees and hot showers for everyone, and it was back down to French Creek.

Hopefully Ian Cole was awake, alert and on board, and if so, it was time to get your stuff onto the old *Captain Vancouver*, find a place to sit, pay the $1.75 fare and roll away toward home.

KILOWATTUS INTERRUPTUS

—Doug

The first inkling that Lasqueti Island was about to find itself at the centre of a gigantic power struggle came in May of 1975. A series of speculative articles appeared in the *Vancouver Sun*, and a week later in the *Parksville Progress*, suggesting that plans were afoot to run a large power line across the Georgia Strait to Vancouver Island.

It was to be the final fulfillment of British Columbia energy giant BC Hydro's long-term dream for the region. The Cheekye–Dunsmuir line would draw its electricity from future dams planned for Revelstoke and along the Peace River. Several routes to Vancouver Island were suggested, one of which crossed Lasqueti. Just how and where it would impact the island was left unanswered.

One Lasqueti resident who quickly grasped the seriousness of the threat was south-ender Kevin Monahan. He had heard the rumour that something big was afoot and independently decided to go directly to BC Hydro planners with further questions. The Crown corporation assured him that the project was only in the planning stage, but the "need" for the line made some kind of crossing likely. Kevin requested a meeting on Lasqueti to allow residents to express their own opinions of the proposal.

And so the matter rested until the spring of 1977, when a new set of more serious rumours and newspaper stories surfaced. In May 1977, Beak Consultants, working for BC Hydro, released a report recommending five potential Georgia Strait crossing points—one clearly crossed over Lasqueti Island. All routes ran overland from Cheekye, near Whistler, to a new substation to be built just south of Qualicum Beach on Vancouver Island. On the surface it seemed a fantastical scheme. The huge, five-hundred-kilovolt line would stretch underwater from the mainland to Texada Island, surface and cross Texada, go underwater again to reach the north end of Lasqueti, cross it on land at Scottie Bay, creep along Weldon Road and then head underwater for a final leg to Vancouver Island.

The meeting with BC Hydro took place at the False Bay School. The representatives from Hydro were surprised to face a day of intense questioning.

It was to be the highest-voltage underwater transmission line in the world. But it was a slash and blast plan.

Giant pairs of pylons would slice Lasqueti and Texada islands in half, leaving a clear-cut swath hundreds of metres wide along the right-of-way. Defoliant herbicides would be used to keep the brush down, and there would be extensive blasting to level the fragile seabed for the cables. Fishing grounds, homesteads, orchards and farmers' fields would be obliterated. This would spell the end of many a dearly held rural dream and level a death sentence against a vital island community. The electricity would supposedly go to power-hungry Vancouver Island, although, bizarrely, Lasqueti itself would receive none of this electricity and would remain off the grid.

Bad news travels fast, and within a few weeks the community took several important steps to avert the coming onslaught. Funds were collected for a sixteen-page informative newsletter that would be distributed that December. An emergency community association meeting was immediately convened, with record attendance. Feelings were strongly against the proposal, and a strategic planning committee was formed to coordinate a letter-writing campaign and start a petition. The Lasqueti Community Association quickly fired off a letter to Hydro expressing the island's rejection of the idea and apprised them that the newly formulated community plan had a clause expressly forbidding such development. Hydro replied in due course, telling the island to relax, as things were still in the planning stage and far from decided. With such a quick and powerful response from island residents, the community hoped the battle would be over before it had even began.

By July 1977, the Lasqueti Community Association's strategy group decided to form a separate steering committee to coordinate the anti-Hydro campaign. A group of six or seven passionate oppositionists formed the core group. Retired professor and island resident Michael Humphries, strongly supported by his wife, Amelia, assumed leadership of the group. And it was these two who were most responsible for what would be the winning strategy.

There was to be no ugly confrontation, demonstration, violence or wild-eyed hippie protesting. There was also no call for ecological purity, preservation of natural beauty or the not-in-my-backyard approach. Instead, the plan was to meet Hydro on their own ground with engineering alternatives and questions about funding and real long-term power needs. To surprise BC Hydro and do the unexpected. Above all, to treat everyone with respect and courtesy.

The island proceeded to educate itself on every facet of BC Hydro's complex energy plans, the dynamics of international politics and the engineering options. A newsletter team organized to publicize the battle through an informed publicity campaign. The island was profiled in the *Vancouver Sun* and on CBC TV and radio.

The Lasqueti Defence Fund was established to receive donations for the cause. Other communities on Texada Island, Powell River and Vancouver Island were steadfastly opposed to the project. The Powell River regional director and the Islands Trust representatives met with Hydro officials and insisted that a two-day public information meeting should be held on Lasqueti in early 1978. Preparations for this meeting immediately moved into high gear.

The Lasqueti Community Association distributed its first newsletter in December 1977. It came complete with maps, artwork, addresses for letter writers, informative articles on the economics of power and the dangers of electrical fields, a technical report by engineer Guy Immega and a strong appeal for funds. This was compiled with the help of an extraordinary contact from deep in the heart of the beast itself: a friend of a friend, who just happened to work in the planning office of BC Hydro, was privy to the latest information about ongoing projects and was willing to share what she knew. A second lengthy Lasqueti Island newsletter appeared in January.

On the weekend of January 27, BC Hydro's second-in-command, Charles Nash, flew in with a nine-person delegation from the Crown corporation to meet the community at False Bay School. They clearly expected a walkover. To their amazement, a three-man CBC TV crew, reporters from the *Vancouver Sun*, the *Province, Peninsula Times* and *Co-Op Radio*, as well as a court reporter prepared to make a legal transcript of the proceedings, confronted the group.

Hydro representatives were seated at a side table facing a panel of dedicated questioners in front, with the rest of the community off to the side. Each member of the Lasqueti Island Steering Committee came prepared, and each specialized in a particular aspect of the project. All three hundred questions had been submitted in advance so Hydro officials could not plead ignorance. Mike Humphries closely watched the proceedings and helped direct the conversation, adding a bit here and there to bring out the inconsistencies.

Questions were raised about the Beak Report and its assertion that the best route ran across Lasqueti. What about alternative routes over less precipitous terrain and sea bottom? Why not run it to Hornby? Doubts were expressed about Hydro's inflated peak forecasts. Was there even a need for a power line, when the logging and fishing industries were dying on Vancouver Island? And where was all this new power coming from—more dams, or even nukes? Was the project really part of a secret plan to carry power south to the United States from future nuclear power stations in Port Alberni, Cowichan or Crofton? How much was the public to pay, including interest, for this extravagant megaproject? What would be the environmental costs and health effects of the massive sixteen-inch oil-filled cables, the 250-metre swath of herbicide-sprayed right-of-way, and the powerful electromagnetic field blasting from the wires? The representatives from BC Hydro were obviously stunned by the careful preparation and self-discipline. Perhaps they had mistakenly assumed that Lasqueti was a sparsely populated backwater that would be unable to raise serious objections to their project.

After an intense half day of questioning by the steering committee and passionate public, the visiting bigwigs were escorted up the road to the Teapot House, where they were presented with an elaborate gourmet meal, featuring a spectacularly glazed thirty-plus-pound spring salmon along with fresh oysters on the half shell, topped off by a flaming chocolate mousse. The plan was to introduce these hard-bitten executives to the reality of Lasqueti life and disarm them with our hospitality. After the unexpected feast, all returned to the meeting, and the brutal questioning continued for hours more.

The group then dispersed to nine different island homes where they were billeted. Mr. Nash proved a gracious guest as he spread his blanket on the floor of the drafty kerosene-lit cabin, regaling the residents with tales of his recent adventures promoting a dam in Afghanistan. The next day the meeting went on until the late afternoon.

Before they left on their floatplane, Hydro agreed to let Guy Immega sit on their planning board. This was a major coup, as it gave the island a strong alternative voice in the project. Guy had previously met many of the engineers at Hydro and was on good terms with them. Both sides shared a common professional interest in the technical challenges of the plan. Billy Ellis, Hydro's chief project engineer, was both friendly and helpful, and the two remain friends to this day.

Guy quickly discovered that the key issue was the limited distance an underwater cable could run before it needed a splice: about sixteen kilometres, which was not nearly long enough to cover the distance from Texada to Vancouver Island. The plan actually envisioned two transmission lines (later reduced to one) composed of three cables each for three-phase power. The seventh cable was a backup in case of line failure. For protection, the underwater portions were surrounded by a thick, flexible sheath and laid as straight as possible—any sharp changes in direction were to be avoided.

Because cooling and insulation along the line were critical, the cables were protected with a special oil that pumped under pressure throughout the line. In the event of a puncture, oil would gush out, preventing seawater from entering the line and short-circuiting it. This meant that all splices had to be made on land to prevent leaks. But what would happen if the underwater line were damaged in some way? How would it be repaired without the splice leaking oil?

Guy proposed using a three-ship system with cranes to allow a splice to be made on shore and unrolled from the spool at sea without breakage. Unfortunately, the engineers at Hydro seemed much more interested in finding out how many Lasqueti residents were living off welfare. They were disappointed and surprised by the low number.

In Guy's words:

> Actually, BCH engineers knew about splicing—they just didn't like it, and kept the option hidden. I asked, why cross Lasqueti when it was obviously easier to go direct from Texada to Vancouver Island? BCH engineers explained that they couldn't purchase a long enough cable without splices. I next learned that Pirelli guaranteed their splices. My role then was to bring the splice option front and centre, because I knew it could save Lasqueti. My professional engineering credentials

helped force the issue. In the end, BCH decided that a splice was more secure, less costly and much less trouble than crossing Lasqueti Island.

While some were working out the technical issues, many others were throwing their energies into creative endeavours to promote the cause and raise funds to aid the fight. The newsletter produced eight multipage issues filled with updates, art and informative articles on energy policy, local and global. (Copies of these can be found in the provincial archives.) Fundraising events were held, with music provided by the Lasqueti Allstarz Band and performances of Donna Creekmore's play *Powermania*.

The play was part *Punch and Judy*, part theatre of the absurd—grossly overacted, with rhymed verse and musical accompaniment. BC Hydro was depicted as a diabolical monster, raping and pillaging everything it touched. Venues were not limited to Lasqueti and included the Errington Hall, a public hearing in Parksville, the Courtenay Renaissance Faire, and even the Van East Cultch. It is said the BC Hydro officials were not amused when they had a chance to view it on Vancouver Island later that year.

The use of humour proved a vital weapon in the struggle. A suggestive t-shirt was produced with the the the words "Bonner's Last Erection—Kilowattus Interruptus," which sold briskly. We heard rumours that even CEO Bonner of BC Hydro ordered several. The school also produced a pro–alternative energy play.

The battle spluttered on for the remainder of 1978 and into 1979, until Hydro finally surrendered. Even a last desperate offer to sweeten the deal with a local power generator for Lasqueti failed to sway opinion.

In the last two newsletters, in August and October of 1978, the steering committee pledged to fight on in support of other affected communities and against the need for the transmission line, but interest waned after the goal of keeping the huge high-tension line off Lasqueti had been achieved. An embryonic British Columbia Energy Coalition was formed to educate people about Hydro's politics and empower the public to resist the utility. It lasted about three years, with meetings held across the province.

In the end, the line was not defeated, but its route was changed. It was a win-lose situation. Hydro's modified proposal stopped the line from crossing Lasqueti, choosing instead the direct underwater path from Texada to Dunsmuir on Vancouver Island. Demonstrations continued on Texada and Vancouver islands with blockades, sabotage and arrests. The ugly scar of that aging Cheekye–Dunsmuir line running across central Texada Island can still be seen today. In the end, resistance from islanders played an important role in the "victory," but the most critical factor was economics. Running the line underwater with splices guaranteed by Pirelli was cheaper than running it over Lasqueti Island.

True to earlier predictions, the newly installed cable soon sprang an oil leak near Qualicum that went on for eight months. It was only quenched after Hydro brought in a special barge from Scandinavia. The long struggle had turned into a bruising defeat for BC Hydro, and there were significant long-term effects at the company. Their ambitious plans for a nuclear power plant on the Cowichan River were revealed and rendered less likely by the publicity. The company remains cool to nukes. The Generation Planning Department was abolished, which removed the Crown corporation's mandate to develop one energy project after another including the Site C Dam. Fifteen hundred engineers and other workers at the utility were laid off. And the corporation's tone became noticeably greener—one started hearing a lot more about energy conservation and alternative energy such as wind, solar and geothermal technologies.

The whole process greatly increased Lasqueti Island's sense of community, as Guy explains. "The fight with BCH unified the Lasqueti community. We worked together, trusted each other, got to know our strengths. This has made Lasqueti much more powerful. We led the Islands Trust initiative. We succeeded in pushing Jedediah Island into marine park status. Recently, we established a successful island Internet system (LIAS). All this and more resulted from the BCH conflict, because we knew the power of working together."

The struggle with BC Hydro also set the island on the path to exploring the many high-tech, low-cost alternative energy resources available—solar, wind and water. This has, in turn, led to the off-the-grid celebrity that the island is experiencing today.

On the downside, the victory did not endear the island to those in power. Starting in July 1978 and leading up to the present day, the island has been annually targeted in large-scale summertime marijuana raids by helicopter and by police and military ground crews. While other areas on the Salish Sea were left pretty much alone in the seventies and eighties, Lasqueti was demonized and dubbed "Pot Island," all out of proportion to its size in BC's annual dope harvest. This anti-drug scapegoating on the heels of kilowattus interruptus seemed more than just a coincidence.

POWERMANIA

—Darlene

While the local political movement opposing BC Hydro's plan to use Lasqueti Island as a bridge to Texada was gaining steam, artistic methods of raising awareness about the Cheekye–Dunsmuir power line were being hatched.

When the hydro fight became an issue, islander Donna Creekmore felt motivated to write a musical play, something that could reach a broad audience and raise awareness about this proposed project and its dire implications for our little island. She also realized that if it was good enough to take on the road, we could use the profits from ticket sales to build a sort of defence fund that would pay for a newsletter and for legal advice. The Lasqueti Defence Fund was born, and I was in charge of keeping track of the donations that were piling up in a glass gallon jar.

Updates and information on the resistance to Hydro's plan were publicized in a weekly newsletter that was printed out on Jack Barrett's old Gestetner machine. The newsletter had a donation form down at the very bottom that you could cut off and mail in with your pledge.

"It was one of those old-fashioned, hand-cranked copy machines," Donna recalls. "We'd work on those newsletters late into the night. My arm would get so tired cranking that thing. Of course, we didn't have a generator back then, as no one could afford a generator!"

Donna became passionate with her first entry into local theatre. She wrote the play *Powermania* and printed the scripts, held auditions and found people to do the sound and the light-

Powermania was the first play Donna Creekmore wrote and produced but she continued on in theatre for many more years.

Charlotte Carey and Darlene Olesko in their roles in *Powermania* as nature-loving clowns, frolicking in a new paradise. Photo Barry Churchill.

ing. She persuaded people to build the sets and paint the scenery. A few local musicians provided the folksy soundtrack. Retired theatre teacher Bill Lynch agreed to direct the play.

She wrote the play in December and asked me if I wanted to have a role in it. I said I did, and we had rehearsals all January. Our first performance was at the public informational meeting on Hydro's proposed project. We opened the meeting with the play, and it set the mood perfectly in our favour. Jack Barrett passed around a donation jar for people to put money into. Shortly afterwards, *Powermania* and an after-play dance with music by the Lasqueti Allstarz was presented at the Errington Hall, another fundraising effort for our Lasqueti Defence Fund.

Later, in July, *Powermania* was presented at the Courtenay Renaiassance Faire. That performance was a hoot, because by then we were relaxed and familiar with our roles, stretching out and improvising with our characters and really playing up to the larger audience that was there.

The play was a one-act musical spoof on a serious situation, and it was presented in an old-fashioned travelling show style. Kevin Monahan, Jack Barrett and all the Lasqueti Seafood Booth gang helped out with moving sets, feeding people and generally adding to the mayhem of the event.

Musicians and costumes for *Powermania*. L-R: Noel Taylor, Barry Churchill, Merrick Anderson, Marsha Andrews. Photo courtesy Merrick Anderson.

The cast included Donna as the woodland fairy, myself and Charlotte Carey as the Goofy Clowns, Howie Siegel as the Foreman and Larry Peterson and Dick Varney as the Logging and Installation Crew. The musicians were Merrick Anderson on guitar and vocals and Noel Taylor on violin. Bonnie Olesko played a bit of concertina ("Drunken Sailor") at the very opening.

From its origins in *Powermania*, the Lasqueti Theatre Company became Attic Theatre, so-called because several of the early productions were shown upstairs in the Teapot House. The space was all wood panelling, with high dormer ceilings and a brick chimney on one side. It could seat around thirty or forty. The front dormer facing the main room was about three metres wide and two metres deep: perfect for small plays with minimal sets. It was rustic, cozy and well located.

Donna continued on as the wellspring of our local theatre into the 80s and 90s, ambitiously producing plays written by Sam Shepherd and Michel Tremblay, among many others. She had the ability to coax and persuade local people who had never acted in anything at all to take a role and try it. She brought out the inner actor in so many of us. She was a dynamo, and when her train got rolling, everyone got on board.

THE JOY OF POWER

—Doug

The problem of how to obtain electric power has dogged Lasqueti Islanders since the 1920s. The nineteen kilometres or so of open water separates the island from conventional sources of electrical power—in this case, BC Hydro. This span is too long to lay a small underwater cable at a reasonable cost. Over the years, islanders have made a number of ingenious efforts to generate their own electricity on the island.

In 1928, Charlie Williams installed a one-cylinder kerosene engine in False Bay to light up the store and government wharf for nocturnal visits from the Union Steamships. Each time the engine chugged, the lights pulsed, but the system was hard to maintain and power was not available to private homes. Later, in 1951, a generator was installed at the school to universal admiration. Again, private homes remained lit by kerosene and candles.

Finally, in 1956, a partnership between Charlie Williams and Lance Johnson created the Lasqueti Light & Power Company to service the area around False Bay. With the introduction of modern appliances in the 1950s—television, power tools, refrigeration, washing machines and, of course, cheap lighting—the company prospered. It was a sophisticated operation with a generator shed, meters, poles and power lines. But it serviced only a small portion of the island, and when the partners retired after a decade, it fell into ruin. In 1972, I remember running across the derelict, empty shed at False Bay that was sheathed in coils of rotting copper wire and cobwebs.

In the years that followed, some islanders bought small generators to serve their needs, but they were expensive and touchy to operate and could not compare to the seamless twenty-four-hour power from BC Hydro. There were a number of appeals to the corporation for relief, but the company cited expense as the prime obstacle.

Tentative subscriptions were offered at ten to twenty thousand dollars a share plus user fees, but there were few takers.

Grassroot politics often sprung from meetings in the local school field. L-R: Mike Humphries, Noel Taylor and Johnny Osland. Photo Merrick Anderson.

The hippie back-to-the-landers were at first highly ambivalent about the "benefits" of electric power. We took pride in using kerosene and candles for lighting. The shine was softer and gentler, and there was no generator chugging away to disturb the peace and quiet. Improved propane lights and kitchen ranges were also becoming a popular alternative. And as for appliances, they were a mere technological extension of human effort, and who needed that? Just do the washing, sanding or drilling the old-fashioned way, with human energy.

But within a few years, cracks began to appear in the facade. It turned out that electricity did have some significant advantages. Kerosene lights stank and were a distinct fire hazard that had to be carefully tended, especially with the Aladdin lamps. Propane was hard to bring onto the island because it was so dangerously explosive. Much to our surprise, power tools for the handyman turned out to be a tremendous labour saver. In summer, refrigeration kept food fresh for weeks. And with young kids, a washing machine was found to be essential for family sanity. But most importantly, electric power brought music into the home. How was it possible to get back to the land in the seventies without Bob Dylan; the Band; Crosby, Stills, Nash & Young; the Stones; Bob Marley; and Van Morrison?

Fortunately, the new-age arrivals included a number of technical geeks and engineers who were quick to see the possibilities for alternative power.

The struggle over the BC Hydro power line had sharpened interest in all forms of alternative energy. Ezra Auerbach started Alternative Energy, one of the first companies to specialize in supplying products for off-the-grid living. He hired island resident Rand Holmes, famous creator of *Harold Hedd* in the *Georgia Straight*, to do advertisements.

It was undoubtedly this early exposure to alternative energy that has brought the island to the cutting edge of this technology today. Wind energy held the most obvious potential. The wind blows up and down the Georgia Strait with monotonous regularity—southeast in the winter and northwest in the summer. In the fall and spring it blows a gale in all directions. A wide-open exposure anywhere on the island will produce a surprising amount of power. Noel Taylor of the Teapot House and engineer Guy Immega were key in bringing alternative energy to Lasqueti.

The following is from an unpublished manuscript written by Guy in which he described the process:

> In 1976, following a series of discussions with Guy, Noel placed ads in newspapers across Canada looking for a used wind turbine. Of the replies she received, the most interesting was from a farmer near Saskatoon who mentioned that he had in storage parts for a large number of 12-volt windmills. He explained in his letter that these were pieces of surplus equipment obtained from the Saskatchewan Forest Service. Unsure of exactly what he had, he invited Noel to come have a look at his collection.
>
> Noel contacted Guy and they soon made plans to travel by train to Saskatoon. She would need his help to determine what there was and whether it could be made to work. Guy couldn't refuse her request or the chance to secure a wind turbine for his own bluff-top cabin. Noel quickly booked train tickets and found a friend of a friend to stay with in Saskatoon.
>
> The two borrowed a truck to drive thirty miles [forty-eight kilometres] out of town across the flat Saskatchewan prairie. The farm turned out to be an ancient and somewhat dilapidated establishment, and the farmer led them to a shed attached to the side of his barn.
>
> Sitting in a jumble on the dirt floor was a pile of somewhat rusted parts; they looked like they had been there for years. Obviously these were old machines, and they had probably been

in use for years on Saskatchewan's fire lookouts. Noel and Guy told the elderly owner that they needed some time to sort out what was there, and that was fine with him.

Over two days, Noel and Guy made piles of parts and then tried to inventory them. Once they were finished, it appeared they had components for seventeen wind turbines, some very worn and others still in serviceable condition. Some of the wooden blades were cracked. Others were usable. Several bearings wobbled. The enamel insulation in the generator wires checked out, but it was hard to tell how these wind turbines would hold up in the wild West Coast weather, with its corrosive salty air. Still, the pile of parts was a goldmine for these two Lasqueti Islanders.

How much, Guy wondered, would he want for this valuable equipment? Purchased new, they would be worth at least $1000 each. When the farmer returned to see how they were doing, Guy made an offer. Putting on his best poker face, he suggested they would pay $1000 for the lot. The farmer immediately agreed. Because the wind generators had been sitting unsold for years, there was no dickering.

Noel was ecstatic and Guy was surprised, but both tried not to show it. While Noel arranged payment, Guy started to pack up the parts for shipment. By that afternoon they had four wooden boxes that were almost too heavy to lift. They loaded these into the borrowed truck, drove directly to the train station and arranged to ship them by rail to Vancouver. That evening, they caught the passenger train west, exhausted but satisfied.

It took several weeks for the shipment to arrive at the BC freight terminal because the boxcar was lost on a siding for a period of time. Finally the wind generator parts arrived in Vancouver. Using another borrowed truck, the parts were driven to False Creek and loaded into Guy's old workboat, the *Sea Ace*. In the six hours of motoring from Vancouver to Lasqueti the weather blew up, leaving them seasick and green, wallowing around in the waves, breathing diesel fumes. They were very glad to finally unload the cargo onto the dock on Lasqueti. After unpacking, assembling and testing, Guy determined that he had ten complete wind turbines plus a lot of spare parts. By this time a general buzz of gossip had developed. It seemed that every resident wanted their own Wind Charger. The decision was soon made by Guy and Noel to sell them at cost to those most likely to use them, of course keeping one each for their own homesteads. The ten were sold within the month.

I might add that I was a lucky recipient of one of those ancient Wind Charger windmills. Guy and I set it up in Windy Bay just a few feet above the high-tide line, next to our beach shack A-frame. It was hooked up to a couple of ancient golf cart batteries, and it changed my life forever. Suddenly there were lights everywhere to chase away seasonal affective disorder—night reading and music once again became a real pleasure. During the powerful winter south-easters when she really revved up, we were presented with a wondrous light show of sparks dancing along the wires from the salt spray. Alas, these antique wind machines were not designed with saltwater corrosion in mind, and mine lasted only a few years. But an important lesson about the joys of electrical power was learned.

Another alternative energy source soon presented itself. Lasqueti Island is a hilly rockpile of cliffs, draws and grades, sometimes as high as sixty metres. In the summer it is a parched desert, but the winters are sodden. This corresponds well to power needs, which are greatest during the dark days of winter. The weight of all that runoff could be easily harnessed by a water wheel. There are numerous lakes and swamps, and a few hundred dollars of machine work was usually all that was needed to set up a reservoir. The system might not run full-time, but with a battery bank, even a few hours a day was often enough.

Mike and Amelia Humphries were the first to install a hydro system. With Guy's help they mapped out a route for the pipe and estimated the amount of power available. But the actual set-up was no easy task. "It took a year of planning and effort before the system was installed," Guy said. "First a local contractor dug a ditch for the water feed pipe. A powerhouse with a concrete foundation and a channel for water outflow was constructed beside the bay, just above the high-tide mark. When the turbine was installed and the wiring hooked up, they found they had plenty of power without needing any storage batteries. This saved expense and maintenance. Mike's brother designed automatic controls to allow them to turn the water turbine on and off from the house. Eventually, they installed a sophisticated electronic governor to regulate the output voltage."

This system worked perfectly, but it had its drawbacks. Hydropower is an old technology dating back to the later years of the nineteenth century,

Amelia Humphries. Amelia and her husband, Michael Humphries, were the first to install a hydro system from their power source, but they discovered the system had some drawbacks. Photo Tom Wheeler.

and most of the models available in the 1970s dated from that period. The wheel was heavy and costly, and it required a lot of water to make it go. There was obviously a need for something cheaper, more portable and smaller in all respects. Enter John Lindsey.

John arrived on the island in the late seventies as a visitor and became an established resident in 1982. An inspired tinkerer, he had long experimented with handmade windmill/hydro systems made of junk. He was quick to grasp the necessity of finding or creating a new kind of waterwheel—smaller and more portable than the giant systems then available. Using such sources as *Mother Earth News* as a guide, he married a small, hand-hammered, Pelton-type wheel made from a cooking pot to an old Honda motorcycle generator. This mini hydro system was hooked up to a small stream producing only 7.6 litres a minute of outflow. It barely produced twenty-five watts, but with tweaking—varying the angle of the flow and the diameter of the pipes and using direct drive—he was able to nudge the power higher and higher. It was a real eureka moment when John realized that this kind of system could actually work to power a small household without a generator. With solar

Energy Alternatives catalogue cover by Rand Holmes, 1990. Courtesy Martha Holmes.

cells for the dry summer months and mini hydro from November to May, it was suddenly possible to remain off the grid indefinitely with no hardship.

John has resisted the temptation to go commercial—no mass-production megafacility for him. He has handcrafted about seventy wheels over the years, each one laboriously built from pieces of junk and cast-off motorcycle parts. Now, he even winds his own coils around permanent magnets for a custom-made generator. He figures that most of the available hydro sites are now taken on Lasqueti and that solar power is the future, since prices have fallen sharply. Beyond that he looks to new and exotic technologies such as thermal electricity and the Stirling engine to provide cheap electricity to one and all.

FOLKIN' RIGHT, IT ROCKS!

—Darlene

The seventies music scene on Lasqueti started with winter evenings around the wood stoves in cabins up and down the island. They were just casual get-togethers with a guitar, maybe a harmonica and a few people singing.

I loved hearing Sam Marlatt's saxophone notes drift through my open window from the forested gully that runs behind the old DiFiore cabin, where we were living at the time, and from Arnie's Corner. Like most singletons, Sam lived by "wolf time," which meant erratic hours and no set schedule, so he'd often play in the early, early morning or late at night.

It didn't take long for organization to occur, and small groups and bands began to meet, jam and perform for events. Aside from playing guitars on summer afternoons on the dry, grassy slopes that overlooked the swimming lake, the first "organized" music days were the Sunday-afternoon jams at Doctor John Mitchell's log house. About a dozen people or more would be there with guitars, maybe a banjo, a flute, some bongo drums and their voices. Doctor John lived in the old Lenfesty place up on Dump Road. The place had rough plank floors, a few old stuffed chairs, a couch and a bathtub in the kitchen where you'd sit if you couldn't find anywhere else.

We'd spend all afternoon playing songs by Crosby, Stills & Nash, the Band, Fred Neil, Joni Mitchell, Pete Seeger, Smokey Robinson, Motown stuff—anything at all. From that group of us, which included Steve MacDougall, Bonnie Olesko, Merrick Anderson, Keray Farrell and Sam Marlatt, someone got the idea to go down and play at the Legion Hall on Saturday nights when it was open. A pretty good group was formed from those Legion nights. There was electricity in the Legion Hall, so we started using little amplifiers for the bass and one or two guitars. At first we sang into a shared little Sony tape recorder microphone fastened to an upright stick with black electrical tape, and if you got rockin' it would sway back and forth. Someone eventually brought a real microphone and a black stand, and it started feeling more professional.

The material got a bit more upbeat, with covers of Little Feat, the Eagles, Linda Ronstadt and the Rolling Stones. Grover Foreman played electric bass, Sam Marlatt played drums, Zootie Drake and Merrick Anderson both sang and played guitar and Ross Hughes, Lenore DiFiore, Bonnie Olesko and I also sang.

LASQUETI OPERA COMPANY

Lenore DiFiore came from Ohio. She'd had vocal training and lots of professional experience and was gifted with a strong, theatrical voice. She could sing anything. She could really belt it out, and it amazed us when she sang "Spanish Harlem" and "Don't You Feel My Leg."

Lenore, along with her brother Alan, his wife, Bonnie Olesko, Tom Wheeler, Ginger Gilchrist and "Brother Richard" Ressenger formed the Lasqueti Opera Company. The Opera Company debut came about when we all decided to put on a Saturday afternoon music fair down at the schoolyard.

Set-up at the schoolyard took place on Friday, with tables for a bake sale, lemonade stand, balloons, a fish pond and a photo display booth. There were lots of musical acts, some comedy routines and some theatre skits. One of the skits, called *Caravan*, was one of the craziest I've ever seen. A bunch of

Musicians from the Lasqueti Opera Company, playing onstage in front of False Bay School, summer of 1975. Photo Tom Wheeler.

local musicians played the Duke Ellington song "Caravan" in a homegrown style wearing turbans, vests and fake moustaches. As the second verse built in volume and intensity, Ross Hughes slowly emerged, twisting like a cobra, from a large woven basket that he had somehow crammed himself into for dramatic effect. His costume was a nylon stocking pulled over his head and as far down his body as it could reach, and then he was swaddled in more tight fabric. He had a bit of difficulty getting the lower part of his body free from the basket, and he kind of fell over. When he was out of the basket, he became the dancing snake. The audience went wild with applause and laughter and started dancing in a Middle Eastern style. There was more music, a film and then an open jam until the wee hours.

The opera company went on to produce a vaudeville show with a play called *The Logger Bride*, as well as some comedy acts and musical numbers.

THE LEGION HOUSE BAND

Bloodsugar Sam and the Watermelon Dance Band was an offshoot of those early Legion nights. The band material was a mix of cover tunes by Stevie Wonder, the Doobie Brothers and Steely Dan, among others. The members were Sam on drums and saxophone, Grover Foreman on bass and guitar, Laurence Fisher on hand drums and Steve MacDougall on harp. Sam tricked out a flat-deck truck in bright colours with "Watermelon Dance Band" written on

Bloodsugar Sam Marlatt and the Watermelon Dance Band performed regularly in the Legion Hall. Photo Merrick Anderson.

the side. He could announce that a dance would be held and drive everything he needed right to the spot.

Grover Foreman recalls playing in Sam's band:

> Sam was living in a shack up behind Arnie Porter's house, and we'd meet up there. Sam was a crazy inventor, and he was the car battery king. He had all this electrical stuff running on car batteries—lights, amps, speakers, everything. Boy, I remember playing at the Legion and it was just stellar. We practised so hard! I'd never practised so hard for any band in my life. All our songs, like this Stevie Wonder stuff, had these amazing changes and diminished chords and major sevenths.
>
> I'd bought this old guitar from Merrick, a 1957 LG-1 Gibson. I got it from him on installment payments. It was $135 in the early seventies and I paid it and paid it and paid it until I finally owned it. Sam put together the Watermelon Dance Band, and we mostly played at the Legion. We did a bang-up job of it! I practised probably fifty hours to get the guitar parts down. We encouraged Sam to play the saxophone more, but he insisted on playing the drums. I don't know why, because the sax really made those songs come alive. We never played off-island; playing at the Legion was our main reason to get together. We played at a few picnics and parties, though.
>
> Sam was a *driver* in that band, an absolute driver, but I didn't care. I just love to play. I care about the music. Every group has to have somebody that pulls it all together. I never said it was a bad thing, it's just what it takes to do it, somebody has to give the orders and get that music sounding right. Like generals in the army—somebody has to do it.

FIVE MINUTES OF FAME AND A CLOSE CALL

Around this time, some of us girls were having fun singing 1940s style. We were inspired by Bette Midler and the Manhattan Transfer and how they recreated those old postwar songs with such pizzazz. We sang a cappella versions of songs like "Lullaby of Broadway," "We Just Couldn't Say Goodbye" and "In the Mood" at events and parties.

We wore slinky thrift-store dresses and stumpy high heels, maybe wigs if our hippie-girl hair lacked the right look, and makeup and jewellery. We worked out the three- and four-part harmonies of those songs and tried to imitate the style of the Andrews Sisters, the Boswell Sisters and the Lennon Sisters. We even went to Victoria and appeared on *Daybreak*, an early-morning CHEK-TV show that featured BC musicians.

That was a crazy trip; we had to do a filming of the show for a later replay, and we were supposed to be at the CHEK station at 6:00 a.m. We were so excited that we hardly got any sleep the night before and we got up at about five to put on our costumes

We loved those 1940's dresses! A Capella Singers, from left: Sue Taylor, Judy Harper, Bonnie, Sherry and Darlene Olesko, 1978. Photo Darlene Olesko.

and makeup and style our hair. We grabbed cups of coffee and bundled all five of us into the front seat of Sherry and Ritchie's old pickup truck and drove off. We were headed through a major intersection, and of course everyone was talking and laughing when all of a sudden one of the girls screamed, "Stop!"

Whoever was driving, I think it was Sherry, slammed on the brakes. We just about went through the windshield when a big garbage truck whizzed past right in front of us. Whew! That brought us right down to earth. After calming down from that near-tragedy, we carried on to the station and had a great time being interviewed and singing to the cameras. It was aired a couple of months later and we had a viewing party. These were the days when just a few people actually had televisions in their little cabins, and we all crammed up close to watch ourselves in brilliant black and white.

GARY LANSDOWN: A STORY OF TALENT AND TRAGEDY

The Spaghetti Island Stringband was another one of the groups that emerged on Lasqueti during the 1970s. This band combined the remarkable talents of three island musicians: Dan Rubin, Grover Foreman and Gary Lansdown.

The beauty of their music, the dazzling talent of this group and the tragic circumstances that ended the Stringband and took Gary Lansdown's life made this band as close to mythical as any small-town band can come. Dan, Grover and Laurence Fisher recall their time with the Spaghetti Island Stringband:

DAN: Gary Lansdown had moved to Lasqueti Island from California late in 1974. He arrived with a change of clothes and a Martin D-28 guitar and was living in a short-frame yellow school bus that he'd had barged over. Tall and thin, Gary was a twenty-year-old happy-go-lucky young man who usually wore a blue stocking cap over his mop of dark brown hair. He had a warm, rich singing voice and knew a range of songs learned from the blues-tinged traditions that were the backbone of country rock in the early seventies.

Gary met Dan Rubin at a supper at Kevin Monahan's house one evening, and after dinner they tried playing music together. The result was only moderately successful, but something must've clicked, because soon the two had found Grover, who played a big old battered string bass, and the Spaghetti Island Stringband was formed.

GROVER: I was the glue that held those two (Gary and Dan) together, because they were opposite personalities. Gary was a free spirit, totally, living in his old school bus like a hillbilly, and Dan was an aspiring college graduate.

To my recollection, we started practising together at the old round house where Greg and Lindsey (Seaman) live now. Gary came to the island and I met him through Kim Laukes. They were going together at the time, but it was sort of on-again, off-again. I heard that he played guitar, so I invited him over to my house. As soon as that happened, as soon as I heard him play, that was it. He was a stellar guitar player—just off the scale. And he really wanted to learn. Like, all day long he just sat in his school bus and practised scales. We got together and played a couple times a week. Dan had a lot of technical knowledge and ability, but Gary sort of superseded it all because he had this absolutely natural talent. Dan would set Gary into a tune and Gary would just run with it, launching into these incredible solos and shit. He had been living in California, playing in a blues band. Bottom line is Dan saw how much talent he had, and I was just trying to hold those two talents together and keep the argument level down.

Opposite: Dan Rubin kickstarts the "Codburgers" chant at the Lasqueti Seafood Company tent. Photo Barry Churchill.

Kim Laukes, 1976. Photo Tom Wheeler.

DAN: The musical blend that began to emerge reflected the diverse interests of the three musicians. With Grover thumping away on the bass, Gary driving the rhythm with inspired arpeggios picked out high on the neck of the guitar and me adding tasteful runs on the mandolin and fiddle, the result was infectious and inspiring. Our repertoire included my original ballads, bluesy standards like "Six Days on the Road" and Gary's own compositions. It was music you could listen to, and it was also very danceable.

GROVER: Gary was a big fan of the Grateful Dead, and you could hear it in his style. When you saw him do a solo it was just awesome. He played all up and down the neck the whole time. Between the chord changes he was doing this real flighty stuff, like, *z-h-o-o-o-n-n-g*! all over the place, then jumping right back onto the next change. I'd never seen anybody do this kind of stuff. He was an incredibly fast player.

He was a real hillbilly, he loved doing songs like that, whereas this was a little beneath Dan—he really didn't want to do this kind of stuff, he liked doing the old standard fiddle tunes and his own original songs, but he did it to appease Gary and me.

DAN: We practised regularly at Grover's round house down in Fisherland, and I would sometimes walk all the way from the south end to False Bay with a guitar in one hand, a mandolin case in the other and a violin wedged under one arm. Grover had this cozy little octagonal house, and we had a great time playing music and sharing his homemade beer and smoked salmon.

Our name, the Spaghetti Island Stringband, came from an island that was in one of "Uncle Ezra" Auerbach's children's stories. Ezra was travelling to local festivals at the time, telling children's stories about a purple dragon who lived on the smell of flowers.

The band's first public debut was at an island dance at the old Legion Hall. There were heady times to come as local audiences, first on Lasqueti and then farther afield on Vancouver Island, heard and danced to the music of the Spaghetti Island Stringband. Within a few months, Lasqueti Islanders would see us down on the ferry dock, heading off for concerts and dances in Errington, Victoria and Comox.

GROVER: Dan wanted to build a band that was going to make a mark. We were travelling, we were doing things, getting gigs in Vancouver and the next stop was ... who knows? And we were all willing to do it. Dan had the drive to make it happen. He was calling people, making contacts, all of that.

DAN: Like the Pied Pumkin, a Vancouver-based acoustic trio, the Spaghetti Island Stringband was part of a move toward what would be known as "alt-folk" three decades later. It was a type of music that was finding its way back to its roots while expressing a lyrical, but also a radical, view of life.

For Gary, who wanted more than anything else to play, the band was a dream come true. There was a growing sense of wonder at what we three were creating. But before we would complete a debut recording, there was a big breakout appearance that loomed in Vancouver: a debut at Gastown's Classical Joint, the small hole-in-the-wall club that was the true litmus test for touring musicians. After that, we were booked in for two nights at the Vancouver East Cultural Centre. It was the spring of 1976 and it really felt like our stars were in alignment.

I dropped by Gary's bus, parked near False Bay, the day that I had to head off to Vancouver for the upcoming gigs. I wanted to go in early and visit some friends before meeting up with Gary, Grover and Laurence Fisher, who had been enlisted to come along and play percussion with the group for these bigger engagements. Gary was sleeping, but he sure didn't look good. A long bout of flu had laid him low, and even after several days of rest he was still decidedly green around the gills. I told Gary he didn't need to go. If he didn't feel up to it, I could probably find other players to fill in. But Gary knew that this was our big break, and he insisted that he was all right to go.

There was a strange feeling in the air; something was really not right. Later I heard that the night before he was to leave Lasqueti, Gary dragged himself up the hill from where his bus was parked to have tea with Hawk, a friend of his who lived nearby.

"I just had the weirdest dream," Gary told Hawk.

"What happened?" Hawk asked.

"In my dream, I died," Gary told him. "There was an accident, and I was dead." It turned out that Gary had been waking up for three nights in a row with this kind of dream before he finally went to see Hawk so he could tell someone.

But when morning came, Gary was down on the dock at False Bay, ready to go. Along with Grover and Laurence, he helped load the gear and the instruments onto the *Captain Vancouver* and the ferry headed across to French Creek. Most of the band's gear was stored in a house up [Bennett] Road, where Dwayne and Donna Creekmore were living. There, they loaded up Gary's old VW microbus with amps and instruments and headed for Nanaimo. Gary was still feeling too sick to drive, so Laurence took the wheel. But halfway there, they realized that they had forgotten a guitar amp, so they turned around and headed back to the house.

GROVER: The way I remember it, Gary and his girlfriend, Kim, had gotten into an argument and we were going back to the Bennett Road house so that they could make up. We were headed to the ferry, and he said, "I just can't go to Vancouver like this. I have to go back and make up with her."

DAN: The island highway, at the time, was a narrow, two-lane road, so apparently as they waited to turn left into [Bennett] Road at Qualicum, a line of traffic backed up behind them. The driver of a fully loaded gravel truck approached from the south. He could see there was a holdup ahead, but it was the last load on the last day before his retirement, so he checked out the line of backed-up cars and decided to just go for it. Pulling around the line of cars on the left, after a single car went by in the other direction, he could see there was no oncoming traffic, so he decided to pass.

The gravel truck was speeding up just as Laurence turned left into the Qualicum Airport Road. When the gravel truck hit the van, there was an enormous shock.

GROVER: It was like I could smell death. There was suddenly this terrible smell. I was standing up, and I had the van doors cracked partway open, trying to get some fresh air. I remember it like it was yesterday. First there was this terrible smell, and then everything went into slow motion, like you see on TV. Everything flew up, and then everything started to just spread apart. I saw it all, and at the moment of impact I already knew what was happening. I could feel things sucking back and ready to blow out, like the tide coming in and going out, that's what it felt like. I had plenty of time. I took the fuckin' doors, in this millisecond before the implosion, and pushed them open, and then the truck hit. My arms were out, and it just blew me into the air about twenty-five feet [eight metres]. I hit the bank and tripped and kept running. I just kept running all the way back to the house. It was like I somehow knew it was going to happen, I had a sort of warning, and I got out.

Bursting through the door of Donna and Dwayne Creekmore's house, about four hundred metres from the accident scene, Grover crumpled onto the floor and began to wail out, "Gary's dead! Gary's dead!" Although he hadn't stayed on the scene, he knew Gary hadn't made it. Someone there called 911, and when the ambulance arrived, the driver of the gravel truck was sitting by the side of the road, shaken but uninjured. Laurence Fisher was also shaken up and bruised, but basically all right.

LAURENCE: I was driving the van, and Gary was sitting in the passenger's seat, sort of snugged in the front corner, where he had almost a ninety-degree view. As we approached Airport Road, I asked Gary if the signal indicators worked. He nodded his head and sort of mumbled something I took for a "maybe," and I decided to slide open the window and use my arm too. It was a really old Volkswagen van, the kind where the driver's window slides open, and it was sort of stuck, so I was steering with my right hand and pulling on this window. Grover was standing up in the back, and he kept fussing with the side door, trying to open it. "Grover, what are you doing?" I shouted back at him. The noise was really distracting. "Just leave it, we're almost there!"

"I need some air! I feel like I can't breathe!" he yelled back.

I got the window open just enough to stick my arm out. When I slowed down to make the left-hand turn, I could see a car coming to pass, but from way down the road, so I began to turn. Gary suddenly screamed out, "Oh my God!" and when I glanced over at him, he was looking past me, and at that very minute an enormous "who-o-o-sh!" just blew me over toward him and we both were propelled right out the passenger door and up onto a grassy bank. I landed higher up than Gary, several feet away. He landed lower, right in the path of the van, and it rolled over and crushed him. All I remember is looking at Gary when he screamed, then coming to in the grass. I was so dazed, I couldn't figure out what had happened for a while …

The equipment was scattered around. Dan's 1927 Martin guitar had come flying out of its case and was lying in a ditch with water and gravel inside it, and the tiniest chip out of the peghead. The van was totalled. Gary Lansdown lay on the ground, face up, looking as if he were sleeping. He was dead.

DAN: Before the accident I had passed through Victoria to visit with an old friend, mandolin player Rick Van Krugel. I thought about asking him to come into Vancouver if we needed a fill-in for Gary. I had this feeling that Gary might take a turn for the worse, no matter what he said, and I wanted a backup. Rick said that he could come over, and to just let him know if we needed him. I went on to Vancouver and found Rick Scott in his studio down on Cordova Street. It was the night before our first engagement, and there was a knock on the door. It was Stephanie Atwater, my wife at the time. Stepping inside, she said, "There's been an accident."

I could hardly believe her words that followed. Once it was clear that everyone else was all right, but Gary was gone, the reality of the accident weighed me down like lead. Gary was gone. Nothing made sense anymore, and I didn't know what to do.

That night I lay awake for hours, just staring into the darkness. My mind was reeling with shock, memories and, eventually, attempted decisions. I remembered driving back toward the Lasqueti ferry from an earlier Stringband performance in Comox, heading south on the Island Highway in my old Morris Minor. It was after midnight and I was determined to get back to Stephanie and work things out. I was barely able to stay awake as I drove along the twisting, winding parts of the highway, and I remember saying out loud, "Life is short. You have got to decide what really matters. It can end just like that!" and as I snapped my fingers, a deer sprang out in front of my car. I saw it framed in white as it passed a few feet in front of the headlamps.

I made a decision to go ahead with our tour. When morning came, I phoned Rick Van Krugel. He came to Vancouver and Rick V., Rick Scott and I played the three nights, dedicating each night of music to Gary's memory.

LAURENCE: I spent some time talking with the gravel truck driver in court. He was such a nice guy, and he was so shattered by this horrible accident. I really hope his life turned out all right, because the day that it happened was the last day for him on the job, and he was retiring the very next day. When I thought of the weird dreams that Gary had been having, I just had to say to the driver, "Please don't feel like this was your fault ... I know it might sound strange, but I believe that somehow, it was written," and I truly felt that it was.

DAN: Gary Lansdown and the Spaghetti Island Stringband are gone, but the music remains, shimmering just out of reach. In recordings made at the time, you can hear the iridescent beauty

Members of the Spaghetti Island Stringband. L-R: Gary Lansdown, Grover Foreman and Dan Rubin.

of the lines he carved out of the air ... notes that dance like fairy dust, filled with transcendent joy.

And I remember the night I was given the song "Wings of Winter." It was during a December rehearsal at Grover's house, and we were down on the beach below his place. The snow was falling thickly and from out on the water came the low tones of the foghorn on Sisters Islets. Little by little a melody, and then words, began to come, falling like snowflakes into my hands. I was afraid they'd disappear, and Grover helped me find a scrap of paper and a pen so I could scratch them down. We climbed back up to the house and I picked up my guitar, and along with Gary and Grover, we began playing the waltz that was the melody of the song. I just kept playing for more than an hour, until every verse, every word, came clear. We played it again, over and over, with the snow falling silently all around the house.

I think of Gary Lansdown every time I play this song, and the magical nights playing and singing, just the three of us, in the Spaghetti Island Stringband.

Home-grown music played in small groups, as in this photo from 1975, can still be found at every festival event on Lasqueti Island.

> If I were a man of the earth,
> I would plant myself deep in the ground
> And I'd stay there through autumn and winter too,
> I'd be there when spring came around,
> I'd be there when spring came around.
>
> —"Wings of Winter"

THE MUSIC GOES ON

Music on Lasqueti continued to evolve as we all played on into the 1980s. Some "folkies" morphed into "folk rockers" when the Lasqueti Allstarz came together, as some of us became interested in playing more rock 'n' roll and rhythm and blues.

People move on, players pick up different instruments or find new musical avenues to explore. Often, musical heights are reached with one group and after a while those players move on and reconfigure, only to find another musical height to aspire to with a new and different group of players.

The music we made in the 1970s was a great mix of originals, traditional songs, folk, rock, swing and blues. Like any kind of immigrant, we brought along our musical influences to Lasqueti and put them out to share and blend with other styles, resulting in an open, active music community that just get broader with every passing decade.

GET A HORSE!

—Darlene

"Who needs to be burning gas?" the islanders of the 1970s said. "Trucks and cars cost a lot of money, then you've got to get them over here on a barge—and when they break down you gotta fix 'em. Think of it—we'll get some buggies, everyone will be on horseback and with all this free grass everywhere, we'll have tons of manure for the gardens!"

Easily said, not so easily done.

But this thinking, not to mention the romantic visions of riders on horseback galloping down the forest trails, was what brought a dozen horses to the island.

It was in the early summer of 1972, and Kevin Monahan, Jack Barrett, Bonnie Olesko, John Gamble, Steve Parent, Chris Ferris and her dad, Jim, all went up-island to a livestock auction in Merville, BC, to bid on horses. They were planning to buy about a dozen horses, get them back down-island and then over to Lasqueti somehow.

Up in Merville, they made an offer of one thousand dollars on a group of thirteen horses that had come over from the Interior. A few of them had "Rocking H Ranch" branded on their hides. The offer was accepted, and they got the animals all trailered down to Parksville, where they stored them at the Red Barn farm, and then to the Wembley Mall K&R grocery store. The Red Barn cowboys had also got a few horses at the auction and agreed to keep the Lasqueti horses there for a few weeks while the Lasqueti gang tried to find a way to get them all barged over.

During this time, Steve Parent's stallion, aptly named Crazy Horse, got loose, and he was so headstrong and wild that the boys at the Red Barn farm had a hard time getting him back into their corral. Under pressure to get the horses off the farm and over to the island, Steve Parent found an oyster buyer with a barge that was for hire. The barge operator agreed to take all the horses

Horses on Lasqueti were used for work, transportation and for pleasure. Shelley McKelvey and Cheryl Lynch out for a ride. Photo Johnny Osland.

over in exchange for a barge load of oysters that the horse owners would harvest and load. It sounded like an almost free way to get the job done, and quickly.

The new horse owners had only one way to get the horses all down to French Creek, and that was accomplished by walking them all down the Island Highway in a line. It took a bit over an hour, and when they arrived at French Creek, the wind had come up.

But the barge operator was on a schedule, and the horses were loaded onto his barge in French Creek in the afternoon and taken across to Spring Bay in a panicky, agitated state. When they finally arrived at Maple Bay, right in front of Tom and Molly Millicheap's house, it was beginning to get dark. Bonnie and Alan DiFiore came down to meet the barge that night and she was surprised to see how big it was. The horses were already off the barge and tied up to trees, and there were people on the beach picking oysters as fast as they could. She saw a silhouette of a person wheelbarrowing across the beach and then up and onto the barge. They joined the pickers and got to work.

The barge operator announced that he was not leaving until the barge was full. "That was the deal!" he snarled. After three hours of cold, heavy work, only part of a corner of the barge was full of oysters. Tired and cold, the horse-owning hippies picked and loaded, picked and loaded, picked and loaded. When that amount was doubled, sometime around 1:00 a.m., the tide began to rise. This signalled the time to depart, and at that point the disgruntled barge owner fired up his engine and took off, heading down the Sabine Channel in a big, loud huff. When he returned a month later to square things up, he was happy with a small number of oysters just to settle the deal and turned out to be a not unlikeable fellow.

The horses were taken to their various homes around the island and were enjoyed, for the most part, for years to come.

Bonnie Olesko kept her white mare, Bree, in a small clearing just off Main Road. She would ride Bree around the mid-island meadows and along Main Road, sometimes with her child Lazarus in front.

Steve Parent kept his stallion, Crazy Horse, up at the Stump Farm. Crazy Horse was a real handful, wild and hard to control. Steve's girlfriend, Maggie Neufeld, got bucked off and suffered a broken leg when she tried to ride Crazy. Once, when Crazy got loose and tried to mount a mare that was being ridden by two local children, the parents called the RCMP in outrage at this dangerous stallion that kept getting loose. The RCMP did come over eventually to investigate the matter, only to find out that the stallion had recently been gelded by a veterinarian. The "vet" turned out to be a local person with a bit of knowledge on how to geld a horse. Anyway, this got Crazy Horse off the hook, and Crazy was afterwards renamed Will. He was later sent over to live out his days on Jedediah Island.

Karl Darwin bought one horse from Kevin, a large half-draft horse. Starting out on a six-month tour of the Interior, he first barged the horse to Pender Harbour, then purchased another horse, Old Red, as a pack animal. He rode them along the Squamish Highway and through Lillooet, then on to Williams Lake. It turned out that his half-draft horse was too slow in mountain trails, lumbering on the uphills and then rapidly clambering on the downhills, so he sold it. He continued on with Old Red and spent six wonderful months exploring the Coast Range on horseback.

Karl kept Old Red on the island, and enjoyed him until the horse finally died here, at age twenty-nine.

Cecil Varney, an old carnival worker from way back, recognized that Jack Barrett's horse was show trained, and he was able to get him to walk up on his hind legs and sidestep. But Jack, along with a few of the others, was coming to realize just how much time, energy and money these animals were costing.

Cecil Varney trained Jack's horse to perform dressage moves.

In spite of the pleasure they brought to the Islanders, the horses were hard work and expensive to care for. By the 1980s the original thirteen horses had all disappeared from the Island. Photo Johnny Osland.

He sold his horse back to Kevin, and Kevin afterward passed it along to someone else.

One by one, the remaining horses were either sent off-island to more capable, appreciative owners or, in the sad case of a few, just abandoned and left to wander around, competing with the free-range cows for grass. When the wet weather came, they stood forlornly in the forest, sheltering under the trees. They developed hoof problems, and all of this together caused a serious controversy that ended up with a minor roundup and removal. By about the early 1980s, this batch of horses had all disappeared from our local scene.

But while they were here, it was a wonderful sight to see people riding up and down the island on horseback. Once in a while, in the middle of the night, I would hear the thundering of hooves as a few of these remaining horses galloped down the road. It was wonderful to be hiking in the forest and suddenly smell the scent of a horse nearby and then glimpse a pair of horses standing together, staring back at you.

MARIJUANA

—Doug

Of course any discussion of Lasqueti Island in the 1970s must include a chapter on the marijuana industry. Being a law-abiding citizen I must disclaim any connection with this illegal enterprise, and the following is based on interviews and the intense island gossip generated during those exciting years.

In the days before Ronald Reagan's War on Drugs, pot farming was a lackadaisical business in British Columbia. Everything was grown outdoors from seed. There was no such thing as clones, indoor gardens, marijuana-eradication teams, pruning for beauty, medical marijuana or high prices. Everything but the roots and stems was sold, and the going rate for rough buds, leaf and even male plants was two to three hundred dollars a pound. Still, that was a considerable sum in those days. The enormous price rise to over three thousand dollars a pound was created by America's prohibition, and it did not come into effect until the 1980s.

In many ways the island is perfectly situated for the production of illicit drugs. It is surrounded by treacherous waters, it is thinly populated, and large parts were at that time an impenetrable wilderness. The island also lies conveniently close to the large cities of Victoria and Vancouver, and the American border.

Lasqueti, and for that matter all of the Gulf Islands, has long attracted those who hold anti-establishment views and is sympathetic to the production of intoxicants. The island has a long history of brewing booze during both the American and Canadian prohibitions. George Hadley, builder of the famous Teapot House, was caught in a nasty police sting operation in the 1930s and sentenced to six months in the provincial jail for unlicensed brewing. Empty antique bottles of Champion Concentrated Embalming Fluid still keep turning up on the south end. There were once thousands of them. Now, what do you think was supposed to go into those bottles? I once asked an old-timer that very question. He replied, "You know, there are some who used to drink that stuff.

Those bottles were intended to contain some of the better moonshine produced on the coast. What better way to flummox the police than to pass their stuff off as embalming fluid?"

In the seventies, Canadian federal laws regarding pot were quite strict but rarely enforced in western British Columbia. A few went to jail for possession, but cultivation carried a much harsher sentence of up to seven years. Still, almost everyone smoked or tolerated it, and pot was considered just another part of island life. However, the police took a dim view of the growing industry and began helicopter raids on island gardens in the summer of 1978. These raids continue to the present day at considerable taxpayer expense with seemingly little effect on supply or demand. One wag even wrote a personal letter to the RCMP thanking them for their attention, calling it a "much-needed price support." Weed is as easy to grow as sweet corn and would be just about as valuable if legalized. Guerilla gardening can be tricky though, requiring skill, knowledge and a lot of sweat.

Along with the raids came Lasqueti's reputation as the dreaded "Pot Island." After the community threw a monkey wrench into BC Hydro's plan to install a power line over Lasqueti, the island's name became mud in some corporate and government circles. Newspapers and radio talk shows revelled in the perfidy of residents and suggested that an army of dangerous organized criminals was growing large acreages. Some have speculated that this demonization simplified the work of the police by implying that clamping down hard on this one centre of evildoers could easily solve the province's drug problems. The cops seemed to play up this reputation, often hitting only Lasqueti and exaggerating the amount seized by adding in the weight of the roots, dirt, water and stems. Ironically, many growers from other areas would profusely thank Lasqueti Islanders for taking all the heat. In the seventies, the island was a centre for the counterculture, and it is true that there were dozens of small plots, but their production rarely exceeded a pound or two. And the violence of organized crime was never part of the picture. It was rather a freelancer's heaven brimming over with entrepreneurial spirit—much like in the days of the rum-runners.

Because of the dry climate on the Gulf Islands in the summer, good growing areas were few and far between. A kind of grower's etiquette quickly evolved. Be discreet and keep a low profile: there were numerous stories of rip-offs and thefts—mostly committed by teenagers from off-island. Don't be greedy: a number of small gardens was always preferable to one large operation, though a lot more trouble. Check out the neighbourhood before you start the hard work of fencing and digging: a concentration of gardens acted as a gigantic heat sink.

Opposite: Ross hiding behind a very healthy pot leaf.

I often wondered if that same amount of effort applied to legal pursuits would not have produced just as much or more profit. Commercial fishing in the seventies was really big money. Anyone who wanted to get rich quick went into salmon or herring fishing. Guerilla farmers had the advantage of working near home with no boss, no schedule, no land/boat payments and no pressure, and they had the leisure time to pursue their own hobbies, art or vices. Rent was free, food was cheap and one quickly learned the skills of getting by. I do not know any grower who struck it rich or lived like a king in those days. But it was a carefree life—now long gone.

This "office in the woods" appealed to a certain temperament. One Vietnam vet characterized it as experiencing all the excitement of being in a war, but nobody ever got killed or even injured. In spite of the heavy police pressure, there were very few arrests or confrontations in the 1970s. In general, when the two sides met each other in the woods, they would nod politely to each other and go about their business. As long as you weren't caught in a garden red-handed or wandering about with a rucksack full of weed, you were left alone.

An example of the relatively benign relationship between growers and the police in the seventies can be seen in this story told by my friend X, who has sadly now passed away. It was the end of a typical three-day helicopter raid in August. Houses had been buzzed, water lines cut, plants yanked up and livestock stampeded. There had been no activity in the air for several hours, so X decided it was time to check on his six plants. They were all small but potent—a one-off mixture of Guatemalan and Thai stick. As he headed across hill and dale to his special swamp, X was in a jubilant mood. Despite the endless drone of the chopper there had been no landings in the neighbourhood that day. Needless to say his level-headed partner pleaded with him to just hold off until the morrow. Why take unnecessary chances? X adamantly refused. Perhaps his plants could be pulled farther back out of sight, giving them a better chance of survival.

The path to the garden was dense with swordfern, alder and native crabapple, a cloying, thorny tree that seemed determined to trip up and entangle at every turn. He was within fifteen metres of his goal when the distant sounds he had been hearing turned into a deafening WHOP-WHOP, causing instant panic. They were back! In seconds the chopper was directly overhead doing short sweeps just above tree level. Being a Vietnam vet, X immediately went into flashback mode. It was the battle of Nha Trang all over again, only this time the chopper was not a welcome ally but one of the bad guys. Even though the foliage was incredibly dense and he was hugging the ground, they seemed able to follow his every move. Later he learned that this was indeed the case as the police were using the new forward-looking infrared (FLIR) spotting devices, which sharply pinpoint and outline anything with a heat signature.

X was sweating profusely. God, what could have possessed him to make this stupid trip in the first place? There was nothing for it but to burrow deeper into the ferns and hope they would lose interest. That is not what happened. The next thing X knew, the chopper had landed on a rock bluff ninety metres away and shut down the engine. Uh-oh ... this was looking serious. Would he be arrested, hauled off to jail or worse? Within a couple of minutes X heard the voices of the two-man eradication team stomping through the underbrush. Mercifully, they passed nine metres from his hideout, loudly chatting and joking about what a great and well-paid job it was to pull up hippie pot. The voices faded and were replaced by the *chop-chop* of two machetes doing their grisly work. This was the time to think about splitting the scene, and X gathered his energies for a mad dash to freedom. Then he hesitated—what was the rest of the chopper crew up to? They could be anywhere in the vicinity.

An air horn suddenly sounded, calling the team back, and they soon packed up their gear. This time, on return, the voices got closer and closer to X. There was no mistaking it—they were heading directly to his little hidey-hole. The crunch of the footsteps got louder, and the jocular conversation was replaced with dead silence. Instinctively he hugged the already badly mangled ferns closer, praying to all the saints of all the religions. Just short of stepping on X's head the two stopped for a cigarette. One leaned a few inches over the trembling grower and said in a loud stage voice. "Do you think he's still here?" The cop took a long pull on the cig, and then they both sauntered back to the chopper. It was obvious that they knew exactly where X had been the whole time. It was also obvious they had no interest in any kind of arrest or confrontation—these guys were just having a bit of fun doing their job.

As an epitaph to this story X waited a full week before checking on the remains of his six plants. Much to his amazement the team had completely missed them in the dense bush and instead ripped up a couple of plants from a nearby garden he never knew even existed. *C'est la vie!*

Sometimes these confrontations led to cat-and-mouse mind games on both sides. Two men I'll call Mr. Mutt and Mr. Jeff were partners in crime. Here Mr. Jeff describes a chance meeting in the woods during a raid:

> Scouting around, I see that Mr. Mutt's little gardens have all been cut down, with only the stubs of his plants left. Garden after garden has been hacked down. Man, is he going to be pissed! My plants are still okay. I feel sorry for Mutt. All that hard work

Illustration "Bud Clippers" by Rand Holmes depicts three generations of a family pruning buds together around the kitchen table. Courtesy Martha Holmes.

and now everything is gone, with nothing to show for it. I get to the top of the hill and look around ... SHIT! Right ahead, about one hundred feet [thirty metres] away, are several cops. Fortunately they haven't seen me, but they are looking around intently. I have about five seconds to hide, or I'll just have to run for it. With nowhere to go I decide to run for it. I leap over rotten logs, bolt across mossy rocks and just tear out. I've gone no more than a hundred feet [thirty metres] when a loud voice rings out, "Lose something, Mr. Jeff?" Holy shit—they know my name ... what to do? I stop, turn around, smile and say, "No." They walk forward. I can see that they are carrying machetes and sweating in their dark blue bush uniforms. The older one starts asking the questions. "Is this your territory?"

"Territory? What do you mean? I hardly ever come up here."

"Well, someone makes these trails."

"Sure, there are sheep up here ..."

"Sheep don't grow these funny-looking plants."

"Well, those plants aren't mine." (True, they are Mr. Mutt's.)

"What are you doing up here?"

And this is where I know that my carefully prepared story will come in handy.

"I came up to see if you left anything behind."

His sweaty face breaks into a tight smile, and then I realize how that must sound to him.

"Like pouches, field glasses, machetes, that sort of thing," I add.

Man, I thought right then that I had blown it bad. So much for my stupid alibi.

"Have you seen Mr. Mutt these days?" the older cop asks in a friendly way.

"No," I lie. "Not in a while, not since he left."

They seem satisfied and ask no more questions, so after a few more feet I stop walking. They just continue on, and I take off in a different direction down the bluff.

GOD! HOW DID THEY KNOW OUR NAMES?

A spirit of mutual respect grew between the two sides. Some of the garden sites were amazingly clever: planting way up in the treetops or staggered across an impassable bog in floating terraces. I only heard of guns being used once, and that was when the RCMP summarily executed a rusty metal water tank in an abandoned cabin. On another occasion someone tried to abscond with a huge bundle dropped off by a chopper near a cliff face. There was a flurry of excitement as the copters converged in a frantic search, but the bundle was too heavy to move far, and it was eventually recovered in a crevice a few feet from where it had been dropped. Only the net was lost.

In the early fall at the end of every growing season in the seventies, a marijuana convention was held to test the various varieties of pot grown on the island. The offerings were displayed on paper plates with only a number for identification to reduce personal prejudice. Everyone was issued a form to fill out listing such things as potency, crystal content, appearance, bouquet, quality of the high and staying power. The only problem with this system was that by the time one got through one's third or fourth choice, it became impossible to judge what was what. These parties always included quantities of wine and champagne and tempting trays of cheese, seafoods and deli meats to combat the inevitable munchies. Attendance was closely vetted, and it was considered an honour to be invited.

They say a very merry time was had by all.

THE LASQUETI ISLAND
SEAFOOD COMPANY

—Darlene

Around 1976, a handful of mostly north-enders (a few from the Mudflats and several from Fisherland) decided to try selling crafts at the Renaissance Faire up in Courtenay. This summer event began as a craft and music gathering, but soon after developed into a straight-out music festival with crafts and food on the side. They brought up small paintings, carvings, hand-sewn clothing, leatherwork and wind chimes, and set up a small craft booth in the fairgrounds. The first year not much money was made, and although it was a fun thing to do, they came back to the island with a new idea for the following year's fair.

They'd figured out quickly that food sales were where the money was at. The food booths were crackin'—they always had at least a small crowd of people up front, and it looked like fun. Lasquetians are foodies—they are now and they were then. So the idea of selling clam fritters, muffins, berry pies and whatever else they could make, along with a few crafts, felt like the right way to go.

So the next July they were back at the Courtenay Faire, this time selling clam fritters, clam chowder, muffins, berry pies and oyster sandwiches. The business was better, but a small booth right next to them was run by two Lasqueti women, and whatever it was that these women were selling seemed to be a hot item. The group was curious. It turned out the women were just selling home-baked muffins, cookies and cakes, and tea and coffee. But why such brisk coffee sales starting in the late afternoon? And why was the coffee from this little booth so popular with the fair organizers? It turned out that they were running the small coffee and muffin booth while quietly providing "special coffees" upon request. A "special coffee" had a good shot of brandy in it and cost twice as much. There was no beer garden at those early Courtenay Renaissance Faires, so in the late afternoon and early evening it

Our big chalkboard at the Vancouver Folk Festival, 1979. Photo Barry Churchill.

became a popular place to discreetly order a relaxing drink.

The women at the coffee booth were ... guess who? Me, Sherry Mateka and Leila Ellis, and we were raking in the bucks. Perhaps recognizing our entrepreneurial savvy, the others invited us to join up with the bigger Lasqueti food booth for the next year.

We agreed to join in, and the next year, in 1977, the Lasqueti Island Seafood Company took shape. The twelve people grew to about sixteen or eighteen over the next several years. Our main gigs were the Courtenay Faire in July and then the Vancouver Folk Festival in August. We did other fairs too, but none were as fun and as accessible as these. They were our steady annual outings. From early June until early August we lived a spontaneous nomad lifestyle, bonded together by the "booth."

We were seasonally tribal, close-knit and focused. We loaded up our trucks with the stoves and work tables, cupboards and boxes of homegrown lettuce, totes of clams, oysters and smoked salmon and headed to the fairgrounds.

Our kids came along too, and they all had little jobs to do in the booth. The small ones played in the back and napped under makeshift sunshades. My seven-year-old daughter, Mopsy, spent most of one June making paper flowers and attaching them to a wired stem. She would spread out a blanket near the front of the booth and sell them there. My son, Hoatie, made batches

Early days of the Seafood Company at the Courtenay fair. Ross Hughes in the centre with youngsters, Hoatie Macy and Uwe Shiek. Photo Barry Churchill.

and batches of Hires root beer from a mix, and we'd carry the heavy wooden boxes (Rubbermaid totes hadn't been invented yet) over on the ferry and up to Courtenay. He had his own area in the booth, way off to the side. He employed several helpers—the Hildred boys, Todd and Aaron, his good buddies Shane and Laz and a few other kids—to tend the booth when he needed a break.

This "Hoatie's Root Beer" booth was very popular and always had a swarm of young kids hanging around it. Hoatie made good money, but when he and the boys got into going around and picking up the empty beer bottles left on the fairgrounds on Monday morning, they made even better money.

Being accepted as a vendor in those days was a pretty easy process. It was done with an open, generous spirit and little, if any, paperwork. We were given a certain amount of ground space to occupy, and it was never enough. Ross and Tony would go and negotiate with the organizers for "just a few feet more" and they'd all return with their clipboards and tape measures and finally give us maybe a metre more on both sides. Once we got to setting up the booth, we always turned that extra metre into two. And as long as no one complained, it worked out.

There were highs and lows, of course, involved in the experience of being with thirteen or more people day in and day out for over a week, and working it all out—sharing your money, kids, toothbrushes and love.

There was the feeling of being a close family: brothers and sisters from the same rock who have travelled into the big city to camp and work. These fairs, and this vendor's life, were a way of temporarily escaping the repeating pattern of everyday homesteading routines and the blandly predictable "home and garden" existence.

But there were hard times too, like the summer of the big, ugly electric stove that Ross bought for fifty dollars and was so proud of. It took four guys to heave and heft it into the booth, and then the damn thing didn't work.

Vancouver Folk Festival, 1979. Saturday afternoon and business was buzzin'. Photo Barry Churchill.

Everybody was crammed around the one working stove, trying to cook everything at the same time. I once sat down and cried into my apron after accidentally burning twenty pounds of rice.

And there were money squabbles and hands coming from everywhere wanting a cut. Arguments. Rain. And that bleak, sodden morning the park was nearly deserted, with only me and Marsha left to disassemble the entire booth while our damp little kids slept in the car—all for the total of two hundred dollars.

But there were fun, busy days too: people lined up, patiently waiting to give their money away for just about anything to put into their mouths. Salmon steaks, at ten dollars a pop, would go like hotcakes, and nobody out there in the city-clean, folk-music crowd seemed to mind the drunken hullabaloo going on inside the booth, as long as those big steaming bucketfuls of clams kept appearing on the counter; as long as the coffee kept being poured for all those hands proffering thirty-five cents ...

Young guys and girls would buy their lemonade and coffee and then hang around the side of the tent, just the seafood people inside, laughing, yelling, spilling and bumping into each other. Carrying paper plates, four at a time, heedless of all that money on the floor or in heaps on the counter, wads of grey, green and silver, gulping that wine and making change, with cigarettes dangling from their lips.

In the early eighties, things began to change and getting accepted as a food vendor was more of a process. The first thing to go was allowing booths to accept straight cash from customers. Up until then, we were to pay ten percent of our profits to the Courtenay Faire, and that was that. Simple, and we did occasionally make justified "adjustments," but we were basically honest and undeniably outrageously hard-working folks, so it was never a case of greed.

Food purchase tickets were introduced at the fair. At first we did not like this change at all, but over time we came to realize that it did take a lot of worrying out of the picture. All those containers of cash that we had to watch like hawks, especially at night, were gone. Tony told me how at the very first fair they did up in Courtenay, they kept all the money in white buckets under the front counter. As evening came on and people in the booth started to drink and party a bit, he and Ross and Barry were standing at the back, toking up and just enjoying the lively scene going down. Then their eyes went to the space below the counter and they could see hands reaching between the boards, grabbing wads of bills. He said they just zoomed to the front and grabbed those buckets, but the robbers had gotten away by then.

In some ways we adjusted to the ticket system, but they also wanted a thousand dollars up front as a vendor's fee. That was about 1985, and we'd been doing the fairs for almost ten summers by then. People began to drop out, move on, and the members changed.

Dazy and I were just starting the Teapot House Restaurant on Lasqueti by then, and we both felt done with the food booth. Others just dropped out. The group had new members, and we always loved hearing the stories when they returned from a fair. We would ask them lots of questions: "So, how did it go? Was Saltspring there? The Choco-Banana Boys? How was the music? Did you make any money?"

For several years afterward, we old, original members would sometimes get together and talk about the possibility of doing just one more fair for fun, but we never did. The day did come when we all got together and cleared out the old cupboards and sinks and stove that we'd stored under a tarp behind the post office, and we had a laugh at the rotten wood, our old signs, the soggy containers of takeout plates and napkins gone all mouldy and ant-infested.

It was time to say goodbye to the Lasqueti Seafood Company, but our sign hangs above the outdoor kitchen at the community hall.

Because, I mean, you never know …

FED UP

—Buckwheat Bob

In the late 1960s, when many young Americans fled to Canada, mostly to avoid Vietnam, they found, at least on the West Coast, fertile ground for co-operative effort. Eventually Vancouver, BC, had a number of co-operative houses, a radio station, a food co-op and finally a credit union.

Back in the US, the movement was beginning to break up, but the Canadians, being a little behind the times, were not aware of this. The Canadian West Coast infrastructure has always been somewhat primitive due to its vast distances, rugged geography and relatively small populations. There is basically one major highway going north–south in the middle of the province and one going west–east. Hundreds of communities are dotted throughout the province with varying access to commerce centres, and coastal communities in many places are only accessible by water.

Because of the difficulty and cost of transporting food to outlying areas, food was very expensive and variety sparse, especially for food groups other than meat, potatoes and oatmeal. A group of politicals got together in Vancouver to attempt to put a food distribution system into operation. This was the genesis of the Fed Up Co-op.

From the beginning, the obvious two political factions formed. The urban co-op members were mostly interested in purchasing politically correct foods. Many of them were expatriate Americans and anything they could do to irritate the American government, such as buying food from China and Cuba, satisfied them. The other group was the "cheap food" coalition. These folks, American and Canadian, lived mostly in the bush.

The Fed Up Co-op included three to four full-time employees and a warehouse. The model was based on warehousing only, except for one storefront in Courtenay, BC. Orders were compiled weekly. Each member community handled the details of food procurement in its own way, of course. The operation on the user end, specifically on Lasqueti Island, where I was

"Buckwheat Bob" Harrison taking a break at the site of the new community hall. Photo Johnny Osland.

a member, was organized in the following fashion: the island we lived on, being long and thin with relatively few vehicles, was broken down into three areas—the north end, where the main island commerce was conducted, mid-island (my group), and the south end. From the list of food available from the co-op, and there were impressive choices because Vancouver had many wholesalers, each member family would select the type and quantity of food desired. This information was compiled as a single order for the group, with quantities compiled as bulk rather than individual orders. The three group orders were then put together to comprise a single island order. Members prepaid the cost of the food plus 10 percent for overhead. The frequency of orders was up to the main group. On Lasqueti, we usually ordered four times per year.

Staffing requirements at Fed Up were met by commitments from the member groups, calculated by the average amount of money spent by the group. At the local level the members who chose to go to town for the current week cycle were given twenty-five dollars and told, "See ya later." Winter duty in Vancouver was a coveted assignment for the dirt-poor islanders. I'm sure that many relationships and lives were saved by this cabin-fever-easing vacation to town.

The twenty-five-dollar stipend doesn't seem like much but the amenities in town were a big perk. The worker was responsible for getting to town and getting back home after the week was up. Shelter was provided by rooming in one of several co-op houses in Vancouver. Having to room with a few other people was no problem with bush-dwellers, and having central heating and hot water and showers was really a bonus. There was one free midday meal provided at the warehouse, which, since we had several tonnes of food

The cover from a Fed Up Co-Op catalogue.

within sixty metres of the office, was not a problem. I still dream about that food. And there was no junk food at all. The work was warehouse work and very hard, but for the bush people, back-breaking work was the norm.

Another advantage of this work-sharing was that it provided a chance to tighten the movement by establishing contact with people who would not ordinarily meet. BC is a vast province with greatly separated communities. The trip to town was particularly good for musicians. The weather was generally pretty good when I was in town and I made a good bit of change playing street music.

At the warehouse the group orders from all over the province and from Edmonton, Alberta, were compiled into a single order. Vendors were contacted, the orders placed, and then we waited for the food to arrive. We set up pallets for each group that was ordering that week. The vendors generally delivered on Tuesday and Wednesday. The bulk food was broken up to fill the group orders. This could be a delicate operation when dealing with liquids such as oil, molasses and honey. Bulk dry food as well as dried fruits such as raisins and currants also had to be repackaged. If a particular product was unavailable we had to decide upon a viable substitute, which was occasionally a bone of contention when the order got back home.

Groups were responsible for transporting the food to their group location. When the orders were finally filled they sat on pallets until the group picked them up. This always required acquiring a truck one way or another, driving to the warehouse and stacking the pallets on the truck. Some locations were very difficult to get to. Terrace, near the coast up by the Alaska Panhandle, was a trip of maybe 1,300 kilometres, very difficult and expensive kilometres during the ice and snow of winter. People in island locations had different problems. The Edmonton group had to truck the stuff through the Canadian Rockies.

On Lasqueti we used several methods of transport during the time I was involved. The most direct was to hire a truck to pick up the food at the warehouse, take the ferry to Nanaimo and drive past Parksville to the French Creek Harbour. There were several options from here. At least once we hired the ferry to haul the food to the island. This required some coordination. It was helpful if the ferry, with willing hands to load the cargo, arrived in French Creek around the same time as the food truck. This actually happened on occasion.

Step two was to have a truck with helpers at the Lasqueti dock when the ferry arrived. When the food came to the north end, the yellow house, often unoccupied, was usually designated as the staging area for the island breakup operation. The food was off-loaded from the ferry onto the truck, driven up the hill and then unloaded at the yellow house.

There would be a work crew from the three island units waiting for the food to arrive. At this point a breakdown operation similar to the breakdown into individual orders at the Fed Up warehouse took place. Each of the three island orders was broken up and orders and quantities and prices were adjusted. At this point there was a lot of anticipation and excitement. Most of us had been living on oatmeal for several weeks leading up to this big event.

Again the food was divided up into individual families and adjustments made to the original order. There was always a lot of participation at the group breakout. It was important to find out who in the neighbourhood ordered what, and who one wanted to visit in the next few weeks at about mealtime.

Of course, each family was responsible for transporting its food to the home location. In our case this amounted to several miles by backpack or by boat if we were lucky and the weather was good. Talk about pigging out when the food got home. Christmas is nothing compared to the food arrival from Fed Up.

During the winter all the transportation options involved uncontrollable variables. Just because someone, say a fisherman who agreed to haul the stuff from Vancouver to the island, promised he would deliver didn't mean that he would. Using boats is always iffy. The trip would be contingent upon the weather, among other things. If the food was loaded in the hold you hoped that it had been cleared of fish guts and rats and the boat didn't leak.

One time a fisherman offered to bring the stuff from Vancouver in his fishing boat. We would save a lot of money and hassle this way. The boat owner had a day job and was going to come across on the weekend. The weather was bad and he couldn't get across the gulf so he docked in Gibsons, a short way up the coast, and went back to town to work. For a week the boat sat at the dock in Gibsons. Our survival was at stake so there were some anxious times on the island. Did the boat leak? God, we hoped not. We finally got the stuff and luckily it worked out okay that time.

Another time, one of the islanders offered to ferry the food from Vancouver. The weather was bad and he lashed the drums of oil, molasses and honey to the deck. The lashings broke loose and all the barrels were lost. Not so lucky that time.

Living in conditions like this we really learned the concept of community. Eventually civilization caught up to some extent and the Fed Up system was no longer needed.

THE LASQUETI ISLAND
REGIONAL DIRECTORSHIP

—Doug Hamilton and John Cantrell

In the early 1970s, Lasqueti Island broke into the local ossified power structure. Both Lasqueti and Texada islands were part of the Powell River Regional District, but there was only one representative for the two on the Powell River ·Regional Board (PRRB)—and he had always come from Texada. That island had a strong redneck mining element who worked in the marble and limestone quarries. They, along with some members of the PRRB, did not take kindly to the alternative hippie lifestyle and the influx of new immigrants flooding into the area. Many long-haired people felt underrepresented, disrespected and ignored by the local power structure. This led the dissidents on Texada, the PRRB and Lasqueti to combine forces and conspire together for a bigger piece of the political pie.

John Cantrell, first president of the Lasqueti Island Community Association, describes how this happened.

> In early march of 1973 I attended a meeting at Nancy and Cecil Varney's house with political activists from Powell River (Bill Fogerty, Len Evans and Harold Lenox) along with Lasqueti residents Mike and Amelia Humphreys. The people from Powell River were unhappy with the regional board and wanted a change, and they were aware of Lasqueti's problems with the PRRB and our lack of representation. So a grand plan was hatched to throw out the old PRRB, get the activists in and get representation for Lasqueti on the PRRB.
>
> The regional board meetings were held once a month in Powell River, and the plan was for me to show up at each meeting

Opposite: John Cantrell.

representing Lasqueti. The meetings were open to the public, and our Powell River supporters would be there to support my demand to be on the board. My friend Ed Harper took me across to Cook Bay on Texada for my first meeting and encouraged me with his positive outlook, which really helped.

I walked up the logging road and got a ride with a logger who took me right to the north end, and I got the ferry over to Powell River. After a few phone calls I got in touch with Bill Fogerty, who I stayed with over the next few days. The Fogerty family was wonderful, and so supportive during the months ahead. Their home was headquarters for the activists, and many nights were spent planning, drinking and carrying on.

At the first meeting in Powell River I was definitely nervous, but I knew I had lots of supporters in the audience with me. We all sat down and the board members strolled in, thinking it was business as usual. After the introductions I stood up in the crowd and introduced myself as the elected representative from Lasqueti Island. I said that I was going to take my rightful place on the PRRB to represent the people of Lasqueti and then moved up out of the audience, pulled out an empty chair around the board table and sat down—to the cheers and applause of the audience. The board members had a moment of stunned silence; finally the chairman stated that he already had someone from Texada representing us. I replied that the Texada rep had never even been to Lasqueti and knew nothing of our needs—our island wanted its own representative! There were a few minutes of confusion, but eventually the board got down to business and the meeting was over. We then went back to the Fogertys' for a celebration and more strategizing.

On my second trip I kayaked across to Texada and walked until I got rides up to the Texada–Powell River ferry where Bill Fogerty picked me up and gave me the update on the meeting that night. The board members were very uptight, but that did not stop me from taking my rightful seat at the table. I put a motion forward that the board write Victoria regarding Lasqueti's desire for our own representative on the PRRD. They reluctantly agreed. When the meeting ended I was taken aside by the chairman and another board member and told in no uncertain terms that my presence was illegal, and if I was to return for a third meeting the RCMP would be there to escort me out of the boardroom.

Back at the Fogertys' we held a meeting and decided we had come this far and were not going to back down now. For the third meeting Ed Harper motored me over to Cook Bay on Texada across a glass-calm Sabine Channel, and off I went to Powell River. A large number of supporters were at the meeting, which was a good feeling, and the evening went off smoothly—without the promised RCMP. This was followed by a ruckus of a party back at the Fogertys' with many supporters feeling strongly that progress was being made. We were finally seeing the people's democracy in action.

My trips to Powell River went on through the summer with visits down to Victoria with other Lasquetians pushing for our own rep on the PRRB. The NDP were in office with Dave Barrett as premier. Rosemary Brown was a member of the NDP caucus, and she also owned land on Lasqueti. We hoped for a sympathetic hearing and voiced our cause in meetings with them. But they did not want to give us a rep because we did not have a big enough population. We argued back that as an island we were a special case with our own special interests, and we needed our own rep because the Texada politico who supposedly represented both islands had no interest in Lasqueti and had never visited the island.

After much lobbying for our cause, we were disappointed by our BC politicians, who refused give us a seat in Powell River. But fall came, and a provincial election was called, which included our regional district representatives. I knew we needed to run someone, even though we would surely lose as Texada had a population ten times that of Lasqueti.

I was also getting tired of all the politicking and running back and forth from meeting to meeting. So we asked a friend and land partner, Dennis McBride, if he would run. At first he was reluctant, but I explained to him there was no way he could win. And we had to run someone as we had been demanding representation. Not submitting a candidate for the election would make us look like a joke. Dennis said, "Oh, sure, what the hell?" He filled out the forms and got on the ballet. Well, two days before the election the Texada nominee was disqualified because he had the government garbage disposal contract, and there was not enough time for Texada to nominate someone else, so guess who got in? It was Dennis McBride—the only one on the ballot.

As you might imagine, this was cause for great celebration not only on Lasqueti, but also for our political activist friends in Powell River who had been elected to the board. There was a wonderful feeling of empowerment. It was hard to believe that our different vision and different lifestyle could actually bring such important changes to our small community.

At first Dennis seemed a little shocked in his new role, but with a bit of coaching he came to love it. He served his community well and is still remembered in Powell River for his flair and dashing presence. On Texada, people now felt they had no representative of their own and, heaven forbid, had to rely on a hippie from Lasqueti. But Dennis charmed them and tried to convince them that he could do a much better job for them than the Texada rep ever did for Lasqueti.

After all this excitement, Victoria began to listen to Texada people's concerns about how they had lost their rep on a technicality. The government decided a year later to have a vote on Texada to allow them to have their own rep. A man named Whitehead got in, and now both islands have a seat on the PRRB.

Dennis McBride served his fellow islanders for two colourful years.

THE SINKING OF
THE GORE ROCK

—Darlene

In the mid-1970s, the herring fishery on BC's West Coast was at an all-time high. The fish counts were staggeringly abundant, the openings were brief but amazingly rewarding and quotas were sky-high. Local fisherman Ronnie Mann made one million dollars in a fifteen-minute opening. Crew share on his boat was eighty thousand dollars. His success was legendary and inspirational.

To quote one fisherman, "French Creek was like the Wild West ... floatplanes were taking off and landing every ten minutes, guys were on their boats partying and drinking, there were cash buyers walking up and down the docks with suitcases full of money. The Boar's Head Bar was packed with herring fishermen every night, the Sea Edge Motel and the Island Hall were totally booked. It was like this for the whole season ..."

This bonanza from an abundant natural resource lasted only a few years before fish populations crashed. A few of the established, experienced fishermen from Lasqueti made good money during this boom and then returned to the lower harvests that naturally followed. Their years of experience had taught them to predict peak seasons and to recognize when they ended. Like the Klondike rush for gold, those few years of mid-seventies knockout herring seasons attracted plenty of less-experienced people who were eager to enter the fishing industry and get in on the boom. They quickly bought boats and licences and found friends to work as crew.

Some of them did well during those seasons: they made it to the areas in time for the openings, worked hard and reaped the benefits. Some people had only their dreams dashed, while others lost their boats and everything on them.

Fishboat Galley. L-R: Gordon Bissett, Ian Ross, Steve Parent, Bobby Nishi, Howie Siegel. Photo courtesy Howie Siegel.

And some lost their lives in the heavy storm that hit the north coast during the late-February herring season in 1975.

This story was told to me by Marilyn and Jan Darwin. Newly married, they were living in a cabin on Jenkins Island, working hard and trying to get together enough money to set themselves up. When the opportunity to work as deckhands during the herring season was offered, they took it, seeing it as the way to make their fortune.

Here they recount their experience as deckhands on the fishing boat *Gore Rock* during a 1975 herring season.

> MARILYN: It was late February of 1975 when Steve Parent asked Jan and me to come along as deckhands on his recently purchased boat, the *Gore Rock*. He really wanted us along on this big opening with him and his girlfriend, Maggie Neufeld.
>
> After talking it over, we decided to come along, and why not? This was our chance to make our fortune! We packed up our gear and and left for Vancouver a few days later, meeting Steve and Maggie down at the Steveston docks. It was early in the evening, pitch black, and cold and breezy. The *Gore Rock* was tied up in the fishing-boat area, with a big welded aluminum herring skiff tied alongside it. After we loaded our stuff

onto the boat, we untied the ropes and began heading south-west toward Victoria. As we went around Race Rocks, we noticed that the bilge pump had been installed backwards! It was pumping water into the boat instead of out of the boat, so Jan was like, "Okay, gotta get this fixed right away," and he had to get out there and fix it. That took a while, but he got it all put back in the right way. So we were following a fleet of other boats, trying to keep up with all these other people in this frenzy to be on time for an opening up in Barkley Sound.

The *Concord* was one of the boats we travelled with. Kurt Carlson was the owner and skipper, and Nick Knott on the *Esperanza* was following him. We stopped in Port Renfrew that night and fueled up, got a few groceries and headed back out. We were travelling through the night, and pretty soon after we'd left Port Renfrew, our radar completely gave out. Whew, that was a sign! So we just kept going north and began to follow a big seine boat, figuring that if we stayed behind the wake, it would be our guide. It was crazy, following this big seine boat up the coast with no radar. Pretty soon two other boats were following us and we found out that their radar was out as well. So there we were, three smaller fishboats, just blindly following this big seiner up the coast, all through the night.

But we eventually made it up to Barkley Sound. In the early-morning light, we saw that all the other boats were tied up side by side. The water was quite rough in there, and I guess that's why everyone was rafted up. We got our boat anchored in and tied up. After breakfast we decided to get into the skiff and have a look around, just to kill time. We went off to nearby little Esperanza Island and there we found a Native burial ground. There were these huge totem poles, right down there on the beach. Then a Native man came down and told us that this was a sacred burial ground, and that we'd have to leave right away. He said that one of the totems had already been cut in half with a chainsaw, and so now no outsiders were allowed to be in this place. I took photos of this island and these totems, but as it happened, they'll never be seen.

We left, walked down the beach and got back into the skiff and took off, but we couldn't even get onto the *Gore Rock*—it was that rough—so we went over to this great big packer.

The guys on it were really great, and they brought us inside where it was nice and warm and gave us coffee. Later, we were able to get onto the *Gore Rock* where we made final preparations for the nighttime opening. When it all looked good to go, we just hung around and waited until opening time. It was in the middle of the night, and there was a full moon with stars glittering in the sky and a light wind blowing.

Now, we had this old herring skiff with absolutely no hydraulics on it, just big compartments where we stood all dressed in our Helly Hansens, wearing heavy gumboots on our feet and big gauntlets on our arms over these heavy fishing gloves. We just stood there and pulled in the herring nets by hand, shaking those nets all night long. We shook until morning light. At one point, Maggie and I went inside for a break. We went down into the galley and looked into the mirror and couldn't believe what we saw! We were covered in guts and slime, with herring scales pasted all over our faces and in our windblown hair. It was incredible!

You know, when I look back, there were very few women out there. I mean, how many women went out to the West Coast and shook herring all night long on a boat with no hydraulics? Those nets were full of herring, and they were heavy, and you had to shake them all night long.

So we pulled and shook nets for another few hours and got all the fish over to a packer. He took it all, so we emptied our skiff and got back to the boat. Believe it or not, after that we were all in a great big hurry again, this time to get up to another opening in the Central Zone. This was up past Cape Scott, near Namu.

We took off that day with several boats following us. It started to get rough out there, because this was the West Coast, remember? And there was a storm warning, but we never heard it broadcast because the building storm caused technical problems on the weather station that day. We were way below Cape Scott at this point, and the waves were getting really big. Maggie was getting pretty freaked out. We would look out the windows and see boats disappearing into the troughs of these big waves, then coming up alongside us, then disappearing down again. We went into Tahsis and we let Maggie off the boat. She was going to fly out to Campbell

River the next day. She was absolutely terrified and was not going to get back onto the boat. I thought about flying out with her, but I didn't, because I figured I'd better stay with the guys for this opening as they'd need me to cook and stuff. Ha! What was I thinking?

So we spent the night in Tahsis, and the next morning the three of us left for Winter Harbour to get some more fuel and food before we headed back up to the Central Zone. We couldn't find anywhere to shop, only this little dive of a place on the dock was open, and there was hardly anything at all in it. All it had was a few wrinkly apples, some stale-looking white bread, some canned milk and a few cans of Folger's coffee—that was about it. I remember Steve telling me to "get some meat, get some meat!" when I left the boat, so I found the rusty old refrigerator that defined the meat section, and when I opened it up I picked up a piece of meat off a tray. When I turned it over, there were maggots crawling on the underside of it. All the meat was crawling with maggots! I still shudder when I think of it. So nope, I didn't buy any. I just got back on the boat.

We continued on our way north, joining in with a small fleet of boats. At this point, Jan reminded me that our CB radio was not on the right channel for weather: we were on a buddy channel where we could talk to other boats. Apparently there was a storm warning out to all marine traffic, but we didn't have the weather channel on, so we didn't know that. And we discovered that the coast guard weather boat had recently been out and it had gotten pretty badly beaten. It had lost some gear and with the technical damage they were unable to broadcast a warning. So there was this big weather system gaining strength and a lot of boats didn't even know that there was a storm headed our way. Only later, when channel sixteen was back on, did we realize what was happening.

Things were starting to feel uneasy as we headed north to Cape Scott. The waves were gaining strength and the wind was whistling through the cables. I went down into the galley for coffee, and when I opened a can of milk, I remember realizing that I'd opened it upside down. It was Pacific canned milk and I stared at it, remembering when Maggie had told me to "throw it off the boat if you ever do that, it's bad luck." We were down to so few groceries that it seemed wasteful to me, and I decided to ignore her words and this silly superstition.

I made my cup of coffee and carefully carried it back into the wheelhouse, trying not to notice that the boat was now really heaving with the wind. Steve had owned the boat for only a year and didn't have much open ocean experience. I had this trust in Jan, though, as he'd worked on fishboats and been out on the water all his life. I trusted that with him on board, we'd be all right. But Steve was in this herring frenzy, just following these other boats with guys that were friends of his. Nick Knott and other guys like Ian Ross were there too, I think, just ahead of us. They called Nick "The Admiral" for fun, because he'd done really well in the past, so these guys thought that they just couldn't lose, following him.

Soon after, I remember hearing all these cans—big, clanging oil cans—suddenly banging around and into each other. I said, "What's all that noise?" and Jan went out to see what it was. When he came back inside he reported that the boat was taking on water, the bilge pump couldn't keep up with the water coming on board, and we may be in trouble. He went back out, tied himself to the mast with a rope and began to use the manual bilge pump.

So it was blowing, it was crazy, it was super-rough, and I was just completely flipping out because I couldn't see him from the wheelhouse and he was trying to bail water out of this boat in this huge storm and all around us the winds were just blasting.

After a while, Jan could see that it was going to be impossible to keep the boat floating with the manual bilge pump. He had trouble convincing Steve that this was all happening, that this boat was in real danger of going down. Steve wanted to stay with the boat, and he had this idea that, as captain, he was going to cut the skiff loose.

We could not let this happen. The skiff was our lifeboat, our only option. So we had to argue with Steve right there, in the middle of a howling storm so fierce you could hardly stand up, on a boat that was slowly sinking.

"I'm staying with the boat!" he said.

Jan said, "No, you're not! This boat is going down and you're getting off of it, now!"

While Jan was trying to convince Steve to get off the boat, I was holding the lever to the emergency pump with a belt. I just stood there and held onto this belt like I was told to do. Stuff was floating all around me: our clothes, our sleeping bags, maps, everything was whirling past me in sixty centimetres of water. And I just held onto that strapped lever.

Finally, Jan turned to me and told me that I could let the belt go, that there was no use in bailing anymore. But this desperate attempt had kept us afloat for another half hour or longer, long enough to persuade Steve we needed to get off the *Gore Rock*, and enough time to make a mayday call. Jan told me to get into the herring skiff. The *Gore Rock* began to heel sideways, with water coming in over the bulkhead and in the wheelhouse door. Then the rigging was going under, and the water began flooding through the gunwales and across the deck. As I crossed the boat I began to lose my footing and had started to slip when Jan suddenly grabbed me. It was a close call, because Jan had this small knife in his right hand, and he could've easily missed and driven it into my ribs. But he turned at the last minute and got me up into the skiff with one big push.

After half an hour of this madness, Steve finally snapped out of it and came into reality and got into the herring skiff with me. We all watched for a moment as the radar was going around and around, and the running lights of the boat started to submerge. The *Gore Rock* was beginning to go down, and nothing more could be done about it.

At this point, we had just made it around to Cape Scott with Bobby Nishi's boat, the *Ensenada*, ahead of us. Jan put out the mayday call. Because Steve was always screwing around on the radio, it was hard to convince the other boats that this was a serious call coming from the *Gore Rock*. When Hugh, a deckhand on Bobby Nishi's boat, didn't believe the call from Jan, Jan yelled into the speaker, "Hugh, this is no joke. We are taking on water and we are going down!" Hugh said, "Oh!" and yelled this out to Bobby, and Bobby Nishi swung his boat right around and flew toward us.

Bobby Nishi was unreal, he'd done it all before. He was a second-generation Japanese fisherman, with a great boat and years of fishing behind him.

When the *Ensenada* came toward us, we were all in the skiff. But the waves were ramming us back against the *Gore Rock*. Jan had to pull the skiff rope up out of the water to cut us free; otherwise we'd be pulled down with it. First, there was this big, heavy chain that he had to pull up, and after that he had to cut the heavy braided manila rope that went from the skiff to the *Gore Rock*. He was cutting like a madman through the heavy rope with this little knife as the waves pounded us back and forth between the two boats. It was like "tight-loose-tight-loose-tight-loose-tight-loose" as he sawed at the rope. The big stanchions on the side of the *Gore Rock* would pound into his upper back and shoulders as it swung out with every wave. He tried to ignore this awful, intermittent pounding and kept sawing away at the rope with his knife. When he heard a loud grunt behind him, Jan turned around for a moment and saw Steve Parent's big arms holding back the stanchions of the *Gore Rock*.

Steve was a pretty burly guy, and this took a lot of strength. But he held the *Gore Rock* away from Jan's back long enough for Jan to make the last cut through the rope and free the skiff.

JAN DARWIN: I could hear Steve grunting really loudly, fighting with the skiff while I was trying to cut the rope, and the waves were going "kah-choong, kah-choong!" back and forth, and I was leaning over the boat, hanging by my gumboots, trying to cut through this rope. Finally it came tight and I got one good cut almost through it, and in a minute it came tight again and I just whacked it with one good cut that went through. We spun away from the boat on a wave. But we looked over, and Bobby was going around and around us in an arc and he yelled out, "You have to get this line now—I can't come in again!"

We understood what he meant. We grabbed the line and tied it on, and he just gave it, right? The last pass he made, we were going on the rocks! That's what he meant: if we didn't get that rope, he couldn't come in again, we were way too close to the rocks. Also, there were these lines coming off our boat and he didn't want to get his prop tangled up in them. It was dark, there were lights from the other boats shining everywhere, so we got this line, and this is the amazing thing: it's gold-strand nylon, right? About the best, strongest line you can get, so I

grabbed it and started tying it up, and Marilyn started screaming, "This line's gonna break! Throw us another line! Throw
us another line!" and I couldn't understand what she meant.

MARILYN: It's like a voice inside of me made me say these
words. It was so bizarre to have these words coming out of my
mouth! Something was speaking to me, and I was just insistent
that we have one more rope.

Jan was yelling to me, "That rope will never break!" and I
just kept yelling at Bobby and Hugh to throw us another line.

JAN: So Hugh throws this little scotchman on a line over to us. I
get two wraps, and *snap!* That first line just snapped, it snapped
right in two.

MARILYN: We got on board Bobby's boat, they took us out
and we had to cut the skiffs loose. Everyone was cutting their
skiffs loose. They had to, they were just smashing into the
boats. They will just rip holes in a boat.

Looking back, you have to think so fast, everything's just
like a blur. You don't even realize that you might die, that your
life is being threatened, because you're in survival mode and
you're doing everything you can to get into that herring skiff
and get away from those rocks and onto that boat.

JAN: At one point Marilyn said, "The pictures! the pictures!"
and I climbed back onto the boat and looked through the door,
but everything was just floating, and I couldn't stay on it.
They were gone.

MARILYN: It was blowing eighty or ninety by then. Freighters
were going up on the beach on the coast and in the Vancouver
harbour. My parents thought we were dead.

JAN: Bobby had reported it, that he'd rescued us, but somehow they got it wrong and said that we'd all perished! So that's
what our parents heard, they thought we were dead. For two
days. And Maggie thought so, too.

So we had to stay on the boat, and the engine could never
be turned off because it was anchored, and we had a boat behind
us. One boat had lost its anchor, I think it was the *Bella Nova*
... Ian Ross's, I think it was him. He was tied behind us, and we
had a spring line with big cannonballs hanging in the middle, so

there was always this *pong! pong!* sound. Bobby had to stay up all night; we had to take shifts. Hugh and I were going up to the bow and wrapping pipe around the anchor chain. The anchor chain was straight out. We had fifty fathoms of anchor line out in nine fathoms of water—that's how strong the wind was.

So Hugh and I would go up in our rain gear, and Bobby would toot when the waves came, then we'd just hang on and we'd go right under—our feet would come right loose from the deck so we'd just hang on, and when we'd come up, we'd tie, tie, tie, tie, then he'd toot and we'd hang on and go under, *splooosh*, come up, and tie, tie, tie, tie. And then we'd make our way back along the boat. We had a rope tied around us so if we did fall over, they could pull us in from the back, or salvage the body.

MARILYN: I remember Bobby told me to have a shower. It was like heaven. He made me, because I had hypothermia. And Bingy made us some hot soup.

JAN: So we anchored for two nights in the blow. We couldn't turn the engines off. Bobby had to go almost full throttle on the anchor sometimes, and he had a huge Cummins. He had a powerful boat. It was twelve metres long, with all the gear on it, but still, in those waves, it would lift right up with those waves and roll right over. That's what we anchored in, for two nights.

I'd have little catnaps, sitting up, and then I'd hear the engine change pitch and I'd wake up, and it was like, "okay, what's up, what's up?"

"It's okay, we got 'er ... no ... oh yeah, we need you! Get another tie!"

We had to sleep in shifts for two nights. At first, Bobby would only sleep in the day 'cause the wind let up, but then it picked up again ... you should've seen the beach.

On the third day the storm left, and we went to shore to see if we could find the skiff. We finally found it on a beach, but we couldn't even see it at first. It was filled to the gunwales with sand. And the undertow in there was so huge, and that's where we would have been going with the skiff. That's where we were headed: we were heading to that reef and that beach, right for those rocks.

I walked up on the logs and I thought, "Wow, the tourists are going crazy, they're putting all these big rocks on top of the logs and up in the trees ... what are they doing that for?" And then it dawned on me, like, "Duh-h-h ... the *waves* are putting the rocks up there." They pitched them up, right into the trees. And that would be the worst, you'd just get propelled out of the boat and smacked onto those rocks.

Maggie was supposed to meet us up in the central area, after the next opening. When she heard on the radio that the *Gore Rock* had sunk, she became suspicious, because they had reported us as being in a completely different location. She began to think that there was a chance we made it off the boat. After two days, someone contacted both Maggie and our parents and told them that we were still alive.

So yeah, this had been our chance to make our big fortune. But in the end, we lost everything—all our clothes, identification, any money we had. It was a real letdown. People had made thousands and thousands of dollars in the previous years, and this was supposed to be another big bonanza season. In the end, some kind of fishermen's welfare gave us four hundred bucks and paid for our flight out of Campbell River.

Devil water took seventeen lives and fifteen boats that year. The *Lady Sylvia* was one that went down in that storm, and on board were a father and his two sons. The mother had search parties out for weeks afterwards but never found her husband or her boys.

Another huge loss of life occurred when a brand new aluminum herring skiff overturned as it came around Cape Scott. The crew didn't bring on water for ballast, so it was high, and it rolled over in the heavy seas. All six men on board clung desperately to the keel, but a quick rescue was impossible. One fisher in the area reported seeing the overturned skiff through binoculars and watching with horror as the crewmen slipped off one by one, into the raging sea. By the time a boat was able to reach the skiff, only one man was still hanging on, but he died a short time later. Exposure suits were available in those days, but the more protective "survival suits" were just coming on the market in 1975.

The weather system that hit the north coast that tragic season of 1975 can be justly described as a freak storm. If Bobby Nishi had been unable to rescue them, Jan, Steve and Marilyn wouldn't have lasted more than three minutes in the water. And, as Jan said, they would've just been ground up on that reef. The ocean bottom was so stirred up that there was dirt in the water at fifty fathoms.

At Cape Scott there is a three-metre tidal fault, resulting in a sudden rise where two opposing currents collide. When a storm hits that area, the wind creates haystack waves as these currents collide. Boats get hit from both sides. These fierce, downward-directed winds were hitting the herring fleet during that storm. These winds literally pushed boats down into the water.

So when the westerly, ninety-knot winds hit the area, the weather ship got absolutely hammered. It lost half its antennaes, and was unable to broadcast on channel sixteen. The crew sent out a PAN, which means they were in trouble, but it is not an SOS. There were PANs coming over ship radios from everywhere. Because channel sixteen was temporarily not operational, fishermen were using the buddy channel to stay in communication with each other. By the time channel sixteen got back on to put out a warning, the storm had already hit. And it hit hard and fast. The prediction was for southwesterly winds at fifteen to twenty knots, a nice sea. But it very quickly turned westerly and went up to eighty knots.

The *Gore Rock* was twelve metres in length, all solid wood, and it may have survived the storm if the fuel tanks hadn't come loose and smashed into the deck. Jan feels that without that, they could have put a sea anchor out and survived that storm.

Afterwards, Maggie Neufeld and Steve Parent built another boat, the *Crazy Horse*, and continued fishing for a while before selling it to Nick Knott.

Marilyn and Jan feel that they just weren't ready to go that stormy night back in 1975. Jan told me that the night the *Gore Rock* was going down, he had the strongest feeling that he was standing on a rock.

"As I looked back and saw the lights from the boat shining and going down in the water, I had this strong illusion of solid rock under my feet ... and I felt so calm. It was weird—we weren't even off the boat yet—but I could feel this rock under me, and I just knew that we were going to be all right."

They went on to have four children, several grandchildren and a small boat, and they live happily and supremely busily on Lasqueti Island.

GHOSTS AND UFOS

—Doug

Most people have seen strange visions, heard weird sounds, found things moving about without cause or experienced a loss of time or "impossible" coincidences. Many years ago I was talking to Ed and Betty Darwin, Lasqueti Island residents for over fifty years. They were both no-nonsense Marxists and refugees from Stalin's Red purges of the 1940s. Betty scoffed, "There's no such thing as ghosts—but those kinds of things happen all the time to everyone."

How true that inexplicable events take place often, but what causes the phenomenon remains a mystery. Are they spirits of the dead, UFOs, creatures from another dimension or even something we generate ourselves? Islands seem to be particularly prone to these events, and judging by the stories I have heard from friends and neighbours, Lasqueti is no exception.

Almost everyone who has lived on the island for more than a few years has some kind of odd tale to tell. I can offer no explanation for the following stories and will only verify that they happened to reliable witnesses—and in some cases to me personally. Some events are so common they are barely worth mentioning. There are numerous tales of footsteps pacing across the floor with a startled dog or cat closely following the invisible walker's progress. Ghostly figures are seen passing through walls, rocking away in a chair or just standing by the roadside. When approached, they fade away or remain in the distance. A neighbour alone in bed was suddenly shocked as his sheet and blankets were whisked completely off and dumped on the floor. There are muffled sounds of a baby crying, boisterous voices or someone singing softly in the distance.

This story by Tolling is typical:

> On the dark of the moon in May I was up reading when I heard
> what sounded like a four-cylinder car labouring up Oben Road
> past Roger's house and starting to descend on the swamp side

of the hill. I got up to see who could be coming to visit this late at night. When I looked through the window I could see the headlights of a car come around the corner on the far side of the clearing. The lights were that yellow of six-volt lights and were bouncing independently of each other, like headlights used to do when they were mounted on fenders that were starting to rust out. I heard the engine rev as the driver downshifted to make the turn to cross the bridge just before the house. The lights from the truck (?) then turned off the road into the parking space in front of the house. The lights went out and the engine stopped. I heard two doors open and close and the voices of two men talking to one another as they approached the house. I went to the front door to greet whoever it was and opened the door to emptiness. There was no car or men anywhere to be seen. The light from the oil lamp I was reading by cast enough light out the front door to see that there was no other truck parked next to my old Dodge pickup.

Or try to explain this story of an unusual water sprite. After almost a decade of squatting in a beach shack, I moved to an inland piece of property. We built our house on the edge of a large, shallow swamp complete with ducks, herons, eagles, frogs, wild crabapple trees, cattails and lilies—a veritable park locally known as the "cow swamp." Initially we had grandiose plans to dig it out and create a water wonderland in the front yard.

A few months after the move I was invited to dinner at my neighbours', and we ended the evening telling ghost stories. Their particular tale revolved around a well-dressed lady who periodically appeared on their hearth in a rocking chair. It was such a vivid description that I felt more than a little nervous on the dark walk home. But I made it back safely and went to bed around midnight. My partner was away at the time, attending to her elderly mother.

A scarce hour later I awoke with the feeling that something was very wrong. The bed was cold, clammy and distinctly sodden from my knees to my toes. My first thought was that I had peed the bed—the first time since my tenth birthday. But it soon became clear that the liquid was not urine with its distinctive colour and smell—and besides, my bladder was full. The bed was sopping wet with at least three litres dumped at the foot while the upper sheet was completely dry. The fluid was odourless and tasteless and appeared to be brownish swamp water.

I dismantled the bed, which took several days to dry out completely, leaving a large, brown stain on the mattress cover. This all seemed weird and impossible—the room was completely encased in drywall. But wait, maybe my hosts of the previous night had decided to play some kind of bizarre practical joke. I called them, and they were as mystified as I was. There was no reasonable explanation so I put the matter out of my head and forgot about it.

Then a month later it happened again, but this time there was a large puddle between my partner and myself at about chest level. Again, the upper sheet was dry with two or three litres drenching the bottom sheet and pad. And that was not the end of the matter. Over the next couple of years we were wetted down on several occasions, but curiously not always in the bed. Several mornings I woke up to find a large puddle of brown water on the floor in a corner. It really started to bother me. Water appearing from out of nowhere just made no sense, and the drenching only happened when I was in the bed, never to my partner alone. It felt like harassment. Was something trying to tell me something?

In Indonesia, people build ghost houses to calm troubled spirits. The haunted householder constructs an elaborate miniature house, places it outside his home and politely asks the spirit to move into it. Something was obviously upset by our presence, but perhaps there was some way to placate our water spirit.

By now the plan to root up our beautiful marsh and convert it into a swimming pool had been abandoned. After living swampside for a couple of years, it was obvious that such a plan would have wrecked everything we cherished about our space and turned the wild marsh into a giant, unsightly mudhole. One evening, after a couple of ceremonial glasses of wine, I apologized to the swamp spirits and promised that we would never consider such a travesty again. The inundations abruptly ceased. That was twenty-five years ago.

One of the saddest series of paranormal events concerned Gary Lansdown, the talented musician who died in a freak car accident in 1976. He was twenty-two and one of the most talented guitar pickers ever seen on Lasqueti Island. He was a founding member of the Spaghetti Island Stringband along with Grover Foreman, Laurence Fisher and Dan Rubin. He and the group hung out practising their riffs in Qualicum Beach and travelling around in an old VW van.

A couple of days after the accident, several of the survivors were gathered at the Qualicum Beach home they had been staying in. They were just sitting down for dinner when everyone heard the sound of footsteps upstairs. The eerie pacing sounds moved from one side of the house to the other but

Ghosts and strange occurences in the Stone House were legendary. Photo courtesy Bruce and Gordon Jones.

were centred around Gary's room. Hackles rose on everyone's necks, and finally someone got up the courage to see who or what it was. He went upstairs calling out and, of course, found himself addressing an empty room.

This happened several times in a row until finally the most fearless went upstairs and forcefully addressed the restless spirit. "Gary, you are dead. You don't belong here anymore. It is time to move on. You were killed instantly in a horrific traffic accident, and your endless pacing is scaring the living shit out of us. Please leave us!" Within a few minutes the footsteps ceased and everyone felt much sadness and relief.

Later on during that dreadful week there was another curious incident. Just before the accident, Gary had offered one of his guitars to a neighbour. He had always been very generous about both lending out his musical instruments and taking time to encourage other would-be musicians. After hearing the news of his death, the neighbour played the instrument many times to honour his memory. She then hung it on the wall with a leather cord to keep it out of the way and well protected. One dark night she woke up to strange sounds. The guitar was being quietly strummed in the next room. This was not a mouse tickling the strings—the instrument was actually being played. Terrified, she crept out to the living room, and the music abruptly stopped. The experience was most unnerving: no more sleep that night. The guitar was reverently placed in its case and removed to the woodshed.

Many of the ghost stories I have heard were from the two dark mansions on the island—the Stone House and the Teapot House. Both were built as a kind of self-made monument to the single-minded men who built them, Ted Sideras and George Hadley. And both buildings seemed to provide the perfect home for a ghost—gaping windows, large dark rooms, no electric lights, huge beams holding up the roof and the decrepit grandeur of someone's private ego trip falling into early ruin. Today only the Teapot House remains.

The new owners of the Teapot land all lived in the house for several months before branching out to their own homesteads. Almost all report strange faces at the windows, the tread of footsteps crossing the floor, musical instruments being strummed and strange lights at night. All felt a "presence" and would actually address George Hadley in conversation from the bathtub. He never answered. Eventually, the building was lovingly restored by the new Teapot House owners and designated as a Canadian heritage building.

Teresa Olson grew up on the island and was a bit younger than the hippie invaders. Gordy was her father and half of the well-respected two-man road crew. She had a weird experience in the Stone House a few years before it burned down. By then, Sideras and the commune were long gone, and the mansion had been sold to an absentee owner. Teresa and three friends decided to visit the Stone House for a bit of sightseeing and to collect some personal effects left over after a friend's breakup. The four walked down the extended porch and entered through the back door that led to the kitchen. Sitting alone at the kitchen table was a strange woman with a haunted thousand-yard stare. She proved completely unresponsive and oblivious to attempts at conversation.

A little taken aback, the four continued warily through the dark dining room with Teresa in the rear. Suddenly someone or something tried to seize her ankle. "Who grabbed my ankle?" she yelled, pushing everyone into the brightly lit living room. "We are in front, how could we grab you?" they asked. But when Teresa pulled up her pant leg there were four clear finger marks on her ankle—and there was no one else behind her. To round out this rather strange visit she decided to take some photographs of the cavernous rooms, secret passageways and gaping hallways.

Several weeks later Teresa was back home showing off her stash of photos to a friend who suddenly exclaimed, "There's something wrong with these pictures—look!" On close examination many of the photos showed bizarre anomalies. A large cedar block near the staircase appeared to be on fire with flames shooting up on all sides. Almost all of the windows reflected strange faces mistily staring at the camera. Particularly disturbing was a man with long hair and beard.

It was so strange that she later sent the pictures to Kodak for examination. In due course Kodak replied that there was nothing wrong with the film and nothing unusual in the shots. In other words, don't bug us.

Teresa told one person about her experience and put the packet of pictures in the kitchen cabinet for safekeeping. A few days later she returned from work to find the back door open. At first she thought it was her own carelessness, but her boyfriend distinctly remembered her locking up that morning. When she went to retrieve her photos, though, they were missing—the only thing taken—and they remain missing to this day.

UFO, Strange Dreams, Tiny Lights.

Some people believed there was a strange kind of energy field that hovered over the little neighbourhood where the Bumps and DiFiores once lived. Both of my children and their friends clearly remember unusual things that happened there in the late seventies—a UFO sighting, strange parallel dreams and a mysteriously powerful light.

One evening there were seven kids (Julia and Shane Bump, Anna and Laz DiFiore, Mopsy Purcell and Hoatie Macy and Sunday Dennis) lounging around in the old DiFiore place that was located not far through the forest from the Bumps' house. An adult party was going on at the Bumps', so the kids were staying out of the way with a little party of their own. It was early evening, and they were generally goofing around, eating snacks and reading comics and magazines. One of the gang came across a magazine article on UFOs, and they all read it with great interest. Julia Bump recalls that night:

> After we were done reading comics and that magazine with the UFO article in it, we all went into the upper level and lay around on the bed up there. A few of us were on the bed, a few on the floor, and we lay there in the dark, pondering about what we'd read and staring out the windows that faced out to the forest. Then we all saw it. It was a saucer-shaped orb that glimmered through the treeline, slowly approaching the cabin. It came closer, and we all watched it in silence as it hovered there. Then, a tripod-like contraption was lowered from it, but it was pulled back inside and the saucer just zipped off in a diagonal direction and disappeared. We were all totally stunned. When Shane and I went home the next morning, we found a large, strange pattern burned into the grass just outside my parents' bedroom window. It was all so weird and coincidental

… We told our parents and everyone we knew about the UFO that we saw, but I'm not sure people really believed us …

Bonnie Olesko remembers that a year before, in that same DiFiore cabin, a mysterious light had appeared at that same window.

It was late at night, and as I lay there in my bed I watched this weird light get closer to my bedroom window. When it floated right up to the window glass, I have to say that this complete understanding—this total awareness—just came over me. It entered my brain and took over my mind. The message was to go. Go into it. Surrender and enter, come away. There was no fear involved, and that was the really creepy thing. It came inside of the house and flittered around the rooms. I was absolutely mesmerized, watching it like a zombie. All at once the vision of never again seeing my children or my family came to me. Resistance gripped me so hard that I almost fainted. My mouth just screamed out the words "No! No! No!" toward the light. The light suddenly stood still, then it got smaller and left through the window and flew out into the night sky.

Parallel dreams between people, both adults and children, happened in that area around that same time. In the dreams a UFO would slowly hover over you, and as it moved, it emitted a deep bass tone. The tone was so low and intense that it went right through your body, vibrating every nerve to the core. The sound waves pushed you down, nearly onto the ground. You tried to run from it, but it had the power. After a while, you surrendered to it and the dream ended. The children witnessed these incidents with completely innocent eyes and minds, and it never bothered them to talk about these accounts. They've been told and retold over the years, always retaining their original shape.

THE ASKING

—Doug

Most of us have seen the extraordinary effect of charisma first-hand—that dynamic person who suddenly enters your life like a thunderbolt, causing you to abandon all those well-laid life plans and suddenly embark on a new path. The Ted Sideras commune on Lasqueti Island during the early 1970s vividly illustrates both the pleasures and the pitfalls of surrender to and trust in a single charismatic individual.

The story begins in the mid-1960s with two dissatisfied residents of Medford, Oregon, who were actively seeking a new future for themselves. Theodor Lewis Sideras (then forty-five) and his friend and business manager George Ralph Orton (late twenties) had come to the conclusion that the bureaucracy and social conventions of small-town America were smothering them. There had to be a better, more fulfilling way to live life. The two were prepared to abandon several successful businesses—a restaurant, an employment agency and a credit-reporting bureau. After a year of thinking things over, they settled on Canada as their new home and travelled to British Columbia in July 1967 in quest of a place to settle.

Ted and George soon found what they were looking for, and they purchased eighty acres of logged-off rainforest on Lasqueti Island. Accompanied by their wives, five children and several friends, they set about building their own little paradise. Ted's brother John and his family also joined them, forming an instant community of around twenty. There were no buildings on the property so a tent village was erected in an abandoned orchard at the end of Gline Road. The structure of the new group was fluid; people did what they wanted, but somehow it all seemed to work out. Sideras described his laid-back world view as "no philosophy," and he openly despised labels like "commune," "leader," "hippie" and "religion" to describe the group's guiding ethos.

A nattily dressed Ted Sideras in the mid-seventies. Photo Gordon Jones.

Communal living was seen as a new and exotic lifestyle in 1967, and word of this interesting experiment spread quickly via the underground grapevine, both on and off the island. Entire families were encouraged to join, to increase membership and to provide a good home environment for children.

"Most who came to see us just want to reassure themselves that we haven't got something they haven't, and they don't understand and go," said Sideras in a 1970 interview published in *Maclean's* magazine. "The ones who come with open minds to look, they initially stay. They don't have to pay anything or do anything. After a while they find no demands of any kind are made on them, and you see them beginning to relax and start relating to the others and doing things they want to do and have to be done anyway. Cooking or cutting down trees, or the laundry, or helping with the house. It's real nifty to see."

Within a few months there was a thriving tent village of enthusiastic members. Most were Canadian, but there were a sizable number of refugees from the American dream. Kids from island families also made up a fair portion. Island life could be difficult for children during this time. Families were fractured by isolation and boredom, and some parents were obsessively controlling. For kids with family problems, there was really no safe refuge. The Sideras group seemed to provide a warm and loving alternative. Sometimes several family members would join the group together.

Teenage islander Karl Darwin signed on in September 1967. "I needed a place to dry out," he said in a 1991 *Globe and Mail* interview. "I'd done so much acid by then, I didn't know whether I was seeing the world stoned or straight. I met Ted on the ferry—God, that man had a magic tongue—and he invited me to camp with them to get my head straight." His younger brother Jan soon followed, along with their sister Gail. Some have claimed that their mother, Betty, never recovered from the sudden loss of three of her six children to the group.

The new commune appealed strongly to disenchanted but successful, well-educated professionals from the city. Largely aged between twenty-five and forty, many were married with children. These people were not low-life dropouts. In fact, it was a highly eclectic and interesting crowd. There was an anthropologist, a sociologist, a medical doctor, a mathematician, a lithographer, a dress designer, a concert violinist, a psychologist and a welder, among others. It is a curious fact that communes tend to attract highly intelligent and adventuresome people. One need only look at the ranks of the Hare Krishna movement, the Rajneesh group in Antelope, Oregon, and many others to find refugees from the best universities and most prominent families in North America. It takes courage, individualism and (let's be frank) money to make this kind of major change in one's life. And as members were to discover, group life also requires sacrifice, tolerance and endless patience.

On Lasqueti, the new commune was viewed at first with acceptance and interest. The numerous visitors attracted to the island were a welcome breath of fresh air. Many were searchers earnestly looking for a new kind of life. The friendly, convivial atmosphere was immensely attractive, and most visitors immediately clambered to join—but acceptance was not automatic. Ted had to personally meet and interview prospective members to gauge their suitability. After the vetting, they would either be allowed to remain or asked to leave. Islanders tell of dozens of disappointed aspirants returning home with heavy hearts, summarily rejected for some unknown fault or indiscreet remark.

While the group was welcoming and open to visitors in the beginning, islanders remember them as becoming decidedly standoffish as the years went by. Members kept to themselves during island gatherings and ferry rides. Neighbours and relatives of members dropping by to visit were treated with increasing coolness. The Teapot House, one of the oldest land co-operatives on Lasqueti, visited one afternoon in a group of about ten. To their amazement, they were not invited in and were instead politely asked to leave. This was a surprising breach of a long-standing island custom. Visitors were traditionally asked in for a cup of tea when they showed up at your door. It was almost as if the non-believing outsiders were becoming a pollution—a dangerous influence to be watched closely and kept at arm's length.

Visitors would ring a bell to summon the gate attendant, who asked their business. Shirley Mann, who ran a taxi service on the island between 1970 and 1975, tells of parents and friends being abruptly turned away, even on holidays like Christmas. "I'm terribly sorry," the gatekeeper would say, "but your son [or daughter or brother] has no desire to see you. You must return home." Some came back many times in hopes of catching a glimpse of their loved ones, but they were almost never admitted. Understandably, these rejections caused dismay and consternation, which were stoically ignored by the gatekeeper standing guard. Today, many ex-members look back on these cavalier snubs of friends and family with shame and embarrassment.

Ted Sideras was at the centre of the group from the beginning. He was both its leader and grand philosopher. Physically, he normally looked like a frumpy Woody Allen—heavy, black-framed glasses, "stoop-shouldered, crinkle-eyed, minus a few front teeth" with a "wind-roughened face fenced by a moth-eaten beard" (*Maclean's*, 1970). But he could dress very nattily, carefully combing his hair over a balding pate, and affected an academic, almost professorial, demeanour. But this belied his power and intensely personal spiritual magnetism. Ted was rarely seen alone. He was always surrounded by admirers—who included many women.

The leader had a glib tongue, and his lively soliloquies were mesmerizing for some. Ted Sideras could spin a story and leave the listener feeling flattered, enlightened and vaguely confused, all at once. He was the ultimate dreamweaver, building castles in the sky to intrigue and inspire. Almost every night after dinner, the frumpy guru would hold forth on the evils of the outside world and the glorious future that awaited the commune. He tended to speak in "cosmic" generalities, which sounded uplifting but were hard to pin down. For instance, he would often compare his "family" to intangible natural wonders like spiderwebs. "It's like gossamer: try to touch it, to define it, and it vanishes" (*Maclean's*, 2002). And Ted insisted on making most of the major decisions. In fact, "ask Ted" was the common refrain when some minor or major question required a solution. Some visitors found this ironically amusing when compared to his frequent assertion, "There are no leaders here."

There was a strong ascetic, puritanical tone to the group, and there were lots of arcane rules to follow. Books, most newspapers, television, radio, music, dancing, most personal property, money and conventional religion were considered useless distractions and discouraged or forbidden. Important current events like national elections, moonwalks and wars were shrugged off as irrelevant and ignored. Members only caught up on these things after they left years later.

A musician friend who spent much of 1970 looking over various BC communes told me he thought that it was the most restrained and least ebullient of any of the groups he spent time with. Meals were eaten in orderly silence while the numerous children were kept sequestered by parents. Loud talking, laughter and emotional outbursts were discouraged. Ted fairly bristled when a lively conversation failed to include him. Discussion of some topics was circumscribed. For example, talking about one's past life was discouraged because obsessing about the past kept one from concentrating on the rosy future. Look toward what will be—forget about what once was. Members were told to leave their "old identities at the gate." This advice was taken quite literally: for years afterwards, islanders turned up pieces of abandoned identification cards, drivers licences, even passports buried in the damp woods around what came to be called the Stone House.

And forget about the counterculture's enthusiastic embrace of free love and drugs—both were roundly condemned here. Pot, LSD, alcohol and other intoxicants were strongly forbidden. For those wishing for something more potent than water, the group provided "Goopa," a sweet/sour drink made of fermented apple vinegar, water and honey.

There was a significant shortage of women both in the commune and on the island at the time. Not surprisingly, membership qualifications always seemed to favour attractive single women. But promiscuity was frowned upon and singles were encouraged to spend time separately, in different areas, during the day. Lust was a temptation to be withstood, except in the marriage bed. On the other hand, having children was a very good thing because they were an important part of the future. Although Ted was married and had strict views on sexual morality for members, he clearly favoured some women over others. It seems likely that he occasionally indulged in discreet affairs.

The commune's finances were murky and, in fact, a tightly guarded secret.

On the surface Sideras and Orton were supporting the whole enterprise with their own funds and "occasional contributions from newcomers." The two were thinking big and planning for the future. They were actively negotiating with the British Columbia government for 640 adjoining Crown acres for future expansion, and neighbours' properties were also considered. The stated plan was to have the Nanaimo solicitors MacIsaac, Clark and Sinclair set up a co-operative that would own everything. Present members would buy a share at a reasonable price, "perhaps a dollar." Newcomers could buy in after they had spent a nominal amount of time in the community. Sadly, this generous and truly communal plan never materialized.

Rules governing property were clear: share and share alike. On joining the group, one surrendered all valuable assets from one's previous life to Ted's control for the betterment of the family. New members were expected to turn over their personal bank accounts, investments and property. Member Jane Anderson remembers that when things got short, people were asked to "kick in some more money. Everyone knew we shared, but I think there was pressure on people who had anything left. People gave a lot, up to $10,000 at a time" (*West: Globe and Mail*, 1991). Certainly, a number of disgruntled members later complained of being "taken" for large sums after things went south. Of course, no records, receipts or IOUs were issued to anyone.

How much was "donated" over the years? It all seems to depend on whom you talk to. Those who contributed large sums think that Sideras made off with hundreds of thousands of dollars. But those who arrived with nothing and left with nothing think he probably went broke feeding the multitudes. The truth must lie somewhere in between.

The commune had a work ethic that can only be called bizarre. Coercion was unknown, no one *had* to do anything: the labour was self-organizing. In fact, work was considered a privilege, and peer pressure to earn the right to labour was overwhelming. Workers were known as the "camp jocks." The jocks had status within the group, and they also received double food rations. The "camp lizards," on the other hand, were the unlucky ones. They were forced to stand around idly twiddling their thumbs while the favoured ones hammered nails and carried stones. Although the "privilege" of work turns the conventional view of labour upside down, it put a powerful tool of social control into the hands of the leader. An army of eager workers was created, all vying with each other for recognition and extra food. Perhaps this is why the commune was able to accomplish so much—at least on the material plane.

Food was a central interest, and all agree that the group ate extremely well. Unlike in many communes of the time, vegetarianism was never seriously considered. The emphasis was solidly on animal protein. They constructed a large chicken coop, and a fishing raft was moored offshore for rock cod and bottom fish. Curiously, vegetable gardening was discouraged because Ted felt that self-sufficiency on the commune would be seen as a put-down of the outside world, and would "turn people off." The commune deeply valued its isolation but did not want to be marginalized as back-to-the-land eccentrics. The local deer and feral sheep population also supplemented their diet. What could not be fished, grown or hunted was purchased on Vancouver Island and ferried over. The fare was upscale. Islanders remember cases of chocolate sauce, crates of condensed milk, quarters of beef, fresh sausage, fall turkeys and smoked pork frequently arriving on the ferry from the grocery stores in Parksville. By 1970, bills in excess of seven hundred dollars a ferryload were not unusual. The typical meals of beef stroganoff, savoury stews, roasts and homemade bread were a major attraction. Plates brimming with fish, island mutton and chicken are still remembered by former members with fondness. "We ate well. Home-baking, great soups, some store-bought stuff we got wholesale, eggs from our own chickens, and all that beef. It was a high protein diet, for sure" (*West: Globe and Mail*, 1991). Some islanders looked askance at this rich, high-fat diet, so unlike the typical hippie fare of sturdy whole grains and rice.

The group was highly spiritual without being formally religious. There was no worship service, no flirting with the fashionable Hindu and Buddhist beliefs of the mystic east, no sacred artifacts or symbols—not even grace before meals. Some claim that Ted was the religion. There was, however, one peculiar "religious" ceremony that played a major role. Complex metaphysical decisions about God, morality and what path to take in life could be answered by performing a ritual called the "Asking."

"They didn't let you see that," Karl Darwin said. "You never did unless you joined us. People used to go off on their own into the bush or some place and ask God or whoever was up there—Ted didn't say if he had a name—for guidance. It wasn't like you were asking for something for yourself, like in a regular selfish prayer in church. You had to say, 'Father, what is your will regarding so-and-so.' People would come back with answers for Ted to interpret ... Anyway, it was impossible to pooh-pooh the Asking. I never heard dick all, but some people got answers" (*West: Globe and Mail*, 1991).

Questing communards would retire to a quiet place in the woods and seek the Papa's advice. His wisdom would then be relayed directly to Ted for interpretation, and Ted would explain the message to the rest of the commune. Gordon and Bruce Jones, neighbours and brothers, tell of running across several members in the midst of an Asking deep in the forest. They seemed to be in some sort of mental trance, oblivious to their surroundings. When hailed, they remained vacant and unresponsive, concentrating on their profound communication with a higher plane. The Joneses described the chance meeting as "eerie." Yet this odd ceremony, rationalized and interpreted by Ted, was to play a crucial role in every major decision the group made.

Sometimes the results were surprisingly prescient. Former member Jan Darwin remembers: "Building the house we had trouble with this giant boulder, and I went into the bush and asked, 'Father, what is your will?' And I heard that I should light a fire on a certain part of this big granite rock. I went back and Ted Sideras was lighting a fire on exactly the place. The rock split" (*West: Globe and Mail*, 1991).

Although the Sideras commune shared many of the communal values of the back-to-the-land-movement, they were not the same. Ted's was a one-man show, a semi-deified leader who demanded devotion, loyalty and assets. The Asking ceremony, the self-imposed exclusiveness and the financial shenanigans suggest a very different headspace from the anarchistic, anti-authoritarian stance of the flower children. Ted was careful to make the distinction. They were not hedonistic hippies seeking empty pleasure but rather a group of serious, hard-working people forging a new world. Ted always went out of his way to disparage the growing hippie counterculture.

By 1970, a number of wild stories began circulating about the group that titillated the prurient interest of editors from Toronto to Vancouver. It was said that Sideras prayed to the rising sun, the Stone House was full of secret passages and surrounded by a three-metre barrier, sex and drug orgies were part of the daily regimen and dozens of teenagers and American draft dodgers had fortified themselves into an armed camp. Rumours of dodgy financial dealings led some to claim that Sideras had amassed a fortune in gold from his followers and hidden the treasure somewhere on the property.

Alan Edmonds, a writer for *Maclean's* magazine in Toronto, was asked to do a story on the commune, and it became one of his most widely read Canadian magazine pieces of the seventies.

Edmonds and his photographer, Don Newlands, arrived on Lasqueti for a visit with the group in the spring of 1970. They soon found the scandalous rumours to be a crock of blarney. Contrary to expectation, everyone was smiling, friendly, happy and healthy. The massive Stone House was nearing completion, an impressive testament to the leader and his vision of communal utopia. Edmonds described it in his story as "a massive *schloss-like* mansion of stone, roofed and half-paneled with hand-split shingles of shakes, and set on the lowest of a series of knolls covered with moss and lichen and struggling brush, all framed, when we arrived, by the deep dark green of the forest" (*Maclean's*, 1970). The foundation and first storey were built of large chunks of stone laboriously dragged from the surrounding hills and set in concrete. The roof and second storey were beautifully finished with cedar and Douglas fir shakes and came together in four graceful gabled windows set on a gently sloping roof. A monumental living room on the first floor resembled a great hall and was surrounded by bathrooms and bedrooms. The second storey held six commodious two-room suites.

My own impressions after a visit in 1976 were somewhat different, and Sideras was long gone by then. Everything showed beautiful workmanship, but the mansion had a haunted feel to it. It was a cold, damp castle. The cedar-panelled rooms felt like dank prison cells dimly lit by high, tiny windows. One felt that this edifice was intended to be an enduring monument rather than a comfortable place to live. And as a confirmation of earlier rumours, the building was indeed full of secret passageways, which accessed what can only be seen as escape routes and hideaways. After the land was sold, the Stone House became a playground for kids in the neighbourhood who were intrigued by the cleverly hidden chambers.

In later years brave souls who spent the night in the deserted palace heard strange sounds and breathed strange smells. Even when completed, the building was never capable of housing all of the members. Most continued to live in the monastic tent village behind the big house. Each tent was set on a wooden platform and came equipped with spartan wooden beds, a thin foam pad, a handmade chest of drawers, an oil lamp and a chair or two. The larger tents were reserved for families with children. Married couples and singles of the same sex shared the smaller shelters.

When they arrived, an attractive young woman named Penny greeted Edmonds and Newlands at the gate and led them to the plastic-covered dining area outside for lunch. Alan and Ted got on well with each other from the start, and the writer was obviously captivated. The two visitors were given a coveted bed in the unfinished Stone House, allowed unlimited access to the master himself and encouraged to go wherever they pleased. Edmonds wrote a long glowing report, enticingly titled "Would You Give up $25,000 a Year to Find 'Peace' in an Island Commune?" Replete with photos and fulsome praise, the article appeared in *Maclean's*, in August of 1970, and compared Sideras and his "family" to those early Christian martyrs and mystics who chose solitude and meditation over the temporal life.

Edmonds and Newlands spent three bucolic days on the commune helping to build a new world. They lived simply, dressed casually and ate communally in a plastic-sheeted mess hall. Although Lasqueti Island was never identified by name in the article, the story generated a wave of interest worldwide. *Maclean's* received thousands of letters and queries, which were forwarded to the island, and the secret location soon became common knowledge. Inspired by the story, hundreds of people flocked to Lasqueti to see this path-breaking social experiment for themselves. The response was so overwhelming that Edmonds remained forever haunted and guilt-ridden when things later soured. Had he inadvertently destroyed the dream?

But the dream was already running into difficulties by the time Edmonds's piece appeared in August 1970. Although the group had hoped for a long-term occupation of their Lasqueti utopia, things were not working out as planned. The grand plan to acquire 640 acres of neighbouring Crown land had bogged down, and there was a disturbing sense of being overrun by encroaching civilization. The land was rapidly filling up with hippies, retirees and affluent back-to-the-landers. Once again, an Asking provided the solution.

> Then one day, Steve Shute [one of the original members] comes in to the meal tent and says that Father talked to him about civilization and pollution getting closer—you could go row a boat and see that; all the crap coming up the gulf—and about the house not being big enough with all the new people and our not having enough land any more, and that it was time to move. Ted said that this Answer was the goods, so we hurried up and finished the house, sold it for $65,000, and moved up to Calvert Island (*West: Globe and Mail*, 1991).

The islets atop Vancouver Island seemed a perfect solution to their growing problems. Calvert Island, a large, uninhabited mountainous tract opposite Rivers Inlet, was far from the inquiring eyes and polluting cities. Eighty-five kilometres north of Port Hardy, it guaranteed privacy and space—for a time. But it was also extremely rugged. The commune purchased a thirty-metre boat, the *William C. Dodd*, packed up and headed north. Their arrival on Calvert was not auspicious. Landing on an inhospitable rocky beach, they were forced to drag heavy gear by hand up a steep corduroy road to a clearing for the tents. This was to be homesteading at its most basic.

Interestingly, the group did not use their communal assets or proceeds from the Stone House to buy property on Calvert. The avowed plan was to squat and raise pigs on ten sections of Crown land (6,400 acres). But the pig-raising scheme soon ran into trouble. For some curious reason, the conservative BC Social Credit government, under W.A.C. Bennett, seemed loath to grant such a large parcel of Crown land to a messianic American guru and his exploding flock. Even with the help of a skilled lawyer, they made little headway.

In fact, the group seems to have lost its way after the move to Calvert. Ted Sideras fell into a funk and spent much of his time alone. Money and food were constantly running short. The familial soliloquies and teaching sessions dwindled to nothing. According to member Jane Anderson, life was "hell, all black fly and muskeg like quicksand, and when he got there he lost a lot of his bounce. He spent most of his time in his tent. We took meals down to him ..." (*West: Globe and Mail*, 1991). Perhaps depression, too, was part of the problem. Dr. Ken Schramm later observed, "I had the impression Ted was unhappy. He was enormously steady, never got riled, but I think he felt the family had got too big to be manageable."

Rudderless, the commune came to be dominated by a clique of Americans led by George Orton and ex-Green Beret Bob Craft. There is no one more possessive about his land than a squatter, and the lack of clear leasehold on Calvert fostered an atmosphere of precarious insecurity. There were no big work projects to unite group energies, and the harsh conditions on Calvert—perpetual rain, cloud, cold, insects and isolation—had a depressing effect on everyone. Paranoid rumours began to fly about eviction, food scarcity and legal complaints from distraught parents who claimed their children had been forcibly "abducted" into the commune. There was even talk of a possible plot against the leader himself. Members began carrying guns and went about their business armed and ready for anything. The group behaved as if it were under a state of siege, and relations with the few locals soured. There were several ugly confrontations with encroaching hunters and fishermen. Jan Darwin remembers:

> Our Lord was patient even on Calvert when we got so paranoid about outsiders. Once, some hunters turned up in a boat, and the word was they were attacking Ted and the next thing I know I'm running down with my .303 to defend my dream. I get there and there's about 30 of our people with guns and rifles and shotguns. Sideras carried a gun you know—a .38 over-and-under Derringer, I put his coat on by accident once and found it, but I don't think anyone else saw it.

William Deverell, a Vancouver lawyer turned novelist, handled legal affairs for the commune on Calvert. In his novel *Dance of Shiva*, Deverell tells the story of a guru accused of murdering his entire following on a small island much like Calvert. Though finally proven innocent, Shiva was a slippery fellow constantly blathering platitudes or playing mind games.

Although an infrequent visitor, the lawyer noted a profound change after the move to Calvert. "On Lasqueti everyone was docile and content, but on Calvert they seemed zombie-like. They were drinking what they called Goopa, some sort of fruit juice concoction, and I thought maybe there was something in it. Anyway, I never drank anything they gave me."

In this climate of paranoia and uncertainty, some crises became inevitable. Without Ted's authority there was no way to settle priorities or make decisions. The final blow fell when long-time member Karl Darwin, then twenty-four, returned after a three-month vacation from the group. Darwin had been a loyal member since the beginning. He was a main builder and architect of the Stone House, and he held a position of respect and authority in the group. But for him the magic was gone. The authoritarian and controlling overtones of the group had become intolerable.

> Maybe I finally dried out. But mostly it was their contempt of anybody who couldn't see that they alone had the ultimate truth, and a feeling that no one should have the power over others that Ted had. Besides by the end, the 'in group' around Ted all had guns and carried stilettos, as well as bush knives. It was dangerous, and I had a younger brother and sister still with them. (*West: Globe and Mail*, 1991)

Darwin retired in solitary to a room where he began to drum on an empty pot. This was an outrageous breach of the rules against music making and was seen as a personal insult to Ted—which it probably was. The full wrath of the community was suddenly focused upon him. "I was immediately classified as mad or on dope."

Darwin was "shunned"—that is, kept in complete isolation, rarely talked to or listened to, and forbidden from participating in normal communal activities. Bizarrely, members told him that he had gone insane; he was no longer Karl but someone else. "You are your roommate" was the line. When Karl continued to resist, "the heavies" trussed him hand and foot and threw him into a bunk for two nights and a day to think about his transgressions. "They were reluctant to untie me and let me go to the bathroom," he later commented.

Conveniently, Dr. Ken Schramm, the family's doctor, declared Darwin to be mentally unfit to handle his own affairs. The RCMP was summoned to Calvert Island by boat, and Darwin was taken off in a straitjacket to Riverview Hospital (a mental health facility), where he remained for two weeks.

Although he was soon released, and no further evidence was ever produced to show him to be mentally unbalanced, the stigma of this confinement in Riverview became an increasingly important issue at the trial that soon followed. But with this kind of harsh treatment from past friends—the shunning, the forced confinement, the mind games and the diagnosis of mental derangement—who wouldn't be a little crazy at the end of it?

Upon his return to Lasqueti in early 1972, Darwin began talking to fellow islanders about his peculiar communal experiences. Vancouver economist and UBC professor Dr. Peter Pearse and his partner, Gary Bowden, owned around 160 of the free-range cows on Lasqueti. One afternoon Pearse happened to be at the Darwin home in Boat Cove drinking beer with the family. He was surprised to find Karl present at the table—it was the first he had seen of him in several years. They casually talked about life in the commune, and Karl began to vent about the darker side of his experience with the group. Pearse, on a sudden whim, asked point-blank about several animals that had mysteriously gone missing. "How many did you take?" he asked. "Oh, about thirty to thirty-five," Karl responded. George Orton had asked for and received permission to slaughter three—thirty seemed hardly credible. With so many cows roaming around it was hard to keep track of them all. Yet Darwin estimated that he had helped butcher dozens of cows for the group in four years. Pearse asked him if he would take his explosive story to the RCMP and the young man agreed.

It seems that while the group was rapidly expanding on Lasqueti, the problem of feeding the growing multitudes had become increasingly critical. The group ballooned from thirteen to almost one hundred members between 1967 and 1971, and that was a lot of mouths to feed, day after day, week after week. After only a few months on Lasqueti, matters became desperate for the commune. The group was flat broke, barely getting by on family allowance checks, and people were hungry. Ted declared, "This can't go on," and George Orton went out to the woods for an Asking to determine God's will concerning the physical needs of the group. Fortunately, God proved both understanding and generous—his "children" needed good, nutritious food, and the semi-wild cattle, which roamed Lasqueti Island's open range, would be their salvation.

Darwin described to police several cattle-hunting expeditions with George Orton, beginning as early as November 1967. Both were good hunters who knew how to stalk their prey. It was said the two became so expert that when equipped with a chainsaw they could kill, gut and quarter an animal in twenty minutes.

The local RCMP was intrigued by these revelations. Darwin's story provided the police with a golden opportunity to expose the seamy underbelly of the counterculture. Darwin was offered a deal. If he would agree to become a Crown witness, he would almost certainly not be charged—even though he had been an accomplice in the alleged crimes. An investigation got under way and the matter went to court.

In all, the court sat for thirteen days, and seventeen witnesses were called. On July 13, Judge Bowen-Colthurst found Ted Sideras innocent on all six counts. The judge was simply unwilling to convict solely on the uncorroborated evidence of an accomplice to the crime. And Karl was the only prosecution witness willing to testify.

Ted Sideras, apparently rattled by the difficult court case, and his cosmic flock did not linger long on Calvert Island after the investigation began. They were swiftly evicted from their tents by the provincial government and sent on their way. For some, the decision was met with relief—Calvert had been a nightmare of paranoia and disappointments. Undaunted by the trial, the shrinking commune's next move was to remote Kingcome Inlet in 1973, which was completely isolated from the outside world. The membership of less than a dozen purchased 346 acres of timberland for sixty thousand dollars and found thirty-five head of cattle to run on it. But the logging/beef scheme required a lot of work for very little pay. With poor soil and miserable weather (1,600 millimetres of rain annually), the family could not sustain itself in Kingcome any more than it could on Calvert.

With typical optimism, Ted came up with yet another new scheme—this time, a life in the South Seas, which he had long talked about exploring. He, his family and the Ortons left Kingcome Inlet and flew off to the South Pacific to investigate, stopping in Fiji on the way. By 1976, the remaining group in BC was down to only eight members, which soon fell to three. Their final act was to sell the property in 1977 and send the money on to Sideras. They had hoped to join him on Fiji, but never did.

The faithful Alan Edmonds interviewed the aging guru for a third and final time in Washington state sometime in 2001. Sideras glowingly described his years on Fiji.

I fell in love with the place. It seemed ideal, so I bought some land. Then it turned out the others couldn't join us because Fiji wouldn't grant residence visas unless you had capital or a guaranteed job. Some came to visit, but we stayed. I got a feedlot operation going and we did all right. We even became a focus; a sort of community centre-cum-hospital, for native Fijians. We came back to be with the kids when they got graduate degrees (*Maclean's*, 2002).

During the interview, Sideras as much as admitted to rustling cattle on Lasqueti—but it was by necessity.

He told Edmonds:

You forwarded those letters, and we answered too many of them and told people it was OK to come. We got people from Latvia, Estonia, Crete, France—we even had three communists who wanted us to go to Cuba and cut sugar cane. We didn't turn anyone away, which was a mistake. We had to feed them, which is why we killed the animals running wild. (*Maclean's*, 2002).

According to friends, Sideras, his family and George Orton purchased a plantation in Fiji for growing fruit and vegetables. Unfortunately, tensions on the island between the native Fijians and Indians made business difficult. Government was paralyzed and the two old friends had a falling out. George left for the States, and Ted followed in the early eighties.

After his return, Sideras published two books under the name Ted Lewis—*Another Paradise* in 1987 about his seven-year stay on Fiji, and *The Keep On Going Spirit* in 1997. Things seemed to have changed very little over the years. In the books, the ancient guru still cast himself in the role of all-seeing teacher with deceptively simple answers to life's perplexing contradictions.

Rumour has it that Ted Sideras/Lewis passed away near Kettle Falls around 2005.

The last physical vestige of the Ted Sideras commune on Lasqueti Island disappeared in the summer of 1987 when the Stone House burned to the ground. A small fire started in an overloaded stove in one of the many small buildings adjoining the main house. It spread along the walkway to the kitchen and then into the upstairs. The bone-dry cedar shakes and panelling quickly became engulfed in flames and within a few minutes all that was left of the dream was a tumble of scorched stones and twisted pieces of scrap metal.

Jim Iverson, one of the caretakers, remarked, "It died hard. Most houses, they burn, the windows crack out with the heat. At Stone House, they melted and ran down the windowsills like it was crying" (*Maclean's*, 2002).

Although tempting, it would be a mistake to completely dismiss Ted Sideras and his grand vision. Most of the people I have interviewed remain conflicted but generally nostalgic, particularly about their years on Lasqueti. To them the commune appeared well organized with a brilliant, charismatic leader. People were living in apparent peace and harmony in a loving group environment. All were united in creating a better world. The guns and paranoia that bedeviled the group on Calvert were absent on Lasqueti. Ex-communards recall that the group spent a lot of quality time together telling each other about how bad the outside world was, and how good it was to build a new world in their own way without the stultifying pressures of society hemming them in. Members of his inner circle still speak of Ted with great reverence and dismiss the rustling charge as a crude frame-up.

Even the curious Asking ceremony seems less bizarre on close examination. What religion does not feature a direct person-to-person dialogue with God? Call it what you like—prayer, worship, meditation, communion, the inner voice—such practices seem to have a commonality with all religions.

In spite of his failings, we must accept that Ted provided his followers with a peaceful refuge of happiness and contentment—at least on Lasqueti Island. In other words, in some strange way, for a time, it worked.

PART THREE:

CURIOUS CHARACTERS

Opposite: Keray Farrell. Photo Tom Wheeler.

HOW DID I GET HERE?

—Darlene

Over the years I've asked many people about the circumstances that brought them here to Lasqueti Island. Was it serendipity? Practicality? Love? Luck? Here, a few of us share the story of how we came to be islanders in the 1970s.

JUDY PETERSON (1974 TO PRESENT)
A CAMPFIRE CONVERSATION

Michael Hugenard and I had both been living in Reno, Nevada. My marriage to my children's father was a victim of the Vietnam war—not because it killed him, but because it killed our marriage. He was a committed United States Marine Corps "fight the Vietnamese and kill 'em" kind of guy, so I couldn't survive the life or the attitude. I was a single mom with four kids living in Reno, where I sort of got dumped the last time that he went to Vietnam. Michael was living in Reno, too, and we became very good friends, as we were both working at the same place. I was cooking and catering for workshops at a centre there. It was a great place to work, and all sorts of fabulous people came through for the workshops. I got to feed the crowd and take the workshops, so it was just what I needed at that time.

Michael was working there and he was a Catholic priest. He and I became very good friends, nothing more. We had a mutual friend who also worked there, John, and this friend invited me to go to Canada with him one year. I had made a plan to go to Mexico with my brother that year, but it fell through because his wife had gotten sick.

I'd gotten all prepared, I had my kids all farmed out, and I

The Peterson/Hugenard family. L-R back row: Michael, Beth, Judy, Larry and Robyn. Front row: Liz and Tim (with roosters). Photo courtesy Pat Forbes.

was all ready for a break and it all fell through, so I was ready to go somewhere, but not Canada! I never even thought of going up to big, scary Canada; from the US perspective it was all ice and snow and big polar bears up there, and certainly no amenities, so I told him, "I can't do that." Well, John turned to Michael and said, "Michael, why don't you come along too? Come up with Judy."

So that was the beginning of a shift in our relationship; we went off together and fell in love on the boat called the *Uchuck II* (ha ha!) that ran from Gold River out to Friendly Cove. The year after that, our lives turned into somewhat of a hassle; Michael's affiliation with the Catholic Church ended and he and I decided to try and have a relationship together. I thought, okay, I've got four kids and all I've been able to afford to do as a single mom is to go camping, so if he can't go camping with us then he's not in. So we took off and we camped in Nevada, California, Oregon and Washington and we told ourselves that we were looking for our island in the sun. What I was really doing was seeing if Michael could blend in with my family and see if he could really take us all, and it seemed that a camping trip was the best way to do it. We ended up camping at Miracle Beach Campground up near Campbell River. We'd been there a couple of weeks, long enough to start a friendship with Paul Capon, who worked at UBC.

In the evenings we'd sit around the campfire and he'd play the guitar, and we'd talk, and one night he said to us, "You know, you guys remind me of Lasquetians!" We said, "What are Lasquetians?" and he told us about the island and the kind of people that he'd met from there. So we came to French Creek on Wednesday, which turned out to be a no-ferry day, and then came back again and crossed over. We met Shirley Mann and her taxi at the dock. We asked her for an island tour to look around, and she agreed, but told us the brakes on the van were bad and suggested that we leave our kids with her family at her house while she took Michael and me out to look at the island.

So off we went, and when we came back we noticed that there was a "For Sale" sign on the funky little log-cabin-type place across the road from her house. At that time we had not seen a single other "For Sale" sign on the island. Also, Ezra had met us on the dock and told us that there was nothing for sale on the island, that we may as well give up and go home right then and there. The next day we talked to a realtor about the place. He seemed to hold a disdainful view of Lasqueti property, telling us it was almost worthless, and to only offer sixteen thousand dollars for the ten acres and panabode house. The owner, Norm Kemp, would only sell for nineteen thousand, so we considered what we both had in our savings accounts and said yes, we'd take it. It was so impetuous; here I had these four kids and neither of us had a job, and we bought a house! Within twenty-four hours we'd spent the two thousand dollars that we had left to get us up to Alaska and bought a house that was on a little island that we'd only just visited for the first time.

We cashed in the traveller's cheques for the down payment, nixed our plans to see Alaska and headed back down to Reno to get jobs to pay for it. The next year we came for the summer and just loved it, and then the following summer, we decided to try and get immigrated and stay. It was where we all wanted to be, all the time.

The immigration process was long, but the officer that worked on our case really seemed to like us, and he did everything he could to help us look good. We had almost eighty pages of documents, references and some job offers, and he used them to our best advantage. We got immigrated soon after, and from then on we never looked back. That was forty years ago, now. You know, it was a remarkably successful, appropriate, and perfectly timed thing that we did then, for both Mike and me, to make that move and bring the kids up here. It took us in a completely new direction in our lives. We just embraced it completely, it was really a dream come true.

Molly McKinna
A Bad Marriage

I was in a bad marriage, and I decided to get out of the city. A friend told me I should go and find a place to stay in her family's unoccupied house on Lasqueti Island. I packed some things up and took my two small sons, Jeff and Brian, over on the ferry. It was in the winter, and the snow was beginning to fall. When we got to the island, we got a ride, I think with Shirley in her taxi-van, up to the corner of Lennie and Mine. I didn't know it was called Arnie's Corner—I didn't know anything at all about where I was going, other than that it was the Livingstones' house on Lennie Road.

Molly McKinna. Photo Tom Wheeler.

The boys and I walked from the corner in the snow and found the place, Edith Livingstone's empty house. I thought there'd be some furniture in it, and I was surprised to see that there was nothing in there, or not much, anyway.

I laid some blankets down and put the boys to sleep. I covered them up with extra jackets and a few towels. I slept in a chair, in my coat. It was a cold, cold night. It snowed all night long, and I sat there in the dark cabin and stared out at the falling snow, wondering if I'd done the right thing in leaving, in bringing my little boys to this.

But the next day we figured out how to use the wood stove, and we found some wood in the shed. From then on, it got better. I ended up staying for several years on Lasqueti Island.

MARC HIRSCH (1971–73)
A RUMOUR

When I was done with my physician's residency, I was ready to move out to the West Coast and up to BC. So were my friends Penny and Doug. We partied together in Berkeley and developed a theoretical interest in communal living. We all hung out together and liked the concept of a commune. We found a commune called Chicken Crest in Qualicum Beach, on the east coast of Vancouver Island. We moved in, and I soon fell in love with a woman who lived there named Betty. But as it went, the people who had the biggest financial investment in Chicken Crest largely controlled the commune, and this did not work out for us. Rumour had it that there was this mellow little island with some really groovy people on it just across the water from Parksville.

Lasqueti Island was everything it was advertised to be, with a winter population of only about one hundred independent souls.

We found the ferry and went over, and someone directed us to a beach on the south end of the island. It was called Windy Bay. There was nothing there but an old A-frame shelter made of beach poles and torn plastic sheeting. It was caked with sand and dirt, but we repaired the plastic and cleaned it up and soon it was "Plastic Shack, Sweet Plastic Shack." Betty, her young son,

Banks, and I lived upstairs, and Penny and Doug lived downstairs.

We cooked on an open fire on the beach. We had plenty of coffee, cheese, sausage, powdered milk and cereal that we kept out in a wooden box to protect it from animals. After a year, Betty and Banks left the island and I moved north to Sandy Cove beach, where I stayed another year before moving on and eventually becoming a medical doctor.

DARLENE KAY OLESKO (1971 TO PRESENT)
ABNORMAL NORMA

I was living in Kitsilano in an apartment on West 2nd Street, along with Bonnie and Alan DiFiore and a few other people who eventually ended up on Lasqueti. Among the flow of friends who came through the large four-suite building was a woman named Norma. We nicknamed her "Abnormal Norma" because she was a bit off-centre. Abnormal Norma came around one day and told us that she'd been spending weekends up at a little island called Lasqueti, and it was so beautiful and quiet and empty, and that there were just a few older people there, and lots of empty houses and cabins where anyone could probably live for free. She told us that there was a log cabin that we could rent for eight hundred dollars a year.

Some of our group had already gone up to Peace River and Haida Gwaii (then called the Queen Charlotte Islands) looking for places where we could all homestead but came back unsatisfied. Too many rednecks and straight people up there, so the sound of this great little isolated island that was right north of Vancouver really excited us. When autumn came, Bonnie and Alan went up to check it out, then John and Dianne Bump, Mark De Roschier and Trudy all followed.

I wasn't ready to take my two-year-old son off to an isolated island by myself, so I went back south to Oregon for the winter months. In late December of 1971 I was living and working in Portland, and a fellow named Ray Purcell came through town. Ray was one of the group of people from eastern Washington that Gordon Bissett introduced us to when we all lived on Kearney Street in north Portland. I'd heard some crazy stories about him but had never met him. We ended up spending a few days together before he went back north to Lasqueti, and a month later I drove up to visit everyone and see how it was all going on this little island. I had an orange pickup truck, a 1955 Chevy.

I remember getting off the *Captain Vancouver* ferry on a cold winter's night and getting into Shirley Mann's Volkswagen taxi. During the ride in the dark, looking out the frosty van window and seeing only the trees and the starry night sky going by, I knew I'd arrived somewhere very different. I was not in Kansas anymore ...

I stayed a few days, long enough to decide that this was a trip that I wanted to follow along on, and then I drove back to Portland, packed up my stuff, picked up my son from my mom's place and came back to Lasqueti. There were six of us living in the panabode, so Ray and I moved shortly afterward to Bull Island, which was very isolated.

DIANA BRILL (SCHROEDER) (1973–80)

A SUGGESTION FROM STEVE AND DIANA

We were young, married, and we had a new baby (Cisco Schroeder, later changed to Ry), and we'd both lived all of our lives in Washington state. It just felt like time to explore other places on the West Coast. We packed and prepared our sailboat and headed off from Vashon Island, bound north for Alaska and hopefully a job. On the way north, we stopped in on De Courcy Island where we met and made friends with Richard Lamb. When we left De Courcy we crossed into Canada and continued north to Cortes Island, where we were offered a caretaking job. It looked like a good opportunity, but in order to be hired, we needed landed immigrant status. Deciding that this was the way to go, we turned back and headed south for the US. By the time we'd done the paperwork and were on our way to getting landed status, the caretaking job was no longer available.

Still looking around, we sailed back up to De Courcy Island and met up with Steve Lamb, Richard's brother, and his girlfriend, Diana Firebaugh. They suggested that Lasqueti Island, where they were living, was worth checking out, so we sailed on up. We had been living on the boat in Squitty Bay for a few weeks when the white house that used to be at the head of Squitty Bay became available to us, so we moved in. That was our start on Lasqueti.

Eventually Bob and I separated, but we both continued to live on Lasqueti. He moved to a place mid-island, and I stayed in Squitty Bay for several more years. After a few years, another relationship gave me my daughter, Selena. Unfortunately, that relationship was brief, but Selena, Ry and I were a very happy little family. Although I had some really tough times being a single mother living way down at the end of the island, both the kids and I have lots of great memories of our time on the island. It got to the point, though, where I just had to make a choice about where I was going in life. The kids were growing, and I was doing everything I could to make a bit of money, enough to keep things together, but I decided to return to Vancouver, enrol at SFU, and complete my bachelor's degree. And that was a challenge as well, but it was a good move: I got my teaching degree, and the kids grew up just fine between Vancouver and Lasqueti (Ry lived part-time there with Bob).

DAZY DRAKE (1975 TO PRESENT)
AN EX'S EX

Zootie (Jim Drake) and I were living in San Anselmo, California. I'd met him through my friend Bob Bayless, who introduced us. Zoot's ex-wife, Helen, was the sister of a man who lived on an island in Canada, a man named Arnie Porter.

One winter, we decided to go up and visit him there. We drove north, and in a week we found our way to the ferry dock in French Creek and took the ferry across. Wow, it was a rough ride, and it was cold. We walked all the way from the ferry to Arnie's Corner in the snow. Just imagine—there was no ferry traffic that day.

As we walked there in the absolute darkness, I felt like we'd come to the end of the earth. Big trees blew in the wind; there was just a little store in the harbour, one gravel road ... It was so rural and felt so isolated. Stormy weather kept us on Lasqueti for about a week longer than we'd planned, but in that

Dazy Drake on the *Lasqueti Sunrise*. Photo Tom Wheeler.

extra week we really had a great time. We were amazed by how people came and went at Arnie's, bringing food, homemade beer and wine. It was like one long, mellow party.

After almost two weeks of hanging around, we met some great people like Ezra and Lorraine, Kevin Monahan, Barry Kurland and Wendy Schneible. Arnie had a little car he called the "Love Bug" and he drove us up to a place on the island called Richardson Bay. It was for sale, and he thought we might be interested. There was a little house up on a bluff there, and we hiked up the trail. It had a fantastic ocean view straight out west and across the ocean, and a really nice bay down below with a gravel beach. This place just really grabbed us, and when we returned to California we got the wheels in motion to buy it. We couldn't get Lasqueti Island out of our minds! We bought tools for gardening and homesteading, and we got rid of what we couldn't use on our new adventure. We came back to the island with our three kids, Gordie, Lisa and Yarrow, and our boat, the *Lasqueti Sunrise*, and built another house up on the bluff in the bay.

Zoot brought up a sawmill from California, and he and Doug Brubaker bought a sawmill and started "Forest Lumber." I worked there too, helping on the sawmill, and I worked on the Humphries' oyster farm down in Tucker Bay. I soon met Ed Harper and he taught me so much, like how to shoot and skin a sheep, and how to make beer and wine. For an anthropology professor, he sure knew lots about living in the bush.

So yeah, it all started from a stormed-in winter holiday at Arnie's Corner.

DOUG HAMILTON (1971 TO PRESENT)
A HITCHHIKER

My long journey to Lasqueti began in the fall of 1969 at the microfilm room at UC Riverside in Riverside, California. I was working on my master's thesis about the Stamp Act levied on the American colonies by Britain in 1765. The chairman of the history department stopped by on an errand and we got into a conversation. He was teaching a course on the history of the Protestant Reformation and had spent the last few classes denouncing the anti–Vietnam War demonstrations as an abject surrender to anarchy and lawlessness. I disagreed and welcomed this chance to explore his views. I used his own course as an example, arguing that just as the Reformation of the sixteenth and seventeenth centuries was a symptom of failed institutions, we were seeing the same kind of thing happening again today. An ignorant, corrupt and racist political elite in the US was waging a hopeless war against Vietnam, and the street demonstrations merely reflected the people's frustration.

The chairman's face flushed and his eyes filled with tears. "No, I'm not crying," he snapped. "My eyes always water during a challenging discussion." I returned to the dorm that night thinking I had made a great impression on a key member of the department. Little did I dream that I had reinvented myself as this man's worst nightmare—a rabble-rousing hippie anarchist bent on the destruction of the American way of life. Two weeks

Doug Hamilton enjoying a well-deserved rest and a cigar.

later I received word that the history department had decided that my plans to continue on to a PhD in American colonial history were far too ambitious for my feeble abilities, and that I should set my sights on teaching high school or perhaps even at the elementary level. My low-ranking friends in the department were astonished and embarrassed but could do nothing. I felt crushed and surprised, having maintained an excellent grade point average for the first time in university. Suddenly, even obtaining my MA became a monumental ordeal.

The war in Vietnam was still on, and I was no longer protected from the draft by being in grad school, so I elected to perform alternative service as a conscientious objector at the Ecology Center in Berkeley. My job as bookstore manager consisted of turning away pissed-off creditors aggressively pushing to obtain payment for debts that had nothing to do with me. At the end of two years I felt a huge burden had been lifted from my shoulders. But what to do now? I had spent much time exploring the California mountains and yearned for life in the country. And the counterculture was all around me—the music, the long hair and the warmth and friendliness of my generation.

It was obviously time to drop out, head back to the land, and join a commune.

At the time there was a lot of social experimentation going on, and my partner and I settled into a commune in Drain, Oregon. A strict dietary philosophy governed the group, and their main fare was brown rice and cabbage. Dairy and most grains were anathema as they drowned one's body in mucus. Sugar was even worse—a undisputed heart and liver killer. Fruit was good because the plant was giving of itself without injury. Unfortunately it was unavailable except for a few scabby apples.

For privacy my partner and I bedded down in a small cave hollowed out under a busy logging road. At dinner someone in the group suggested expanding the diet to include the odd rooster and billy goats that were being given away. That sounded great to me until I discovered that there was a strong faction in the commune that believed eating meat was tantamount to murder.

I remember one communal meal where there was incredible tension between the veggies and the chicken eaters. They refused to hold hands for grace and clumped together in two sullen groups. Suddenly one turned to his opposite and snarled with poisonous vehemence, "Daryl, I LOVE YOU SO FUCKING MUCH!" Daryl returned the compliment. "YOU WORM—YOU WORM!" When we returned to the cave after dinner we found that someone had relieved us of a contraband stash of cake smuggled in the day before. They left us a tiny wedge and anonymous thank-you note.

The next day (it was early '72) we left for British Columbia. The two of us arrived in Qualicum Beach on Vancouver Island just in time to see another commune break up with acrimony and financial hijinks over the critical question of vegetarianism. Please God, I thought, deliver me from this puritanical insanity! Several weeks later a hitchhiker named Kevin pointed to a distant, fog-shrouded island in the Georgia Strait called Lasqueti and suggested I give it a try. The place was supposedly full of empty houses with fields for animals and gardens.

I followed his advice, and have been here ever since.

Morley lived here for a couple of years in the late 1970s. I don't recall his last name, but he had a partner and a couple of kids and he held the job of school bus driver for about a year.

MORLEY THE SCHOOL BUS DRIVER
A CROW

We were just driving up the Island Highway, driving all over the place that year, and we were thinking about going clear up to Port Hardy and checking out all the places along the way there. Well, just when we got a bit past Parksville, I looked out the car window and noticed a black crow sitting real cutely on the wooden sign that says "Lasqueti Island."

Somehow, it just made me feel that we should follow the arrow and go that way. It felt cosmic, like the crow was showing us where to go. I turned the car down Lee Road and we waited around, then we got on the ferry when it came.

Morley and his family found a vacant house and lived here for a few years; then they moved on.

WENDY SCHNEIBLE (1976 TO PRESENT)
THE ARROWSMITH STAR AD

Pure chance! In around 1976, I was living in Errington with Barry Kurland. I thought Errington was okay, but Barry thought it was too suburban. We went along on a friend's fishing boat and looked all up and down the coast, but we didn't find anything that really thrilled us. One January day, we were looking in the papers and we saw an ad for about 2.6 acres for sale on Lasqueti. We decided to go over there and have a look, so we got on the ferry and went over and found the spot, then spent a few hours walking around it and looking for the pins and surveyors' posts. It started to snow, and it got seriously windy.

We got down to the ferry, and Ian Cole was the ferry captain, and of course he's drunk and doesn't want to make the run. So we stood there in False Bay not knowing what to do. Well, Dana Darwin came by and he knew Barry from being one of his students in the school where Barry was working then on the other side. Dana was kind of a "bad boy" in school, but Barry had seen some special spark in him and had taken him under his wing, so he and Dana had this kind of friendship.

Dave Miller was there too, and I remember him saying to us, "What are you doing here? Schoolteachers can't afford to buy land on Lasqueti," and he drove off. Then Dana came by and he said, "Come on home with me." So we got in his car, and as we drove south, Dana stopped along the way several times and introduced us to people. We stopped at Arnie's Corner to have another look at a piece of land that was for sale, but again, we could not seem to find the property lines. After a while, Arnie Porter came over from across the road and helpfully showed us where the corner pins were. After that, he invited us over to his place for a drink. His daughter Lhasa was born three days earlier, and he was celebrating ... Oh, and there was Gwen sitting in a rocking chair with nothing but a silk Chinese robe on, nursing the baby. A beautiful sight!

After that, Dana drove us south toward Boat Cove, stopping all along the way to introduce us to people. Dana took a salmon out of the freezer and brought out some beer and cider, and we had quite a party. That night, we decided to buy the land.

The next morning Dana drove us north in the snow to catch the ferry, and I remember that his car did a big sideways slide right off the road at the Teapot corner. For some reason we went into the school, maybe to use the phone, and we met Sheila and Peter and they offered us breakfast. After that, we used their phone to call the real estate agency and told them that we wanted to buy the land on Lasqueti.

When we finally made it back to Errington that afternoon, the people where we were living told us that everyone on Lasqueti was crazy, totally insane, and that even if we moved there, we should never talk to anyone. We bought the 2.6-acre place for $6,600, and everyone told us that we were stupid to pay that much money, that you could easily buy ten acres for that amount. But we didn't want ten acres, and the little corner place felt like enough land for us. Besides, my share was my entire life savings. We built a little cabin there and stayed for several years before we sold it and moved north to one of those lots in Johnson Lagoon.

L-R front: Bonnie Olesko, Bo Columby and Alan DiFiore. L-R back: Dennis McBride, Tony Seaman and John Bump. Victoria Day Picnic at Douglas Field, 1975. Photo Tom Wheeler.

REMEMBERING
COUNTESS KOLBASSA

—Darlene

"**F**uck *art!* Let's cook!"

These are the very words that Julie yelled out once, at an early-summer food-booth planning meeting. The conversation had somehow veered off into a long, drawn-out discussion about art, and she was getting hungry. "Fuck *Art!* Let's Cook!" said it all. Just stop already with the chin music and get down to the basics, and right now. It became our mantra that season.

Julie Skulsky (or Countess Kolbassa, as she sometimes called herself) came to Lasqueti from Vancouver in the mid-seventies, and before that she lived in Toronto. I'm not sure what brought her to the island, or even where she was actually born, but I know she was of Ukrainian parentage and that she spent her younger years in Toronto totally immersed in the jazz music scene there. She became interested in jazz as a teenager and began picking out simple riffs and standards on the home piano. Her Ukrainian mother was not very fond of this music and would say to her, "No more jazz band music! No more!" in a thick accent.

She fell in love in her twenties with a fairly conservative Jewish man. They had two sons, but after ten years the marriage ended on a bad note. She couldn't conform to his lifestyle or his religion, there was disapproval from his family and tension began to build. She began drinking, and it was a problem. When the divorce went through, her husband fought for and won custody of their sons. For a while she had no visiting rights, and Julie had to move back into her mother's apartment.

One day while they were both away, there was a fire in the building and their apartment was completely gutted. They'd lost everything, and they had no insurance. She said her biggest loss was the photos of her sons as they were growing up. After a few more years in Toronto, Julie decided to go to the West Coast. By then she'd stopped drinking, she'd resumed contact with her sons and had watched them grow into young manhood and she felt that it was time for her to expand her horizons. She arrived in Vancouver, immersed herself in to the fringe jazz and art scene there and met a professional fool named Kim Foikus. Together they came to Lasqueti.

Friendly, and with an earthy, wicked, East Coast sense of humour, she made friends with people very easily. Especially if they had a piano in their home. Then she'd stop in for a visit, always bringing some interesting food to "knosh on," and proceed to play the piano for awhile. Between songs, she'd lapse into hilarious stories and little recollections of people she used to know, musicians she'd admired, adored and sometimes had love affairs with, just great peeps into her old world of 1950s and '60s Toronto.

This world was inhabited with eccentric Ukrainian uncles and aunts, crazy hipster musicians she knew, jazz clubs she'd gone to as a regular when she was only in her teens ... and food.

"Oh, Darzo, you gotta try this!" she'd suddenly say, often stopping right in the middle of a piano tune.

"Take some fresh spinach, cook it just a little—you know, steam it, that's what I mean—and put some butter in it, then add a pinch of salt, some basil and garlic—garlic from the garden—throw it all in the blender and ah-h-h. You gotta try it! It's so simple."

Julie was one of those old-school beatniks: funky, uninhibited, crazy and forthright. She cared for her friends; she mothered us if she thought we needed it. In her heart she was soft and sentimental. The lyrics to the old jazz standards could cause her to cry.

"Here's that rainy day," she'd croon, leaning over the piano keys.

At island events, she would show up wearing bizarre outfits: rough hiking boots under a silky Pakistani dress, then pearl earrings and a babushka. Gumboots under stretch pants, a colourful apron with a purple polyester shirt, shoulder pads and all. She was a grab bag of bizarre fashion trends, a mix of downhome gypsy gal, wicked witch, bad grandma and strange, stoned seductress.

Millie recalled an event at the community hall that everyone was going to. The Mudflats crowd all canoed and boated over to Lasqueti. Julie was living in her floathouse at that time, and everyone met at someone's cabin. They had snacks and a few beers before setting out on foot for the community hall, but right as they were leaving, Julie asked, "Has anyone got any acid?"

Someone said, "I do," and brought out a box of blotter acid. Everyone had a little dot and headed out for the hall, where they danced with wild abandon all night long. The evening was so good, Millie recalls that they walked home on the gravel road, laughing and singing all the way in the dark to False Bay and into their little boats. Under the dark, moonless sky their paddles dazzled with great swirls of bioluminescence as they rowed across the bay to their floathouses.

Julie's was right at the top of China Cloud Bay. There was a trail leading down the slope, right off the Main Road. From there, she just had to walk out on a plank and get onto the floathouse. But it was a bit rough for her there in the uninsulated little plywood place with no amenities. Millie came by one winter day and found Julie inside. The place was cold and smoky, and Julie was fanning the feeble flames inside the little wood heater. It seemed dismal; all she had for firewood that winter was green alder. There was a pan of soba noodles on the stove top, and Millie remarked that they needed to boil.

"Oh, they kind of cook, if you just let them soak in lukewarm water for a while," was Julie's remark. It was then that Millie began a conversation with Julie, encouraging her to consider moving to an affordable place off-island. After that winter was over, she did just that.

Peter Lironi recalled one of Julie's favourite Ukrainian sayings. When a visitor would stop by, she'd welcome them in with "Eat, eat, eat! We was gonna frow it out anyhow."

And she was a stickler with cooking methods. "Warm up the milk *before* you slowly whisk it in" and "Stir it slowly, in a figure eight" were among her many cooking tips. Julie taught many young girls how to make "bow-knots." They were simple little pastries that are rolled out, tied in a knot, and then deep-fried in oil and sprinkled with powdered sugar. Here's how I described them in the *Lasqueti Island Cookbook* that Sue Taylor and I put together in 1977:

Mrs. Skulsky's Bow-Knots

Anyone with a young daughter who knows Julie must be familiar with these goofy little morsels. They're somewhere between a cookie and a pastry, crunchy and not too sweet. Mopsy's first attempt followed Julie's teaching of using "four of each": four eggs, four cups of flour, etc. She was up past midnight rolling out the cursed delicacies.

On one of my mother's early visits to the island, she was staying with my sister Sherry in her cabin up along Teapot Road. My mother was a fairly conservative Christian woman who also had a great sense of humour, but when she happened to see Julie strutting down the trail one afternoon, all smiling and waving to her, she just about fainted. Here was a woman (about her age in those days) with a shaved head, wearing nothing but a rag wrapped around her waist as a skirt. And right out in public!

Julie was bringing Sherry some turnips from her garden up at the Lironis', and she proceeded to sit down with my mother, introduce herself and just yak away comfortably, like an old friend. Mom had never seen anything like it, and she laughed about Julie for days.

Millie Aites also had a funny story about her mother meeting Julie in the late seventies. They were taking a Sunday afternoon stroll in Beacon Hill Park: Millie, her mother and Julie. It was a sunny day, and quite busy. At one point, Julie

Julie Skulsky as Countess Kolbassa. Photo Barry Churchill.

needed to find the ladies' bathroom, but it was a bit farther along the path. Julie just went into the bushes, pulled down her pants and peed away. Millie's mom turned to her and whispered sharply, "What is she doing?" Then Julie emerged from behind a large camellia bush, smiling and whisking sawdust mulch off her hands. Julie, of course, thought nothing of it at all.

Julie's spontaneous comments were outrageous. Once, as she unexpectedly entered the Lironi household after being back in Toronto for a few months, she pulled off her heavy backpack and announced, "Well, I fucked my way across Canada," to everyone within earshot, and that included some surprised visitors who'd never even met her. Later on, she remarked to Millie that Toronto didn't feel right anymore, and that she'd missed BC, the island and the song of the Swainson's thrush as it emerged from the forest in the evening. (The true flower child she was came out in that last comment.)

I remember how Julie stood on the dock along with a dozen islanders as we waved bye-bye to the RCMP boat one summer. They were pulling out after their annual three-day weed raid and had gone only six metres from the dock. As we waved them good riddance, Julie pulled out some rolling papers, rolled a big fat joint and sparked it up, laughing like a maniac as the smoke wafted its way across the water.

Julie eventually moved down to Victoria, where she found a place to live in one of those big old shared houses in James Bay. Of course, she became a regular at the jazz clubs in town and entered the local music scene as a devoted jazz groupie.

Her "digger" spirit was always there, though. When Millie met up with Julie once in downtown Victoria, Julie suggested they go for lunch at Pagliacci's Restaurant. They went inside and sat at a table, waiting for a server to arrive. It was then that Julie began eating whatever was left over on the plates that hadn't been picked up yet. "Perfectly good garlic bread! Wow, Millie, have some!" Millie watched as Julie casually walked across the floor and high-graded the better pieces off abandoned lunch plates. And it didn't stop there: zeroing in on tables that looked like they were finished, she'd approach the diners with a friendly, "Are you finished? You're not going to eat that piece of chicken?" When given the okay, she'd thank them and waltz back to Millie with the plate.

And she was so generous! Maybe it was because she had already lost so much in life that material things didn't hold much importance to her. But I remember when a friend complimented her on a sweater she was wearing, and Julie insisted she have it. Pulling it off over her head, she told her friend to wear it, right then and there. "Look how it matches your beautiful eyes. Oh, your eyes! I could just pluck them and eat them like grapes!" Julie fawned.

During those last years in Victoria, Julie continued to play piano, weasel her way into jazz concerts (she adored the piano style of George Essihos and always sang his praises), hang out at cafés and generally enjoy all that Victoria had to offer her. I always appreciated how she kept in contact with my daughter, Mopsy, visiting her and tutoring her on the piano.

When a close, loving relationship with a local saxophone player suddenly ended with his death in a car accident, Julie slowly went into a long depression. and eventually she also developed Alzheimer's disease. She died in Victoria in 2008, with devoted friends at her side.

Long live the Countess!

ROGER RAMJET

—Doug

I first met Roger on Good Road in the spring of 1972. He had a dead sheep on his shoulder and immediately offered me a leg.

Like me, Roger was in his mid-twenties, with a love for the woods and a profound distrust of authority. With his bushy red beard, florid complexion, significant paunch and frantic, indomitable energy, he counted himself as a proud member of the redneck Irish working class that had helped settle the province since its earliest beginnings. Rog's attire was always West Coast casual—baggy wool fisherman's trousers held up with suspenders, a baseball cap and the ubiquitous red Chinese flannel shirt and tattered sweater. He was generous and good-natured when sober, but contrary and argumentative when otherwise. Like many on the Gulf Islands, he was appalled by the changes brought on by rising land prices and the sudden influx of rich professionals looking for summer homes. Known as "The Ramjet" to those who liked him, and Roger Rectum to those who didn't, he always seemed to evoke strong feelings.

When queried about how he had acquired the peculiar surname "rectum," his stock reply conveyed both humour and honesty. "Because most people think I'm an asshole—why do ya think?" Roger was among the first of the hippie longhairs to colonize the empty south end of Lasqueti.

Self-sufficiency was the much-repeated mantra of the day. Dozens of beach shacks were artfully constructed in remote places from the plentiful milled wood and shake logs that washed in with every southeaster. Some families got by on less than a thousand dollars a year, even obsessively knitting, weaving, sewing and tanning their own clothes.

The south end was a very tight society of around twenty, which depended on good-neighbourly relations day to day, and cooperation on big projects. Everyone knew just about everything there was to know about everyone else.

For us novices from the city, Roger's woodland skills and encyclopedic knowledge were an inspiration. Rog knew how to butcher a sheep, split shakes, plant a vegetable garden, jig up a cod, smoke a salmon, brew beer, build a roaring fire out of sopping green alder and scrounge building materials on land and sea. I quickly became one of his most avid pupils. The Ramjet possessed an amazing physical stamina, usually covering many kilometres a day restlessly roaming the island. His base was an ancient but comfortable log cabin left from logging days, but he was rarely found at home. Roger would breakfast at our place (three kilometres), lunch at the government dock (five kilometres), work on his boat in a protected bay during the early afternoon (six kilometres), then hoof it into the Bull Pass house for a happy-hour homebrew (six kilometres), finally returning to his bachelor home in the wee hours (five kilometres). He never connected with a lady for long—they all found him to be hopelessly uncivilized.

Sometimes his frenetic wanderings proved costly. During one of those long hikes after midnight with only a candle lantern, he stumbled from a cliff far off in the bush and broke his ankle—an ugly compound fracture. With bone exposed, Roger somehow dragged himself back several miles on his stomach in complete blackness. Miraculously, he was discovered barely conscious on Main Road after a rare all-night party broke up and the merrymakers were returning home.

Perhaps because of his mobility, Roger always knew the best places a squatter could set up a temporary homestead without fear of being hassled by irate landowners. In this area he had lots of expertise. Rog had only recently arrived after being evicted from a shack on Texada Island. One stormy afternoon, he had foolishly shared a joint of homegrown with the garrulous crew of a stranded tugboat. Loose lips sink ships. The captain got wind of the crime, and in due time Roger received a visit from the authorities. His court case, heard in Powell River, took a dramatic turn for the worse when it was discovered that in addition to the illegitimate pot smoking, the accused had also somehow racked up $1,700 in unpaid parking tickets over the preceding decade. Justice was served. He was sent down to Oakalla Prison Farm for ninety days—it was the hardest three months of his life.

The Ramjet was always a fount of grandiose plans and schemes, which he would share in great detail with all who would listen. Sadly, few of these ideas ever came to fruition. For a while he was going to build a large hutch and breed pedigreed pigeons, then it was a plantation of saskatoon berries and later a fishing charter operating off the government dock at Squitty Bay. The high-end boat fantasies were the worst. It started with a plywood dory, which transformed into a ferroconcrete sailboat, which metamorphosed again into the conversion of a rotting clinker lifeboat into a world cruiser. Every winter

Rog swore he was going to head north in the boat in a few months—or maybe it was west to Hawaii or Fiji. At first we believed him, but after a few years it became apparent that these optimistic predictions were merely a harbinger of spring and should never be taken seriously.

On other occasions, Ramjet's projects seriously backfired. The south-end pig caper was a fair example. One spring, he and Jim Ferris went in together on three cute black piglets to be reared and slaughtered in the fall. The future hogs were all going to live happily together at Roger's place in a flimsy pen of rusty page wire strung on alder posts. However, the pigs had other ideas and disappeared into the woods within minutes of their arrival. All was quiet for a month, and we assumed that the porkers had either been rustled or met some other untimely end. It seems, though, that they adapted very well to island life—too well, in fact. As the weeks went by there was an increasing number of unconfirmed sightings here and there around the south end. At first, we all thought that he had stumbled onto a rather sensible and original idea. What could be sweeter? Free pork in the fall without fencing, labour or feed. Just harvest when ready. But the sightings quickly degenerated into full-blown attacks on vulnerable winter gardens and root cellars. The three escapees struck hard and fast at anything that might contain calories. Hunger made them merciless and audacious.

I remember one incident in particular. During a lunch with friends at Lehman's Corner, we were just tucking in to a halibut feast when there was a sudden infernal racket from below. A cacophony of crashes, clattering and thuds echoed through the house, followed by the sound of shattering glass. Throughout, an ecstatic chorus of grunting and snorting accompanied the commotion. After a moment of dumb confusion, we ran down to confront the culprits with two-by-fours. Of course by then they were long gone, but they did grace us with a calling card. In seconds they had gobbled two sacks of potatoes, knocked over untold cases of home-canned halibut and sprayed several boxes of winter carrots and apples with dirt and shit. I think it was this final atrocity that spelled their doom. A hunt was hastily organized, and after a few days the infamous trio was brought to earth. They were small, tough and delicious.

While Roger was fond of pigs, he had a different view of the cows on the island's open range. There were over a hundred at the time, most owned by absentee landowners, who returned only briefly in the fall to harvest their herds. Ramjet viewed this as a simple case of class warfare. Rich outsiders were burdening locals with a plague of bovines to make a quick profit. Open range was fine for the little guy with a cow or two, but it was a very different matter when someone owned scores of them. One morning in July, he awoke to find an immense brown bush bull finishing the last of the corn in his extravagant garden. Without taking time to think matters through, Roger snatched up his trusty 1918 Lee-Enfield rifle and slew the offending animal.

Unfortunately, other pressing matters distracted him, and he didn't get around to dealing with the mass of meat for several days. This proved to be a fatal mistake. July is not exactly an auspicious month for slaughtering, and the Ramjet was soon faced with an odiferous dilemma. The yard was strewn with illicit rotting beef in various states of butchery, with the nearest fridge twenty-four kilometres away. To make matters worse, the cops were on the island checking out the cattle rustling at the Sideras commune. Anyway, it was obviously high time to get rid of the evidence. How he was able to cajole anyone to ferry that foul carcass over to the other side remains a mystery. Even today, friends there still describe their horror when confronted with Roger's smelly truck and his insistent pleading for freezer space. Chagrined, he eventually hauled the bull off to the dump—almost a total loss.

Now, the Ramjet was a generous person, and he expected to be treated the same way by others. Whatever was his was also yours, and vice versa. The cow episode certainly illustrated that. But this curious standard of behaviour became the basis for one of his most annoying habits. If you were at home and he needed a tool, Rog would always ask. But if you happened to be off somewhere, he would simply grab whatever he wanted, never leaving a note. This was certainly not theft in the normal sense of the word, but just about everyone in the neighbourhood had a story of searching high and low for something and then finding it six months later sitting on Roger's workbench. Yet he always happily admitted to taking the missing object, and then thanked the lender profusely for their generosity, throwing in a chunk of mutton or venison to sweeten the deal.

Roger left the island sometime in the mid-seventies and headed off to Campbell River to make his fortune in fish farming. I ran into him occasionally over the years, and although the fish gig turned out to be a bust, he was still optimistic and full of piss and vinegar. When I last saw him in 2005, he complained of tightness in the chest and a "small attack," but everything seemed under control.

A year later we heard the news. Rog had keeled over in Campbell River and died of a massive heart attack. Remembering his incredible endurance, vitality and vigor, Roger's death still seems improbable. No doubt he is still hatching schemes and working the angles in that better place. I just hope God doesn't get tired of hearing about those endless projects over a bottomless jug of plum wine.

BOHO RON

—Darlene

Among the "water people" who lived on the small outer islands and secluded bays and coves of Lasqueti's north side, Ron Lawton is one of the most memorable. Ron and his girlfriend, Ida Jane Stobie, were hired caretakers of little Boho Island from 1970 to '73. Following up on a help-wanted ad in the *Vancouver Sun*, they left the city, came up the coast and settled into the cozy one-room cabin that sits on top of the Boho bluffs overlooking the bay.

Boho Island's owner, Dr. H. Minor Nichols from Portland, Oregon, paid a wage of one hundred dollars monthly, and for this you got a furnished

Boho Ron Lawton lived with girlfriend, Ida Jane Stobie, on Boho Island, just on Lasqueti's east side. Photo courtesy Jenny Proctor.

Ron's boat the *Maritimus* performed well in the stormiest of West Coast weather.

cabin to live in and an island all to yourself for nine months of the year. Not a bad situation in 1970s Lasqueti, and you had the choice to stay on in the summer as a helper or take leave until September, when the Nichols family and entourage left.

Ron and Ida always welcomed friends who dropped in at Boho, and often the visits were several days long if a storm raged outside and it got too rough to leave. We'd pass the time hiking around the little island, storm watching through the big windows that frame the front wall, swapping stories, cooking up feasts of baked cod, snapper and clams and eating and drinking beer well into the long winter night.

Ron would be out on the water in his boat, the *Maritimus*, in all kinds of weather. Living on nearby Bull Island, there were many times I'd be standing out on our bluffs, storm watching in a southeast gale, only to hear the distant sound of Ron's Johnson 9.5 outboard engine coming through the Bull Pass toward us. Soon enough, he'd pull into the bay, anchor out and be scrambling up the trail, arriving at our door all smiles and dripping salt water. He would say he was "just coming over for a coffee and a visit, on such a lovely day." Ron told me that he took the *Maritimus* out in stormy weather to see how much she could take. "You have to know how your boat handles in all kinds of weather. It's the only way you'll ever get to really know your boat," he said.

Ron had the appearance of a mischievous seafaring elf, with twinkly blue eyes and scraggly, reddish hair. Always open to self-improvement, he reached into his pocket one day and pulled out a harmonica. Leaning toward me, he said, "I've been noticing that people who carry and play little instruments seem to be calmer and more centred than other people, so I'm going to learn to play this." He was a talented woodworker, inventive and visionary in his ideas. He loved books, poetry, music—especially songs with rollicking lyrics—and he loved messing around with boats. He was a pirate, too, in league with Bull Island Ray. Exclusive members of the "Robin Hood Club," these two would often leave for days at a stretch, liberating boat motors, short-wave radios, household articles of value, you name it. They would return at dawn with their booty (at least whatever wasn't cooling off in the various stash points they had along the way) and wild tales of unexpected winds in overloaded boats, misread tide charts that had them stranded, tales of near misses and almost being caught red-handed.

An Easter visit to Boho Island by the RCMP convinced the entire membership of the Robin Hood Club to disband and cease operations. Although everything was cool, and no evidence was found, it was a turning point for R&R Removal Service. They immediately quit their business.

After leaving Boho Island, Ron and Ida moved to nearby Sandy Cove, between Tucker Bay and Lennie's Lagoon. They resurrected an old cabin, put in a garden and a boatshed and lived there happily for a couple of years. Ida got restless and moved on, getting a job with Parks Canada, and after a while Ron moved on too, back to Vancouver. He sold his beloved *Maritimus*, got an apartment and started up a house-painting operation. Soon after, he created a niche vintage boat restoration business for himself and did very well at it. When he wasn't redoing the interiors of vintage yachts and sailboats, he continued to explore, camp, hike and cruise the waters and lakes around Vancouver and the Interior with his new love and partner, Jenny Proctor. Ron passed away in 2009 at age sixty.

GOD HATES A COWARD

—Doug

Captain Ian Cole was a fascinating and commanding figure. He was a man of incredible talents. A master mechanic who could fix or improvise his way through any problem with machinery, he was always available to help anyone with a stubborn Briggs & Stratton. As ferry captain he knew everything there was to know about the sea and seamanship—no small feat when facing off against the treacherous nineteen kilometres of rough water between False Bay and French Creek on Vancouver Island.

At the monthly Legion gatherings and local parties, Cole loved to dress up in a fancy tux, or women's clothes and wig, and grab one of the young hippie ladies for a turn around the dance floor. Ian was also a fabulous cook and was devoted to his two children, Gwyn and Gregg, who affectionately called him "Poopsie." He offered his kids "liberty but not freedom," which included playing loud marching band music at 6:00 a.m. to get them out of bed and detailed daily instructions left on the kitchen table. He could be very thoughtful and generous to fellow islanders, and always made it a point to hire the most needy (and attractive) for odd jobs and ferry maintenance. If you missed the ferry and were stuck on Vancouver Island, he would often make a special trip over to get you home. Cole enjoyed company, and it was not unusual for him to invite in the RCMP and Jehovah's Witnesses for tea when they visited the island.

He arrived on Lasqueti in 1962 with his wife and family at the suggestion of his sister, island resident Betty Darwin, who urged them to take on the general store and mail contract. It was not a demanding job as the island population at that time was sixty-eight. In 1965 he purchased the newly established ferry, the *Captain Vancouver*, and founded the company Western Ferries Ltd., a variant of which exists to this day. All went well for a year until 1966, when his wife ran off with his best friend and moved to Parksville.

This event marked a major turning point for Cole. He had always enjoyed a few drinks but suddenly his capacity and appetite for booze exploded.

Captain Ian Cole at the helm of the *Captain Vancouver*. Cole was proud that he could make the crossing even in sixty-knot winds, but his passengers were in for a bumpy ride.

He could down a 750-millilitre bottle of vodka in minutes and often would start his drinking bouts in the early morning just before the eight o'clock ferry crossing. His favourite saying when facing adversity was "God hates a coward." It was a matter of personal pride that he would make the ferry crossing in the worst gales carrying the most dangerous cargos—though some said it was his need to secure more booze that led to the most risky crossings. But all agreed Ian was completely without fear, on the water and off. Onlookers would only shake their heads when he took the ferry out on a deserted sea in sixty-knot winds. The *Captain Vancouver* was a small, round-bottomed tub with a vicious roll guaranteed to bring up your breakfast. The seats were overstuffed sofas unsecured to the floor, and they and the overflowing trash cans gravitated wildly from one side of the main cabin to the other as the little ship laboured through its crossing. On rough days the stench of vomit was overwhelming, and the tiny fantail at the rear of the vessel was usually crowded with escapees from the fetid interior.

During the seventies it was common for the *Captain Vancouver* to mysteriously remain at the dock for an hour or more after sailing time because the captain had passed out on the floor. Invariably the mate or someone wanting to get home would take the wheel and guide the good ship home. In the dark and foggy days of winter, a crossing could take several hours as the ferry meandered up and down the Georgia Strait searching for a harbour. I remember during one particularly long, foggy passage when someone chirped up, "Isn't that the Nanaimo breakwater?" We were thirty-two kilometres off course.

Merrick Anderson recalls one of the many crazy incidents that took place while he was Ian's deckhand in the seventies:

> Ian would do anything for an animal. We were coming into French Creek one morning, and here's this deer swimming in the water. Ian says, "Goddamn dogs, chasing these deer into the water! Come on, let's herd it onto the riff raft!" And sure enough, we herded it on, then Ian hops out and wrestles the deer into the ferry, and when we got into the harbour, we managed to get it into his little Datsun and we took it up to the vet.

Ian's drinking also took a toll on the docks, into which he regularly crashed—sometimes taking out a neighbouring vessel in the process. But he always cheerfully paid for the damage when he sobered up. There were frequent complaints, and a court appearance or two, but the police rarely did more than occasionally chain the ferry to the dock. In those days alcoholic impairment behind the wheel was considered no more than a quaint idiosyncrasy. How times have changed.

Perhaps because of his fondness for liquor, Ian was not prejudiced against other intoxicants. But he politely refused offers of pot and LSD, saying he much preferred the bottle. There was one memorable ferry crossing where almost everyone but him was tripping on psychedelics, and several had to be forcibly pulled off the fantail as they watched the phosphorescent, shimmering wake dancing behind the ferry.

But when drunk, Ian Cole's generous, kindly nature gave way to a gruff, impatient exterior and a flushed, perpetual scowl. He became highly volatile and moody—even cruel. First mates quickly learned that it did not pay to show up late for work. Captain Cole would wait patiently as the tardy victim walked down the dock. Then, just before boarding, he would suddenly gun the engine with a sneer and leave his co-worker standing alone on the dock as the ferry started its run. Few mates made that mistake more than once. But once you had proved yourself, Ian would go to any length to support you.

Convention and legalities were anathemas to him, and he conveniently ignored them. As passengers held their breath Cole would drive one or even two vehicles from the dock onto the narrow top deck on a track of flimsy boards, with a milk cow sometimes thrown in for good measure. And forget about the rules governing fuel runs, from which passengers were supposedly strictly barred. A can or two of gas or kerosene could almost always be found on the fantail along with the refugees from the vomitorium.

One mate remembers a stormy crossing with eight passengers in the cabin and eight 150-litre barrels of fuel lashed to the top deck. In the rough sea the barrels broke free and began rolling around with an ominous rumble. Cole pulled into the wind and sent the mate topside to investigate. It was a horror story. All of the 135-kilogram barrels were rolling back and forth, and one had a gaping eight-centimetre puncture spewing volatile gasoline everywhere. A single spark would have blown the whole thing sky-high. One false step on the slippery deck and the mate would be crushed or knocked overboard. This incident should have ended in tragedy, but somehow they managed to dump the leaking barrel over the side and tie everything back together. Cole had coolly stepped outside the cramped cabin and guided the ferry with one hand from the poop deck.

The required safety equipment was never quite kept up to snuff. An ancient diesel engine was set up to run the auxiliary pump and generator in an emergency. If the main engine failed, the ferry could be kept afloat and lit with this vital piece of equipment. Unfortunately this little diesel engine had a very nasty habit. It was started by a heavy hand crank, which remained stuck on the shaft for a while after the motor started. The motor would spin the crank wildly around at 100 rpm for about ten to twenty seconds before sending it flying off, bouncing around the engine room like a Ping-Pong ball. The engine being exceedingly difficult to start, the mate knew he would be risking both life and limb in a real emergency—which fortunately never materialized.

In another incident Cole was working with friends on a surplus landing craft to be used for carrying freight. Diesel engines are curious beasts. If you feed them too much ether for start-up they can become very difficult to shut down. The engine accelerates up to an impossible rpm rate, and it can literally explode from excessive speed. This is exactly what started to happen. His assistants wisely fled the scene as the runaway engine began to scream. Cole frantically tried to shut it down, but nothing seemed to work. At the last minute he threw himself bodily onto the raging motor's air intake, cutting off its oxygen supply. He could have been killed, but instead the protesting motor abruptly coughed, stopped its mad gyration and died. "God hates a coward."

Around 1968 or '69, Ian's sidekick, Harold, showed up on the island. Harold was a longshoreman from Vancouver who had at some time received a severe head injury. Rumour had it that he had fallen through an open hatch on the job and never fully recovered. He was sandy haired, small, shaky and good-natured, but seemed to be in a perpetual haze. Like Cole, he loved to drink, and it was a common sight to find Harold passed out in a ditch on the way to or from the ferry. We often wondered how many times the iron plate in his skull had saved his life in a fall. One dark night he was found face down in a puddle of muddy water, and a good Samaritan gave him mouth-to-mouth resuscitation. Harold sat up, regurgitated on his rescuer and continued on his way, none the worse for wear.

Ian knew him from way back and promptly hired him as a general handyman. The two were great friends and drinking companions. "Thick as thieves" was how several described them. Both moved near Scottie Bay, on separate properties but in close proximity. Ian's house was always ablaze with light, with the diesel generator thumping in the background and the radio blaring 24/7. Various machine parts lay strewn everywhere, and the front of the house was full of metal filings from a lathe set up on the kitchen table.

After Ian sold the ferry to Sandy Gillespie in the early 1980s, he fell into hard times. He and Harold were living on Harold's meagre disability and

Heading for the island. Howard Dennis and Sandy Gillespie loading Sandy's barge in French Creek. On board are some cattle and the sawmill that Howard and Ray Purcell owned.

what they could scrounge from the grocery dumpsters in Parksville. It is said that they even occasionally rustled a cow off open range. At one point Harold created a small scandal when he was discovered butchering up an elderly donkey that had recently died of natural causes.

As the years went by, both developed unusual ideas of sanitation, preferring to shit in buckets rather than bother with an outhouse. Often a full bucket was strategically placed in a walkway in hopes visitors might be inclined to dump it for them. During periods of excessive binging in the late eighties, they were known to hang it all out and even relieve themselves on the front steps of their domiciles. Yet these esoteric practices were accepted without rancour from fellow islanders.

Imagine everyone's surprise when the electrifying news spread that someone had shot Harold! He had been hit in the side by a .22 rifle bullet, which had passed through his abdomen and almost exited his left buttock. We all wondered: was it a jealous lover, or perhaps someone with a grudge about those nasty buckets? Harold was typically vague and named a possible suspect. He claimed that someone had taken a potshot at him while he was on a walk in the woods. The RCMP were called in, and the truth finally emerged. Harold had simply gone to bed with his loaded rifle, anticipating a dawn hunting expedition. Somehow during the night the gun had discharged under the bedclothes, causing the injury. Fortunately it was minor, and the island was quietly relieved.

But neither man could endure this kind of alcoholic self-abuse forever. In June 1991, Captain Cole was sitting at his kitchen table when he died of a massive heart attack at age sixty-one. One Halloween night three years later, Harold followed him in a raging fire that destroyed his life and trailer. With their passing, a legendary and exotic chapter in Lasqueti Island history ended forever. I hope there are boats and booze in heaven.

FOOD OF THE GODLETS

—Laurence Fisher

My eldest daughter was born in 1974, in the middle of the back-to-the-land/personal independence movement. She was, I believe, the fourth baby born on or near Lasqueti during the renewal of home-birthing that this movement entailed. It wasn't that we needed to have our babies at home; we just wanted to own the birth of our own children. This is something most of us take for granted today, but in the 1970s hospitals and doctors owned virtually all births, and I probably wouldn't even have been allowed in the delivery room.

As Sarah was ripening in Kathy's belly, we got ready as best we could. This did not make for a pretty picture, as we were of course preparing for the worst. If it all went as it most often did, little preparation was necessary. But the tomes of diagrams and stories of breach births were horrifying.

Then Ina May Gaskin's book *Spiritual Midwifery* appeared. What the home-birth movement would have done without Ina May and the Tennessee Farm, I can't imagine. We wolfed it all down; I read the book from cover to cover. I was particularly fascinated by Ina May's discussion of the placenta, and what a marvellous organ it was. In fact, as all other animals know, the very best thing for a new mother is to eat the placenta. It is so packed with nourishment that hospitals sell placentas to drug companies!

At that time, we lived in the farthest reaches of the north end. It was even more isolated then. So we figured that for the event, we'd better move closer to phones and roads. Rosa Schumach had died earlier that year; her empty house, still fully furnished, was now owned by Keary and Allen Farrell.

Kathy and Rosa had been great friends, and I had known Rosa since childhood, so it seemed appropriate that our first child be born in her house. Keary and Kathy were good friends too, and he was happy for us to move in. So, off to Rosa's we moved. Once there, we settled in and began the wait.

The house was a classic, built with loving care in the 1930s. Unfortunately, as with all houses built in the thirties, neither insulation nor draft barriers had been considered. But still, the kitchen was a warm, solid, useful room, and that is where we all congregated, as people have done since kitchens were first built.

A month and a half later, Sarah dutifully arrived after twenty-four hours of hard work on Kathy's part. After the birth, Kathy had a small rest, from which we woke her (with some difficulty) to start the process again and get the placenta out. Once she had been successfully delivered of it, I put it in the cold room at the back the house, with the intention of burying it later.

Larry Fisher with his daughter Megan.

The next morning, I was up early admiring our brand new, oh-so-innocent-looking reason for existence. I stood, amazed as only a fresh parent can be, staring down at my first child. Then, while I was checking to make sure that uncomfortable-looking clip on her belly button wasn't bothering her soft, plump tummy, I suddenly remembered the placenta. I went into the cold room to really have a good look at this remarkable factory—this bloody, messy, life-giving lump of flesh. Here was the ultimate gift from a mother's body to her child, formed by the blood of both, now belonging to neither. I gazed at it for a moment before beginning to sort it out.

I discovered that it was contained in a remarkably tough bag of membrane, with the umbilical cord coming out of one end and an opening at the other where it had been attached to the uterus wall. I was easily able to separate the bag's sides and expose this remarkable, incredibly beautiful orb of life.

Staring at it, all I could think was, *incredible!* With its endless tributaries—perfect fractals covering the surface of this miniature planet—it lay at the bottom of the bag, clearly still full of life.

The other thing I had learned from Ina May, with great delight, was that placenta is the only meat you can eat that has not been killed. Part mother, part child, not killed. I liked that. So back I went to the kitchen for a good, sharp knife. Taking two or three finely carved slices of this beautiful thing, I popped

Kathy Fisher with Grover Foreman and Bo Colomby. Photo Tom Wheeler.

them into the frying pan with my eggs. It was the very best, most tender meat I have ever tasted.

Kathy, whom I felt should really be the recipient of this traditional mother's first meal, wouldn't even look at it. I didn't blame her; I, too, was still mostly under the sway of our wasteful, middle-class values and taboos— hence the few, thin slices. However, the word spread, of course. And I became, for a moment, the local epicure of birthing.

A couple of months later, our neighbours were having their child. This turned into one of those births where a dozen or more people showed up. The energy was fabulous, and they were both fully accepting of all the guests. It is an unusual opportunity when a mother is able to share her birth that openly. For many, it was their first chance to witness the evolutionarily questionable, painful, gory, unbelievable event of a human birth. The mother had a good, relatively fast labour, and a lively baby girl was born that afternoon.

Everyone was excited, to say the least. Mother was lying with child on the bed, the look on her face at once both exhausted and goofy. Father was on cloud nine, and we all had a contact high; there was so much love and joy and laughter in that room. I had the placenta in a bowl and asked Dad what he wanted to do with it: "Would you like to save it to bury under a tree? Or do you want to try tasting a little beforehand?"

Looking at me askance, he replied, "Let's have dinner." Everyone split in various directions to gather the makings: wine, bread, veggies and whatever could be scrounged up. I started to carve part of the placenta up (the whole thing would have fed a cast of hundreds) and proceeded, with the dad, to make a placenta stew.

Soon, all and sundry were gathered once more, and the dinner was coming together with wonderful energy. The stew came out well; at least, I found it tasty, and I felt that it was an honour to be eating what, on a moment's thought, I could only consider sacred food. I have to say that I'm not sure how many people actually tried it, though quite a few did. I do remember that, once again, the person most deserving of this rocket fuel—the mother—would unfortunately have none of it.

The sun had set by the time we ate, which made things a bit tricky for the squeamish. Later, Howard Siegel did a comedy routine about how he was terrified to eat anything at all, because it was too dark to see exactly what he was putting in his mouth.

The story quickly spread and soon reached Parksville. Lasquetians were the darlings of Parksville in the early seventies; we had long provided them with endless material for wild rumours and laughter.

BOBBY THE PROJECTIONIST

—Doug

I slands have a well-deserved reputation for attracting odd and curious characters. Certainly one of the strangest was Bobby the projectionist. Bobby
first arrived on the remote south end of Lasqueti in the mid-seventies, a
refugee from the city and his irregular job as a theatre projectionist. Soft-
spoken, of medium height with laughing, watery eyes, he was always more
than willing to pitch in and help, yet at the same time he remained distant and
remote. But what really set him apart was his bizarre affect and appearance.
Bobby invariably appeared in public draped in a coarse, black horse blanket
tailored like a priest's habit, which he wore rain or shine. His long, grey hair
was done up in a neat bun on the top of his head, which was capped by a
peaked hood. The flowing robes stretched discreetly to his ankles, often seriously impairing mobility. Like Friar Tuck in the movie *Robin Hood*, he secured
his ample belly with a piece of frayed manila rope. Bobby made no secret of
his disdain for shoes, and almost always went barefoot—even when it was
flooding or there was snow on the ground. We wondered about frostbite, but
he never complained. The impression from afar was that of a stooped, elderly
penitent preparing to celebrate Mass.

One summer's day, a group of us were chatting it up on the back of the
Lasqueti ferry, the *Captain Vancouver*, as she slowly rolled her way toward
French Creek. Bobby seemed uncomfortable and was fumbling with his thick,
woollen habit when there was a loud clank as something heavy and metal-
lic hit the deck. Startled, we all peered down to see a sixty-centimetre military bayonet lying at his feet. Without missing a beat and carefully avoiding
eye contact, Bobby bent down to retrieve his pigsticker. Alas, Captain Cole,
who just happened to be passing by, was quicker and smoothly scooped it up.
Depending on his alcohol level, Cole's mood could vacilate wildly between
a mellow love for mankind to a testy intolerance for all warm-blooded creatures. Fortunately he was in a good mood that day. He held up the piece of

heavy steel for minute examination, grinned blearily and said to no one in particular, "I'll just be holding this for safekeeping upstairs. The owner may collect it in French Creek from the captain's cabin." With that, both Cole and the bayonet exited majestically into the wheelhouse. We all turned to Bobby, waiting expectantly for an explanation or jocular remark, but he simply smiled vaguely and remained mute. When we reached French Creek, all watched in fascination as Bobby dutifully headed up to the captain's cabin.

Just what our companion intended to do with this war relic remains a mystery to this day. It could have done serious damage had it had fallen on someone's foot and must have been a heavy and awkward burden to lug around Parksville on a day's shopping trip. While eccentric, Bobby seemed a peaceful person incapable of hurting a fly. Perhaps he saw himself standing off against a group of young toughs at the Rod and Gun beer parlour. "Back off, gentlemen, or taste the cruel steel of my hallowed blade." Or perhaps those thousands of kung fu movies he had projected over and over in the movie theatres had finally taken possession of his psyche? Whatever the case, we were all left wondering.

Bobby combined his sublimely rich fantasy life with a dark desire to mortify the flesh. This took the form of a kind of self-abuse in which he attended to the normal routines of life with a special handicap to make things just a little more interesting. One afternoon, while helping his neighbours with a cabin-raising, his horsehair cloak fell away to reveal a curious sight. His upper torso and arms were wrapped tightly in serpentine strips of black innertubing. Care had been taken not to cut off all circulation, but the skin surface was covered with angry red welts. Again, Bobby avoided eye contact and replaced his habit without comment.

Several days later he was seen limping around the local clam bed, laboriously collecting dinner. He seemed unsteady on his feet—almost drunken—and was having real problems stooping down. A group of us approached to offer assistance and have a neighbourly chat and we discovered the problem. Bobby had nailed a one-by-four-inch board to his right leg with finishing nails. Saintlike, he was mortifying the flesh like someone right out of the Middle Ages. It was a surreal moment, and a little too much for some—the crowd quickly faded away. Bobby neither asked for help nor offered to explain his predicament. Were we supposed to comment, or pretend not to notice? No one wanted to intrude, and after a bit of desultory conversation the penitent returned to his solitary clam digging. In those far-off days many of us liked weird people, the weirder the better. Life on remote islands encourages tolerance. Nowhere else on the planet will one encounter a more eclectic assemblage of misfits, geniuses and dreamers. But in retrospect I wish we had been a bit more aggressive in helping this fellow confront his demons.

Bobby's stay on the island came to an abrupt and surprising end that summer. He had become good friends with Keefer, one of the owners of Rouse Bay, who encouraged him to stay on as a part-time caretaker. Keefer asked for only one thing in return. He wanted Bobby to vacate the house once a year so he could spend a few weeks in solitude at a truly beautiful and remote island paradise. Keefer arrived as planned and drove Bobby to the ferry, where he was to connect with a projectionist gig in town. The happy owner returned home, doffed his clothes and ambled down to the beach for a refreshing swim. The peace and quiet was just what Keefer needed to shake out the wrinkles of urban life, and he passed ten days and nights in blissful reverie without a single visitor. On the last day, while he was packing for a return to Seattle, the phone rang. It was an urgent call offering another projectionist job for Bobby. Keefer apologized, saying he knew that his caretaker would be happy to take the job, but that he was booked up until the end of the month. He was about to hang up the phone when there was a soft scuffling from overhead. The trap door to the attic slowly slid aside, and a cloud of cobwebs cascaded onto the kitchen table. "No," a muffled voice called out. "I'm here, and I'll take the call." It turned out that Bobby had been living incognito in the dusty attic for the entire duration of Keefer's vacation.

WHATEVER HAPPENED TO BROTHER RICHARD?

—Doug (special thanks to Alan DiFiore)

Richard Resseger, or Brother Richard, as he preferred to be called, was an inspired teacher, actor and musician with a clear and resonant tenor voice. Richard had majored in philosophy and theology at Kent State in Ohio in the late fifties and took God very seriously in all his/her forms. Perhaps this was what drew him to the novels of C.S. Lewis and J.R.R. Tolkien and led him to the practice of white magic with its obsession with spells, rituals and ceremony. He knew a lot about religion but tended to favour monastic Catholicism over the rest. And there was nothing Richard liked better than to discourse on some abstruse theological subject like transubstantiation or the true meaning of the Eucharist.

Before his arrival on Lasqueti in the mid-seventies, he had made several concerted attempts to adopt the religious life, first with the poet and monk Thomas Merton and then as a solitary of St. Benedict, herding sheep in Colorado. He was a portly fellow who dressed for effect, donning a modest woman's dress or monastic robe that went from his greying hair to his sandal-clad ankles. His flushed face often bore traces of makeup, and it was difficult at a distance to tell whether the stooped figure was a man or a woman.

He was also prone to sudden mood changes. One minute he could dominate the crowd with his rye (misspelling intentional) humour and belly laugh, and the next lapse into self-conscious silence and social invisibility. But Brother Richard could almost always be relied upon to be amazingly helpful, thoughtful and charming. He was much loved by many and soon became a fixture at island happenings, often taking on the role of emcee in flagrant drag.

Richard also had a great sense of the ridiculous. When Captain Ian Cole collapsed on the ferry deck in an apparent fit, no one was particularly surprised because of the captain's infamous drinking habits. But Richard stole the moment after he solemnly began to administer last rites in the original Latin.

Richard Resseger and Marge Harrison enjoying a summer libation. Photo Alan DiFiore.

Who knows—perhaps Richard even saved Ian's life, for the patient soon recovered.

But there was a darker side to his character too. As time went on Richard became more and more enamoured of drink. Both his parents were alcoholic, and he clearly shared their enthusiasm for God's libations. On hot summer days he could often be found stretched motionless on the sand by the ferry dock, beet-red with sunburn and semi-comatose, half in, half out of the water. Friends said that poverty was his best friend because he was healthiest when too broke to buy booze.

An ambiguous sexual orientation added to the bevy of harpies that haunted him. Richard freely admitted that he was bisexual, but as the years passed it was clear that he preferred being with other men. He loved to dress up and flirt with the few young gay men on the island. But this was not something that he could accept in himself without guilt and internal conflict. When someone crudely joked about his "stable of catamites," he was horrified and left the room in tears.

Although there was no bar on Lasqueti at the time, the store and restaurant in False Bay was owed by a family of legendary toughs from North Vancouver. Alcohol could only be sold with meals, and it was common to see a table heaped with several dozen empty beer bottles surrounding an ancient plate of untouched fries. With nowhere else to go, the store quickly became a centre for the rowdy drinking crowd.

Perhaps this is why Brother Richard accepted a caretaking job at the hostel just across the street—a fateful decision. People living around the bay during those years describe the store as being a dark and debauching presence, with a host of desperate and seedy characters passing through on various errands and assignations.

One night in August 1980, that malignant alcoholic haze exploded into violence. Longtime resident Terry Beck got into a brawl and pitched a fellow punter off a balcony. Threats were exchanged and Terry was followed home

Brother Richard showing the Lieutenant Governor Walter Owen the entrance to Dennis McBride's dome on the Teapot House land. Noel Taylor at right. Photo Merrick Anderson.

and shot dead at the White House with an ancient .303 rifle. One man later confessed to the killing and did time, but others said the confessor was simply too drunk that night to manage anything as complicated as a homicide.

Whatever the case, within a few weeks of this high-profile Gulf Island murder, Brother Richard suddenly vanished. He left everything behind—his beloved blind dog, empty wallet and ID, even his expensive glasses. Nothing further has turned up in the thirty-odd years since, and Brother Richard is still listed as an unsolved missing persons case by the RCMP. Yes, it might have been an unfortunate accident on the water, but there have long been rumours that Richard's disappearance was somehow connected to Beck's murder.

Richard had helped with the cleanup after the killing, and had been hanging out with the combatants. Did he know too much about Terry's end, and was he himself murdered in turn? An old friend commented, "As far as his (Brother Richard's) murder goes, the cops had the motive and the right guys on their radar years ago, but never had enough direct evidence to do anything about it."

A third intriguing possibility also exists. This was not the first time Richard Resseger had disappeared. In the middle of the 1950s he had joined the American Air Force to escape the draft to Korea, and on his way to boot camp he went missing. Several months later Richard surfaced in rural Louisiana sporting a monk's robe with a rope belt and long hair. The trucker who picked him up thought he was a girl. He was incoherent, with no memory of where he had been or even who exactly he was. Identified through his fingerprints, military psychiatrists diagnosed him as having full amnesia. It took months to get his memory back and figure out what happened.

Apparently Richard had entered a men's room during a bus stop and mistook a can of lye for lens-cleaning solution. Crazy with blindness and pain, he had wandered the country talking in German (a language he barely spoke) and telling acquaintances he was a member of the Hapsburg family on the run from assassins. Years later he retraced his journey with a friend and discovered he had also worked on a farm and stayed at a monastery.

Although it is possible that Richard was once again overcome with amnesia, or something similar, this seems unlikely. Thirty-three years is too long for such a distinctive human being to go unnoticed in any society, and his fingerprints are on file. The general consensus among islanders is that he knew too much about Terry and paid the ultimate price. But for those who remember Brother Richard with fondness, the jury remains out, and we are still waiting.

DENNIS MCBRIDE

—Doug

Dennis McBride, or Bad Louie, as he was known to friends, was one of the original partners of the Teapot House at the north end of Lasqueti. He was a strikingly handsome Gemini who loved to party, and who always managed to find and win the prettiest girl in a crowd. Chameleon-like, he could be all things to all people—adapting his outfit and world view to the situation (or woman) at hand. One day he was a motorcycle tough, the next a sensitive vegetarian.

Dennis McBride enjoying a cool puff on a sunny day. Dennis was a reluctant politician who won his first election by default. Photo Merrick Anderson.

"He was just so much fun" was how many described him, but charming Dennis was certainly not all fluff. It turned out there was a serious side to his character as well.

Dennis ran as a representative for Lasqueti and Texada when new elections were called for BC's regional boards in 1972.

At the very last moment it was revealed that Director Fox of Texada, who was favoured to win, was disqualified from running for office. By then it was too late to find another candidate anywhere else in the district, and Dennis won his seat on the Powell River Regional Board by acclamation, much to the horror of voters on Texada Island.

In his new position as the Texada/Lasqueti politico, Dennis blossomed. I remember him earnestly heading off to Powell River by seaplane, briefcase under his arm, dressed in fetching hippie attire. He loved to schmooze with fellow politicians, and his immense charm made him many friends—among them the mayor of Powell River and Lieutenant Governor Walter Owen.

Dennis McBride in False Bay, ready to hop on the seaplane. Photo Merrick Anderson.

As a member of the Union of British Columbia Municipalities he was invited to a reception for Owen and his entourage at the posh Government House in Victoria, where the Lieutenant-Governor found Dennis to be a delightful companion. Addresses were exchanged, and several weeks later a naval convoy arrived in False Bay bearing Owen and the all-male entourage. They came ashore and headed up to Dennis's small dome for tea. It was a great success as well as being a surreal juxtaposition of cultures.

Dennis's charm was not confined to politicians. At one point he disappeared for several days during a holiday political gathering in Vernon. "Where's Dennis?" everyone asked. The answer came when Dennis was sighted at the head of the closing parade in a shiny red Cadillac convertible with his arm around a beaming Miss Okanagan.

He pulled a similar disappearing act in Parksville when a crowd of Lasqueti friends found themselves stuck off-island in bad weather. Dennis went off on an errand, and the rest all headed off to the pool at the Island Hall for a swim. One thing led to another and everyone took their clothes off for the dip. A few minutes later Dennis showed up with a gorgeous blonde who gamely removed her clothes too, and they all frolicked together in the pool—until angrily ousted by the management.

After his term ended in Powell River, Dennis started getting restless. He travelled to Hawaii and the Philippines, where he had a serious motorcycle accident. Then in the late seventies McBride left the island and moved to Vancouver. There, he entered the movie business and made a name for himself as a hard-working union representative. Although he reputedly settled down with a single woman partner, in many respects it was the same old Dennis. One informant described an 8:00 a.m. visit to an apartment in Vancouver. Dennis appeared bleary-eyed in a robe. "Come on in for a coffee," he said. "The girls just left." When his friend entered he found the flat completely devoid of furniture, except for a bed and a half-dozen heat lamps. Everything was dripping with baby oil.

Like most of our generation, Dennis enjoyed the intoxicants of the day in moderation—booze, pot, cocaine and the rest—but he was not an IV drug user. We were a little surprised when he became ill with AIDS in the mid-eighties, but he blamed no one but himself. "It was the cocaine and questionable women that made me sick," he lamented. We all assumed this to be the case, and he passed away quietly in 1992. Later it was revealed that Dennis had had several transfusions in the Philippines after his motorcycle accident. According to his mother, this was most likely the cause of his death.

BIG WAY RAY

—Darlene

Raymond Elroy Purcell, the eldest son of Wenatchee, Washington, orchardists, came north to Canada in the early 1970s. His childhood home and the orchards were located along the Wenatchee River, and Ray grew up hunting in the Chelan forests, hiking and fishing along the many rivers in that area and working in his parents' orchards.

In his midtwenties, Ray became friends with the Portland/Spokane group of Gordon Bissett, Alan DiFiore and Mike and Danny Gerrior. Disillusioned with US politics and having an independent streak, Ray was attracted to their plans to leave the States for the wilds of Canada where he could homestead, hunt and generally live unhindered by the rest of society. He arrived on Lasqueti in the autumn of 1971, living in the panabode for the winter with the rest of the Portland/Spokane group. Ray's rural upbringing in eastern Washington and his innate hillbilly savvy made him an especially helpful member of the panabode group. He knew how to hunt, make his own bullets, hotwire a truck and can food, and he had all sorts of valuable backwoods talent that we city kids had no clue about.

It was 1970 when I first met Ray in Portland, Oregon. It was late December, almost the new year, and he was passing through town on an errand to pick up some things that I was storing for my sister Bonnie and her husband, Alan. Months before, we had all heard about this great little island from Abnormal Norma. Everyone around me made plans to move to Lasqueti right away, but I didn't feel ready for that and I returned to the US with my infant son, Hoatie. I was living in a big communal house in northeast Portland, working part-time at a low-paying job and trying to save enough money to join them up there. When Ray arrived at my house for the pickup, he introduced himself to us and then ended up spending a few days at the house. As I got to know him, I found something very attractive in his willingness to help out my sister and her family in this way. A deeper connection formed and we became friends and lovers during those few days together. This was just the motivation that I needed to return north and finally join the rest of my old Portland friends and family in their new adventure in Canada.

On one of my first island hunting trips with Ray, we hiked way up over many bluffs behind the panabode looking for a sheep. He finally spotted a ram high above where we stood, and then quietly turned and motioned for me to be dead still. He slowly crouched down and held his .30 calibre rifle steady. I was barely breathing as I stared

Ray Purcell at work demolishing an old wooden building in False Bay, 1975. Photo Tom Wheeler.

up at the young ram standing in the sunlight above us. In one moment his life would be over, but for now he was to me a gallant young male animal enjoying his life, and perhaps deserving to be left alone. Ray's back was turned to me as he concentrated on the ram in his sights, and I could see the pressure on his trigger finger just starting to build. Slowly I lifted my arms and silently waved them in a wide overhead arc, back and forth. The ram looked sharply at this motion and then turned away, rattling the dry salal bushes before disappearing into the pine forest. Raymond just stared at the spot where the ram had been, in a kind of disbelief that the animal had just bolted like that.

"Damn, I can't believe it! How did it see me?"

I faked my own disappointment and he was so puzzled and pissed off about missing that shot that he pondered aloud about it all the way home.

We spent several months living in the panabode. When the others in the group slowly began to move on into their own nuclear dwellings, Ray and I inquired and got permission to live on Bull Island. There was already a small shack there that we lived in for a few months, and when that unfortunately burned down, we moved into an army tent and lived in it for a year.

We also bought a fibreglass boat from some friends in Nanaimo. It was four metres long and bright yellow, with Chinese characters on the bow. We called it "the Chinese boat," and always thought that the boat's name meant something exotic in Chinese. Later on, Ken told us that it was just something

Ray Purcell and Ritchie Stewart. Photo Tom Wheeler.

off a menu in a Chinese restaurant that he liked the look of, and so he painted it on the boat. He had no idea what the translation was. "You're probably motoring along in the *Fresh Eel with Steamed Noodle*," he laughed.

Ray was always on the water in that boat, either out looking for good logs to salvage, beachcombing, jigging up a cod or a red snapper to bring home or getting into some kind of misadventure with his friend "Boho Ron" Lawton. A few times these misadventures proved dangerous. On more than one occasion, a middle-of-the-night crossing on the Strait of Georgia became very rough with a sudden wind change, and twice both men came very near to capsizing and could have drowned.

For the most part, our life on the small outer islands was one full of adventure. We lived in wild solitude amidst stunning natural beauty. My young son, Hoatie, and our daughter, Mopsy, grew up toddling along the shoreline, playing on the sunny bluffs above the sea, fishing and riding in boats everywhere in all kinds of weather.

After spending a few years living on both Bull Island and Boho Island, Ray and I returned to Lasqueti. He and his father, Kenny Purcell, framed up a small cabin for us on Nancy and Cecil Varney's land, down along the back trail. After two summers, though, we changed our course and moved north to False Bay. Ray went into a partnership with Ed Harper and Nancy Varney. Their idea was to develop the property across the road from the Sea Shell Store and Marine. Ray had a working share and Nancy and Ed actually owned the land.

Ray's first idea was to put in a small laundromat, which it seemed that the island could have used at that time. Even though he went through all the appropriate environmental procedures and got the permits lined up, the island voted it down. The next idea he had was to create a type of bar and restaurant up on the hill.

Even though the Sea Shell Store and Marine already had a small café area where you could get simple food or a cheese plate if you wanted to have a beer, Ray, along with some others, thought that it would be cool to have a place that was more in step with the times: a fun place with good food where you could have a beer (and maybe a toke) with friends. Something just the opposite of the Sea-View Room, with its suspicious-eyed owner. His vision was to create a typical small West Coast bar that had a relaxed, hippie vibe.

In order to begin this, he had to first apply for a type of business licence that would allow this establishment to serve food, beer and wine. This type of licence was called a cabaret licence. Well, when word got out that Ray Purcell was planning to build a *cabaret* in False Bay, it did not go over well *at all* with the skeptical "straight" inhabitants, or with the new back-to-the-landers who came to the island to get away from it all. At an informational meeting held in the Sea-View Room, it was soundly voted down, most energetically by teeto-taller Johnny Osland, who was nearly foaming at the mouth with the very idea of a drinking establishment being even considered here. Yelling and with fists waving, he had to be ushered out the café door.

Disappointed but undaunted, Ray turned his energy toward cleaning up and reconfiguring the bunkhouse (where MaryJane's Kitchen now resides) and we worked it as an unofficial motel. After that, he tore down an old shack on the property and started a propane distributorship business. He went into Steveston during that time, along with John Bump and Gordon Bissett, and together they purchased the *Wee Geordie*, a nine-metre pilot tugboat made of welded steel, painted dark green. The guys salvaged logs with Ray's log-salvage licence, they beachcombed, and it became a sort of communally shared workboat, warts and all. It had a ridiculously loud diesel engine and pitched in any kind of a wind over twenty knots. Raymond told me that when he and the guys went into town to buy the *Wee Geordie* they negotiated hard with the marine yard salesperson who was selling the boat. They finally got him down to a real lowball price, and when it came time to do the cash transaction, the guys went out and stood in the office hallway and literally turned their pants pockets inside out to meet the agreed-upon price. They were twenty-eight cents short but got the boat anyway, borrowed enough money to fill the diesel tank and motored it back to Lasqueti Island.

At this time we lived in a small, green house in False Bay, right on the waterfront. And when Ray arranged for the little green house to be moved off the beach and pulled up to the top of the hill in False Bay, it was then that he was nicknamed "Big Way" by some of the locals, I guess for his style of doing things.

Soon afterward, the green house on the top of the hill became our first island "Free Store." But running the bunkhouse and the propane service and doing the occasional backhoe job was not enough for Ray. He had bigger aspirations for himself and, in a commercial way, for False Bay. Seeing that neither Nancy Varney nor Ed Harper would ever share his vision of what their property could become, he removed himself from the partnership and we left False Bay. Right about that time I'd befriended a young woman from Nanaimo who would come up to Lasqueti on weekends to be close to nature. Together, Bonnie Smith and I would hike the forests and bluffs picking wildflowers, identifying mushrooms and discussing everything under the sun. When a quarter section of land came up for sale on the island, Bonnie Smith was eager to buy into it with us.

The land was in the centre of the island, way up the dump road, and we spent the next two years building a road into it, clearing a home site and blasting stumps. We did most of the work by ourselves. Ray would dump the gravel on the road using Bill Riley's dump truck, and I'd walk behind with a sledgehammer, smashing the bigger rocks into road gravel.

Ray eventually found work driving trucks up in Alaska on the Alyeska Pipeline project. He worked for one month, had ten days off to come back to Lasqueti and then he'd leave again. The money he made in Alaska enabled us to frame the house and pay off any debts we had racked up. His colourful weekly letters from Alaska told me of working in sub-zero temperatures, meeting interesting Alaskan characters, the politics surrounding the pipeline, camp life and big ideas that he had for our life on Lasqueti.

When he decided that our family should pull up roots and move to Alaska, I decided that it was time to part ways, and we did. Ray Purcell did move to Alaska and continued working on the pipeline. He bought property there, then he fulfilled his dream of travelling to Africa and finally he settled back in eastern Washington state for several years before moving back to Errington, BC, where he lived very contentedly until his death in 2007.

"Big Way" Ray Purcell did indeed attempt things in his own big way, and in those times when we all held a generally laid-back approach to life, his style was a bit puzzling. Ambitious and always on the go with one project or another, Ray seemed to have a big picture of what was possible, no matter the vision. And like every one of the characters in this book, there are dozens more anecdotes and stories about Ray Purcell that will go unwritten, only to be spoken of quietly in congenial circles of old friends and enemies.

DEAR MOM, DAD AND DIARY

Letters mailed home to such far-off places as Oregon, New York City, Calgary and Toronto were often written by candlelight or kerosene lamp and sent off on mail days with an eight-cent stamp.

These letters carried news back to our families and friends. They told of our day-to-day life: the joy, the surprise and the struggle that we experienced living out our dreams here on this isolated island.

In 1976, Bonnie Smith was in her early twenties. Originally from Guelph, Ontario, she was living and working in Nanaimo for Malaspina College when she discovered Lasqueti Island. After a year of weekend visits to the island, she purchased a ten-acre share of land. It was love at first sight, a tree-hugger's paradise that she fully embraced.

Following are some excerpts of letters that Bonnie wrote to her parents back in St. George, Ontario, in 1975–76.

February 22, 1975
Dear Mom and Dad,

... I guess this was what was happening to me this weekend on Lasqueti Island: I felt so free there, I remember walking in and out from my land several times, about three miles [five kilometres] each way, with no sensation of being tired or of having to get somewhere or to do something. Just nothing, nothing eating at me. I can hardly stand it when I get a peek at what life can be ... I guess what really gets me going is how close the time to move (April 18) is approaching.

I've gotten an old Army tent from some people that were living on Jenkins Island, and Ross, a guy in our land group, has a wood cookstove to give me. All set!!

Darlene and I have arranged to plant a garden with her sister Bonnie, as they've just cleared it and there's too much to cultivate on her own the first year. The land division was insane! We drew lots, which I was completely against, and even as we were doing it, I didn't think it was for real. The ridiculous map I've drawn here shows that I know next to nothing about the actual land lines. The piece that Mike Regis got was horrid! So help me there's not a square yard on it that is level enough to build a road on, or a house foundation. He'll have to carry water at least two hundred vertical feet. No soil even, just solid rock, rock, rock! We were very lucky that he was the one pushing for drawing the lots, or I'm sure that he wouldn't have accepted it.

I was so relieved to have gotten a good piece. There's this beautiful ridge that runs from Jenkins Creek. It's long, wide, flat, and covered with big trees, but clear underfoot. Unfortunately, I didn't get the nicest piece of the ridge, that's on Ray's half. Due to the shape of our block there was no way I could have gotten it ... I considered it mine ever since I first saw it, and I always end up walking there, no matter what part of the land I first start out to explore.

It's spring time, all sun and catkins and pussy willows and everything else that spring means to me.

January 2, 1976
Dear Mom and Dad,

I saw the "Messiah" in Parksville in the middle of December. It was really excellent this year, which was a surprise after last year. Their soprano was just beautiful, and she sang like an angel. Me and the young man who sang tenor solo seemed to be the only people in the whole building who really appreciated the wonderful performance! Everyone else sat like rocks all the way through.

The Christmas Eve mass on Lasqueti was sure a different bag, we were jammed into the little church so tight that I couldn't move enough to scratch my nose! All throughout Brother Richard's chanting, the audience was doing "Om" (which would surely freak a regular priest out) and hollering "Amen. Praise the Lord." (or "Praise Lasqueti Island!"), or anything else that popped into their head. Afterwards we all started singing, a few were dancing, and it turned into a regular Lasqueti party. They had a piñata … it was a big paper bird full of candies and toys, hanging from the ceiling, and George gave me a green dinosaur from it. It was about the nicest Christmas Eve that I've ever had.

Right now I'm looking after Brother Richard's cat, which hates my two cats. My dog, Rufus, has been trying to eat my two cats all day. I'm beginning to hate all my animals and I would gladly eat them all right now if I could. The dog chases sheep as well as cats, so he always has to be in the house with the cats, and the cats have to be kept in the house because they will tear all the insulation off under the floor if I don't let them in. (However, they won't bother going to all the trouble to get outside to go to the bathroom, they just shit all over my rug.) So, I'm going to throw all my animals out of my life, and dump the whole lot in Parksville next week—(heh, heh.)

Bah! Humbug! And Merry Christmas!

Love, Bonnie.

Barry Churchill was twenty-six when he sailed north from Vancouver. His aim was to explore the northern Gulf Islands and to hopefully find a place to either homestead or just squat on. Following are some excerpts from his 1975 journal, where he recorded his first impressions of Lasqueti Island.

May 13, 1975

Got up early to catch the tide to head south again for the tip of Texada and around it to Lasqueti. I heard there was a lot of good weed and young people living there. Had a hell of a sail up the strait on the other side of Texada. It took me all day to sail to the northern part of Lasqueti, and I didn't see anyone on the island yet. I got to the northern part when the wind died, and I had to row around that tip until I got to the post office. A young guy gave me a tow into False Bay. I asked him about the people. He told me they're here, but hiding all over the island. I pitched my tent in the church yard up the street.

May 14

When I awoke I went for a walk down the dirt road. Saw a lot of cabins with many young people. Friendly folks. I talked with one who gave me a lot of information about how much land costs here. Then I sailed to another part of the island to Long Bay. Had a very strong westerly behind me. The boat has never gone that fast. Met some very groovy folks and had dinner with them and they asked me if I'd like to housesit for them for a week. Vic and Irene and their baby. I think he told me how to solve the land problem: a miner's certificate. We talked a lot about ourselves and became friends. They have chickens; that means fresh eggs every day for a week. Very happy.

May 15

Raining when I got up and went over to Vic and Irene's house. Got last-minute instructions and walked down to Vic's boat. Came back, then went for a walk down to see if Ed was in. He's the guy who owns a lot of land, including where Vic lives. He and Ben had gone to Victoria for supplies until Saturday, but I met Doug, who is building a floating house on a scow. Later, Ed's wife Sue came by with her two kids, and we had a fantastic dinner of macaroni and cheese made on her wood stove.

Celia King arrived here in 1974, a young elementary teacher newly married to Roger and immersing herself in island life. Here are a couple of letters that she wrote to Roger's parents, Barbara and George King.

False Bay
Thursday, 4 September, 1975

Dear Barbara and George,

It's too bad you missed the fair and fireman's picnic. It was a fine day, so everything including the Logger's Bride melodrama and dance could be held outside. The whole event was very successful. The firemen will have made approx $300, The Opera Co. probably an equal amount. Our ice cream stall was

Celia Parker on the day of her marriage to Roger King, 1974. Photo courtesy Celia King.

the most popular item. We sold homemade cakes and cookies too, and made $60 profit!

Roger is up on a wobbly aluminum ladder putting up the remaining shakes on the back of the house. He's doing the worst bit now, right up in the apex of the roof above the bedroom windows—I'm just waiting for the crash!

For the past week I've had miserable backache and muscular aches under my ribcage. I suppose it's the extra strain. I'm certainly expanding rapidly now!

Love, Celia

Lasqueti Island
Monday 2 of June 1975

Dear Barbara and George,

Just before five this a.m. I woke up as I heard several loud bangs. I told Roger someone was shooting. He listened, and said they were explosions. We thought maybe someone was blowing stumps, but then we heard the fire department pump running. We rushed out of bed and saw black smoke from up the road. It turned out to be Laing's house—that's the white one right on the road beside Mud Bay, just below the school. When we got there it was a wall of flames and propane tanks were exploding like fireworks! Several tanks were pulled out before the shed caught fire. Ian Laing has just started hauling propane over here to sell. He had about a dozen tanks, but most were empty. The volunteer fire crew did their best but the tide was going out, so they couldn't pump much water from the bay. At least they controlled the blaze and saved it from spreading to the trees. Rog and I eventually came home for breakfast at eight o'clock.

All for now

Love, Celia

Dianne Bump wrote this letter to her mother five months after she, John and Shane (her son) first moved to Lasqueti in April 1972.

September 30, 1972
Hi Mom,

I still haven't got the glass cutter, but I did get the mangoes you sent quite a while ago. I got the stained glass and plaster books. I already know what my birthday present from John is—a harmonica and a bag of some nice lavender flower tea (I know because he asked me what I wanted). He also got me a nice big artist's notebook (the really good kind of paper) and a box of water colours—twelve colours and they come in tubes. I'm going to Vancouver tomorrow for a "holiday" and will stay until Friday. I'm going so I can "do nothing" or whatever

I like, so I think I'd like to paint while I'm there. It will be weird since this is the first time I've been away.

No diapers to wash and I'll be sleeping in. I'll probably worry a lot about the guys. I made up an easy menu for John for dinners but I still hate to leave him with so much to do. Oh well, it may be good for me.

We got 65 chickens yesterday—fifteen are ours, and Mark (Desmarais) and Alan (DiFiore) got 25 each. We're going to can some of them soon because there's so many in the coop right now. They're "eating hens," not "layers" anymore. Out of all of those hens we only got six eggs before noon. Of course they had a ferry ride and are in a new place so we will wait and see how it goes.

Our cat Linus is sick. The vet said he has a really bad cold. The vet prescribed a bit of [tetracycline] for him, and for Bonnie's horse, who also has a bad cold, he prescribed a pound of [tetracycline]!

Anyway, I'm going to go and bake up some cookies for John and Shane now.

Love,

Dianne

Darlene kept journals on Boho Island in the 1970s. Here are some excerpts.

September 20, 1972

Mopsy Jane Appletree is four months old today! It's a crazy, really stormy day. A big tug pulled into the bay last night at about midnight. Since we hadn't had any coffee here for about a week, Ray rowed out this morning to see if they maybe wanted to trade oysters for coffee. He brought a fellow back and they sat here and talked until about noon. When he rowed him back to the tug, another crew member wanted to come up to the cabin, so Ray ended up rowing him back over here, and he walked around the island and visited with us until about 3:00. Then Ray took him back over to the tug in the yellow boat.

When Ray was down in the tug cabin, I saw that our yellow boat had broken loose and was drifting fast and free down alongside of the tugboat, just skirting the edge of the boom of logs. A guy jumped off the tug and ran across the boom, caught up to the yellow boat and motored it back and tied it up again. The wind was really howling by now out in the strait, even white-capping in the bay. When Ray came home later he tied the yellow boat up really tight, but it broke loose again from our front dock! Ray had to row out in the [fibreglass] boat and jump in again and bring the yellow boat back to the dock. The winds have just been howling all day long. Then, to top it off, the lines that hold the front dock out straight to the east, they all broke.

As Ray was down there, fighting the rain and winds, I heard a loud crash on our back porch. The wind had blown our big outdoor cooler right over! Mopsy chose this moment to have a big scream. My God, I was cleaning up sour cream and split pea soup with the rain pounding down on my back and a baby crying in my ears ... It was just wonderful. Like a fool, I put the cooler back up, put the eggs and everything else all back in, and within twenty minutes it blew down again. Beautiful British Columbia! Fuck! Later on, I had a dizzy spell, and had to [lie] down. Way too much excitement. Ray kind of felt sick, too. Now the kids are asleep, the cabin is warm and quiet, and my coffee cake is baking in the oven. It's 9:30. The wind is still howling and the tugboat sits anchored in the bay like a big strong bulldog. The deck lights shine softly, glowing red and green, rocking up and down, up and down, through the stormy night.

January 28, 1973, Boho Island

Ted the clam man returned to grace our shores once again, this time bringing along a first mate, his 18-year-old daughter. I've yet to meet her. I took Mopsy and we rowed over to the Joneses' yesterday. We went to the Lasqueti Island Community Association meeting at the school. When it was over at 3:00, Ida came home with us. We had a dreadful and emotionally disastrous—to me, anyway—walk home from the road by the Stone House.

The cold afternoon turned quickly into a moonless early evening, and we got really turned around on the trail from the Stone House to the Joneses'. We found, then lost, then found and lost the trail over and over again. My flashlight batteries were going dead, down to a dim little yellow beam. It began to snow, and we were lost and going in circles. Mopsy was like dead weight in her slippery snow suit, and the thought of being lost in those frozen woods overnight with her just freaked me out. I tried to remain calm but I was really faking it. Ida seemed calm, though. Eventually we found those marks on the tree trunks that Ron had carved last summer. We followed them carefully, and after a while we saw the lights of the Joneses' house. I was so relieved! We found our way down to the bay, got into the Davidson and rowed back to Boho. By then it was pitch black, and we bumped into the rocks out by the point twice. That's the last time I go out in the afternoon in winter.

August 25, 1974, Boho Island

My friend Luella Appledorf killed herself today.

She wrote a note saying her boyfriend was not the cause of her suicide. Then she took his .22 and shot herself in the heart and lay down dead in the ferns near his house. Arnie and Sam found her. The cops came and Ray drove them up to Arnie's in Bill Riley's truck.

I stood on the dock tonight with a policeman waiting for Ray to arrive in the speedboat with the other cops. I thought of Luella herself, her face, voice, her clothes. She was just here, and now she's gone. I thought of the day that I moved her from Maureen's tipi and into the white house, and how we laughed as we carried the boxes and bags of stuff she had to move. Luella. I heard her name over the police radio-phone. It sounds alarming, like trouble and injury, when you hear a loved one's name spoken over a police radio-phone. Luella. Luella is gone.

October 1975, Lasqueti Island

I now have experience as a "powder monkey." Last Friday, Ray and I wanted to remove those three large stumps that are right in the middle of our house site. They were still smoking away, all stinky and big and black and refusing to disappear even after three days of burning! I had the job of [lying] stomach-down in the mud and packing the stumps full of dynamite sticks. When the stump had maybe six or eight sticks jammed into it as deep as I could push them, I crawled out and got as far away as reasonable. Then Ray had the less desirable job of carrying the primer cord and caps and setting it off.

It was a bit freaky the first time; we'd hide down low, wait and wait, but you don't dare go near it to see if it got hooked up alright. Then ka-boom!! Shit flew everywhere. The last few times were easier, I wasn't nervous at all after a while. Today we planted two young apple trees along the little creek that runs up by the old logging road.

April 1976, Swamp House

The frogs chirp so loudly here that it sounds like a permanent U.F.O. landing strip. Just me and my precious children here in this little brown house in the middle of some big swamps. But I'm so grateful to be able to get around in the Blue Ghost (our 1958 Chevy pickup truck).

Today is April 19. Leila, Dianne, Angus and I went to Rena's and got plants from her beautiful garden, because she's moving to the Stump Farm. I felt strange today; Angus and I had taken the .22 out to hunt for sheep in the big swamp. We didn't get a sheep, but it was fun just hiking around looking for them. When I got back to Leila and Dianne and their babies I felt bored and uninterested in their conversation, like a tomboy around girls with dolls. I couldn't stand all that baby talk and wet diapers and crying. I just wanted to get out and go look for more sheep with Angus, and that's what we did, we went down to Conn Bay. Again, we found no sheep, but it was a nice hike out to the point, and I got some oysters and we kicked around the old homestead that's across from the ravine. This has been a beautiful day ... it is my twenty-ninth year.

SEVENTIES CHILDREN

—Darlene

Growing up as a child of the 1970s on this somewhat remote island was a unique experience. Many of these island-raised "kids" are now around forty years old, and while many of their childhood recollections are similar, a few had one or two outstanding memories.

HIPPIE FOOD

My daughter Mopsy remembers hating duck eggs. I had to lie to her about the eggs that I scrambled. They were duck eggs, big ones that always had extra goop in them. I disguised them with a little grated cheese, but she was still wary. She'd poke at them with a fork, searching for hints of their origin.

"They're chicken eggs, from our Barred Rocks! I saved the duck eggs for the cake," I'd lie. It would usually work.

And there was this great-tasting powdered milk that my sister Bonnie would buy from Buckerfield's. It was actually calf starter, but it was whole milk, nice and creamy. It came in big brown bags that weighed about fifty pounds. I'd get a bit off her now and then, but she used lots of it. Years later we found out that it contained small amounts of tetracycline, which unfortunately mottled her daughter's teeth in the following years. It made great hot chocolate, though.

Some staples of the Lasqueti diet as remembered by the kids:

• Rough whole wheat bread, a bit on the dry side, sliced into slabs, which promptly crumbled into thirds when you bit into your lunch sandwich, which caused the sprouts and the big fat slice of co-op cheese to drop into your lap. In fact, whole wheat everything. Soft, white store-bought bread was a real treat.

• Goat's milk that could have been fresher, could've been colder, or could've been from a cow.

- Apple juice that had started to ferment and gotten fizzy (we'd pretend it was Coca-Cola).
- Mom picking a few tiny bugs out of the cornmeal before she dipped the measuring cup in. ("They're just little bugs, nothing wrong with that! It won't kill ya. They don't hurt anything. In other countries, people eat bugs.")
- Oysters and clams. Good memories and bad.

Good was the late-night hikes out to the beach helping to pick oysters and dig clams. The low tides, holding a flashlight or candle lamp and exploring places way out on the beach that you'd never been to before. It was kind of spooky, but fun. The crunchy, spicy taste of fried oysters and the hot clam chowder on the next day.

Bad was wanting to stay in your warm bed, but having to go out to the windy beach and maybe wait in the car while your parent(s) picked oysters. All you could see from the foggy car window was two little lights way out on the beach. It was cold. Would they ever come back? And the next day, those slimy oysters that they tried to get you to eat, or the awful, rubbery little clams that had sand in them.

HIPPIE KID FASHION

Grandparents often sent packages of brand new clothes in the mail, but we frugal hippie parents dressed our kids almost exclusively in "S.O.S. Thrift Shop, by Design" fashions. Little black gumboots, the Hebo brand. Jeans with elastic waistbands, and later on, the adored rugby pants with striped T-shirts. They always wore a white shirt for the False Bay School Christmas play.

The mix of second-hand duds with brand new bits resulted in a sort of "Huck Finn meets Luke Skywalker meets boy raised by wolves" look. The girls dropped the Holly Hobby dresses when they turned about seven and went for a preteen look that included shagged haircuts and patent leather accessories. Mopsy, Fohla and Jennie were all over Pat Benatar and Linda Rondstadt in 1979, with big sunglasses, stretchy tube tops and the flimsiest little shoes.

Opposite: Cousins Anne DiFiore and Mopsy Purcell, both aged four. They absolutely refused to put down their apple slices for this photo, 1976. Photo courtesy Darlene Olesko.

FREE-RANGE CHILDHOOD

Seventies kids were blessed with the freedom to roam up and down the island in packs. Riding on bicycles or walking miles of dusty roads in summer, they could wander from homestead to homestead and play with their friends until dinnertime, or until wearing out their welcome and simply moving along. The island was, and remains, a wonderfully safe space for a child to explore. They knew which houses had the mean dogs, and how to either approach them or go around them. They held onto sticks in case a herd of cows was around the corner. They built secret forts in the forest, had trails up on the bluffs and shortcuts down to the ocean. These kids were free-rangers.

Eight-year-old boys playing on the front gate of False Bay School. In front L-R: Simon Linori, Shamus MacDougall. Back L-R: Dominic DuBois, Little Alan, Shane Bump, Omar McBride, and Hoatie Macy.

CHORES

Some seventies kids recall the chores they had to do around the house:

> After school I had to cut kindling and fill the kindling box with it. I had this great little hatchet, and it was my own special hatchet. After that, I had to carry in firewood if the box was low. I had to wear a special little old jacket for that job. My mom wouldn't let me wear my school jacket.
>
> I had to help in the garden, mostly. In the summer I would water plants with a small watering can. I knew morning glory, red dock and plantain, so I had to weed all through the garlic, all through the tomatoes, all through about everything except potatoes. They never needed weeding.
>
> Oh, firewood. I had to carry in arms full of firewood. I had to take a soapy rag and wipe down all the kerosene lamps after my dad filled them, cause he'd spill it down the sides by

Enforced child labour: Hoatie Macy and Shamus MacDougall happily split alder for their masters.

accident sometimes. If it was summer, I had to help out in the garden digging up ground with a shovel, raking places. There was this horrible push mower that I had to push around in our little garden. The ground was all bumpy and I hated that job. Oh, and I had to help carry buckets of water up to the bluffs for the pot gardens, too. That was hard work, and it was always done early in the morning, which I didn't like. But it was sort of fun, too, being with my dad and his buddy.

I had this job of bailing out the two rowboats, but only if it had been raining. I had a fat sponge and a white plastic bucket and had to go down the funky driftwood dock every morning and soak up any rainwater that was in these rowboats. I didn't have to do it in the summer.

My job was to go to the chicken coop in the morning, let the chickens out and then look through the nests for eggs. I had to gather them up and put them into a little basket. There was always a few. If it was spring, then there was always a hen sitting on a pile of eggs and I was supposed to leave her alone.

That was easy! She was sitting there all puffed up and scary and would make a kind of chicken growl if I even went near her. Sometimes an egg would have a bit of chicken poop on it—ugh, I hated that ...

FUN

I also asked these now-forty-somethings what they remember doing for fun.

MAKE-BELIEVE: We would get out all my mom's costumes that she kept for parties and Halloween and put them on. Then we'd go out under the apple trees and pretend that we were in the city, working at jobs as secretaries, bartenders, models, movie stars. We'd get real virtual lives going, too, with boyfriends that we fought over, money that we gave away, snits of all sorts. Every time we got into those costumes, the soap opera picked up again. It was very dramatic.

TRAPLAND: We loved jumping off logs and into the deepest slash-piles of branches and sticks that we could find, stuff that was up to our waists, and challenging ourselves to get out of the mess. There'd be four or five of us in there, all up to our chests in snapping branches, yelling and screaming ... and it was *really great* if suddenly we heard buzzing, because it meant that there was probably a wasp's nest down in there. Wow, did we ever move, then ... Ha!

BINGO: We loved Bingo! I felt so cool when I could play more than one card at a time. And we had these old cards—over the years the little round marker things all got lost, so we used pennies to mark the numbers. It was a hot game when we played for money, like twenty-five cents a game.

Karl Darwin recalls a visit to Bull Island:

STILTS: First time I saw Aaron and Todd, I was on Bull Island for a party. The boys were only about eight and ten years old

Opposite: Hoatie Macy (foreground), Shamus MacDougall, and Mopsy Purcell take a break from splitting and stacking wood.

then, and I saw them way off in the deep salal bushes, up on these six-foot-high [two-metre] stilts, and they were sword-fighting! It was an amazing sight—they looked like giants, and it took me a minute to figure out what I was looking at.

PITCHBALLS: I recall three boys who were fascinated by tree pitch, and they would create big balls of it, rolling the collected fir and balsam pitch into balls about the size of apples.

HIGHER LEARNING

In the late seventies, these same kids were approaching adolescence. The necessity of going off-island for higher education loomed dead ahead. False Bay School went up to grade eight, but a few kids just did the distance education program and chose to stay here until grade ten, eleven or twelve. That, combined with special tutoring if needed, seemed to serve some island kids very well. For the others, the entry into a much bigger off-island school was usually fraught with all of the insecurities that go along with any major life transition.

"Will I know anybody? Are my clothes okay? Will they all be way ahead of me and will I look stupid? Will I get lost inside the building? What should I say when they ask me where I'm from? Should I tell them that I go back home on most weekends? Can I remember the right bus to take? I can't wear these old hiking boots to school!"

Lasqueti parents were not always able to move off-island for a child's schooling. The option of boarding with friends or relatives was, and remains, one choice. One group of island parents collectively rented a house in Victoria and took turns being the house parent. Nowadays, other parents do the same thing, but closer to home, usually in Parksville. Looking back at my own experience, about the only positive aspect of not moving into town with my kids was that they became more self-reliant in those early teen years. Because they were boarding in other people's homes, they had to adopt better behaviour and better work habits. They both had after-school jobs and came home when they could on weekends. Outside of that, I feel that I missed out on the precious day-to-day part of those years when they were in town from September until mid-June.

For the parents who chose, and still choose, to move to town and rent or buy a house, living in town had its benefits, and it is often this seemingly temporary move off-island that becomes the gateway to a permanent return to the "Other Side."

Understandably, it can be hard to give up a good job, close contact with

Hoatie's tenth birthday at the Stump Farm. L-R: Hoatie Macy, Mopsy Purcell, Shane Bump, Anna DiFiore, Fohla Burton, Julie Shalman, Jamie Shalman, Laz DiFiore, and Shamus Mac-Dougall, 1979.

your teens who are now young adults, new friends and creative connections and return "back to the shack" when the four or eight years are over. For them, leaving the monotonous chores, perhaps the still-unfinished house, the endless firewood hauling, the rough ferry rides, is the better choice. But most parents could hardly wait to return to Lasqueti once the schooling years passed. With high school over and the kids moving on with their own lives, these parents were glad to be back on the island, away from traffic and noise, the high cost of living and the commuting.

Close bonds formed between all of the kids who shared their formative years here. Many have been connected since birth. Nearly all of them still communicate and keep up with each other (pretty easy in these internet days), hang out in town together and continue in these strong friendships through work, travel and their own children. They enjoy the memories they all share of their crazy adventures, playing in the forests and on the beaches, False Bay School, the parties with real live music and real live food. Most of all, they share the fondest memories of each other.

Eli Haukedal grew up on Lasqueti in the 1970s. He was a wild guy with a heart of gold, and when he died three years ago of a heart problem it struck that generation of close-knit friends hard. The now-thirty-somethings had a huge burial reunion in Nanaimo to celebrate his life. His friend Marisol remembers him in this poignant Facebook post:

> Mum and I were talking about you and your dad and the fun our parents had when we were little ones. Your dad came back to the island with an old ringer washer and he installed a gas motor in the back so he and mum could wash our diapers. The things they did for us, Eli … when they were young and we were so small. I remember so much of that time, chasing the chickens, tiptoeing on the sharp rocks to jump into the dark water at your house, we were terrified of spider crabs grabbing us if we dove too far. The parties, the sauna and kid's root beer. Don't know if the path to your old house on Wolf Rock is just a deer trail now but I bet I could follow it in the dark even if it is. Love you.

SUMMER SOLSTICE
by Hoatie Macy, 1990

Back to the night:
laying in this field,
We breathe perfumed rain.
The water here is so clear that
My reflection is perfect.
Even with our flaws,
it mirrors the truth, the beauty
of our wholeness.
The nature of this island is so giving;
The outside world just crumbles
around this dream.

Opposite: Bringing home the Christmas Tree. L-R: Mopsy Purcell, Burke Gillespie, Hoatie Macy, 1978.

THE SWIMMING LAKE

—Darlene

The swimming lake up on Centre Road was our main meeting place on warm summer afternoons in the 1970s. It was here that we would gather with our children, picnic baskets and guitars. We'd play music, eat and just lie around relaxing under the old, craggy apple trees shading the grassy hillside that led down to the lake's banks on the north side.

Officially named Lambert Lake, it was an old homestead, and not much aside from an old tumbledown shack and some apple and plum trees remained. But it was paradise, and we had the time in those years to meet there nearly every afternoon.

Just off the hillside, a trail led through an alder grove down to the banks of the lake, where a very large log, about a metre in width and perhaps nine metres long, ran from the muddy bank right out into the water. We'd either leave our clothes up on the hillside or undress down on the banks and hang our things on the tree limbs.

Stepping out onto the mossy log, we'd walk out to the end and dive right in.

The air held a taste almost like water hyacinth and lemon. Insects buzzed and hummed around us while the summer breeze caressed our backs, drying our long hair. Dragonflies mated while suspended in the air, and water walkers strolled between the lily pads. You never lingered in the shallows, where the cattails were thick, because there were small leeches in there that might attach themselves to your skin.

The water looked dark, but once you dove in, the immersion into a cool, green underwater world was pure bliss. I loved swimming way out to the middle of the lake and then floating on my back, watching the clouds pass above. I would bring my kids over there for baths, sending the peppermint smell of

Opposite: Chris Ferris enjoys a cool dip.

The lake in winter: Hockey games, sledding, all styles of ice-skating took place on Ogden and Lambert Lake, 1978.

Dr. Bronner's castile soap into the air. The lake served as our spa, our picnic beach and our networking area.

In winter, a stretch of freezing weather would turn the swimming lake into an ice-skating rink. Lively afternoon hockey games were played out in the centre, while casual skaters glided along the lake's edge. I loved skating way out on the far edges of the lake, exploring places that would be too far to swim to in the summer: the rock walls of the bluffs on the lake's south side and the smaller, distant shorelines on the north side. The ice made it all possible. At times, the ice would flex and make loud popping sounds, a kind of muffled "whoop-whoop-whoop" that came from below and travelled across the top. These sounds were scary and everyone would stop and pay attention to them, but since the thickness of the ice was usually around thirty centimetres or more, it was very unlikely that it was going to just suddenly crack. It was just adjusting. Figure eights, hockey and sliding around on a cardboard box would all resume after the noise stopped. In spring, the lake was home to millions of chirping frogs, migrating geese and travelling ducks. Spring squalls turned Lambert Lake into a hauntingly beautiful landscape, with low graphite clouds dancing above the rippling lake water. Steep rock walls and long stretches of cattail reeds waving one way and then another as the wind shifted.

My earliest swim there was one late March day. It was during one of those unseasonably warm stretches that sometimes happen, and I remember the sun coming out really strong in the afternoon. We were living at the Stump Farm, and I got really hot working out in my garden, so I jogged through the alder trees over to the lake. I just stripped down and jumped in, right off the big log. The water was bloody freezing, so it was a quick one, but the air felt so good on my skin as I dried off with my towel. Shaking the water out of my hair, I marked that day in my head the way people do: "earliest swim in lake ever, March 25, 1979." After that chilly hallmark day, no further warm spells came, but when summer did arrive, the swimming lake was again ready to welcome us all.

In an unpublished poetic memoir, Arnie Porter also remembers the swimming lake:

> They water the garden and pack small bags to go to the lake. Her brown skin glows in the autumn sun. At the lake they take off their clothes and sit naked on the grassy hillside that slants into the angle of the sun. Little by little other people trickle in: single people, couples, families with children, all refugees from the heat and dust of their small farms. They take off their clothes and sit in the dappled shade of the old apple trees. They eat apples from the trees and pick blackberries from the vines at the edge of the clearing. They share the simple food that they have brought, bread and cheese, leftover brown rice, carrots from the garden, a chunk of salmon.
>
> He looks around and sees a re-creation of the paradise panel from Bosch's *Garden of Earthly Delights*: the nakedness, the slim European bodies reaching to pick fruits that dangle freely from the bounteous trees. There is an openness, an amazing peace and harmony.
>
> When it gets too hot, they walk naked through the small alders to the edge of the lake. There is a great old fir log fallen on the lake; they walk out on it, past the margin of reeds, and dive into the cool clean water. They play games on the log, wrestle each other and fall in with great splashes. The children splash and shout, bobbing about in their life jackets and inner tubes.
>
> For this moment it is a song of innocence, Eden, the world before—or after—guilt, shame, and vengeance have had their time.

Carolina Foreman leads three toddlers across the Douglas Field during a picnic. (Sarah Fisher, Jesse Foreman, Emily Thompson).

LOOKING BACK, LOOKING FORWARD

—Darlene

Forty years later, Lasqueti Island remains a forested, green island of refuge nineteen kilometres out in the Salish Sea, but time has brought some significant changes. Now, when you walk off the *Centurion* ferry at False Bay, there is a throng of people to get through on the dock. In summer it can be a madhouse, but a friendly, bustling madhouse as residents and visitors haul plants, totes and tools off the ferry and up the ramp.

Standing at the top of the dock you see that the Sea-Shell Store and Marine of the 1970s is now the Lasqueti Hotel, with eight rooms, a café, bar and fuel pumps. Lively Mary-Jane's Kitchen is across the road in a pretty yard with picnic tables. The Judith Fisher Health Centre is now built to lock-up stage, thanks to incredible effort by the Last Resort Society. It includes a health clinic, a recuperating room, a permanent Lasqueti Internet Access Society internet centre and cleared areas for future elder housing. The Teapot House still stands, beautifully preserved. Farther south lie various bed and breakfasts, shops and a farm and garden store.

You see a few people on bicycles, in cars, on motorbikes. You see

Wintertime in Goose Hollow, 1969. Darlene Olesko holds her infant son, Hoatie Macy. Photo Tom Wheeler.

unique home-based businesses in pretty, rustic buildings, paths leading off to small houses and cabins. You see yellow ditch irises, blackberries and wild roses clambering between the tall firs. You see children playing games and running in the schoolyard. Many of them are the grandchildren of people whose stories appear in this book. Their parents ran in the same field for years, climbed the same trees.

Look closer and you'll see a close-knit community, one that is working toward as much independence as possible. Among the general population, you'll see the grey-haired graduates of the "University of Lasqueti, 1970s and '80s Class" as they bike and walk past you on the gravel road. You see them using their degrees as they hammer, saw, excavate, landscape and install systems at the health centre. You see them using their degrees at community planning, land conservation and informational meetings. You see them playing golf and running across the disc field. You see them checking the lines on their boats in the winter, and you see them at the Blue Roof Bar having sunset drinks in the summer.

So what don't you see?

You don't see cookie-cutter plastic houses on tiny logged-off lots along the road. You don't see BC Hydro wires strung up like drip tubes on poles along the roadways. You don't see "smart metres" on gateposts. Even though the provincial and federal economy was quite good in the 1970s and '80s, and generous offers of "rural improvements" were offered, you don't see wide, paved roads or a car ferry running seven days a week.

What you do see are the remains of an ancient civilization. The young, earnest, long-ago, long-haired generation, "the hippies" who arrived here in the 1970s, left a visible influence as evidenced here. Today's Eden owes much to their visionary efforts and hard labour. In today's Eden, patience remains a necessary trait for residents and visitors alike, and convenient inconvenience is still the rule. Our Eden was no accident.

—Doug

Life is an adventure with many unexpected twists and turns. All of us who arrived in the 1970s were seeking a new and different life from our parents. The hippie/back-to-the-land movement was one of those strange social upheavals that seem to periodically ripple through the human experience. It had its foolish, frivolous side, but a good part of the value system remains as relevant and useful today as it was back then. Even though the movement was consigned to the waste bin years ago, many of those ideals continue to reverberate.

Among them are respecting the environment and using as little as possible; the value of a close-knit supportive community; the recognition that rampant economic growth cannot continue forever in a finite world. I could go on, but I'm sure you get the point.

Following spread: Hangin' out on the edge of Douglas Field during a 1975 May Day picnic: L-R: Carolina Foreman, unknown, Jerry Curle, Audrey Alsterberg, Steve MacDougall, a young Aslan Carey, and Merrick Anderson and Grover Foreman with guitars, "Doctor John" Mitchell on fencepost, and Trey Carey, 1975. Photo by Tom Wheeler.

Caitlin Press Inc.
8100 Alderwood Road,
Halfmoon Bay, BC V0N 1Y1
www.caitlin-press.com

Text design and cover design by Vici Johnstone.
All known photo sources have been credited where possible, but if the source
is unknown the image appears without credit and was provided by the authors.

Printed in Canada

Canada Council   Conseil des Arts   BRITISH COLUMBIA
for the Arts   du Canada   ARTS COUNCIL

Caitlin Press Inc. acknowledges financial support from the Government of
Canada through the Canada Book Fund and the Canada Council for the Arts,
and from the Province of British Columbia through the British Columbia Arts
Council and the Book Publisher's Tax Credit.

Library and Archives Canada Cataloguing in Publication

Hamilton, Douglas L., 1945-, author
    Accidental Eden : hippie daze comes to Lasqueti Island / Douglas
Hamilton, Darlene Kay Olesko.

ISBN 978-1-927575-52-9 (pbk.)

    1. Lasqueti Island (B.C.)—History. 2. Lasqueti Island (B.C.)—
Biography. I. Olesko, Darlene Kay, 1947-, author II. Title.

FC3845.L38H34 2014   971.1'31   C2014-904118-7